THE PEOPLE FACTOR

STRENGTHENING AMERICA BY INVESTING IN PUBLIC SERVICE

Linda J. Bilmes
W. Scott Gould

BROOKINGS INSTITUTION PRESS
Washington, D.C.

Library of Congress Cataloging-in-Publication data

Bilmes, Linda.
    The people factor : strengthening America by investing in public service / Linda J. Bilmes and W. Scott Gould.
        p.   cm.
    Includes bibliographical references and index.
    Summary: "Presents a blueprint for reinvigorating the public sector based on 'The People Factor.' Shows why the U.S. personnel system needs reform, revealing the high price of inaction. Lays out specific steps to achieve the necessary gains, focusing on implementing 'best practices' from successful companies, the military, and high-performing government agencies"—Provided by publisher.
    ISBN 978-0-8157-0141-5 (pbk. : alk. paper)
    1. Civil service reform—United States. 2. Civil service—United States. I. Gould, W. Scott, 1957– II. Title.
    JK681.B55 2009
    352.6'323670973—dc22   2008051173

3 5 7 9 8 6 4 2

Printed on acid-free paper

Typeset in Sabon and Strayhorn

Composition by Cynthia Stock
Silver Spring, Maryland

Printed by R. R. Donnelley
Harrisonburg, Virginia

For our families
Jonathan, William, Stephen, and Owen Hakim
Michèle Flournoy and Alec, Victoria, and Aidan Gould

The only sure bulwark of continuing liberty is a government strong enough to protect the interests of the people, and a people strong enough and well enough informed to maintain its sovereign control over the government.

Franklin Delano Roosevelt

Contents

Preface

This book sets out a bold vision for strengthening public service in America. Our proposal will transform the way people work for the government—and how government works for people.

A new approach is badly needed. The monolithic structure of the U.S. federal government—with its top-down management hierarchy, its stovepiped job classifications, and its slow, ponderous method of making changes—is based on an organizational model that is a relic from an earlier age. The enormous advances in modern management have largely passed it by. Consequently, the federal government is poorly equipped to cope with rapid technological change and a looming wave of retirements. These problems threaten the government's ability to deliver the critical services on which our quality of life depends.

The people factor blueprint set out in the following pages can transform the civil service into a leading-edge "people system" equipped to tackle the challenges of health, education, security, and economic stability facing our society. World-class companies understand that managing people effectively is a source of competitive advantage. That is why the director of human resources occupies a pole position in the modern executive suite. The civil service needs to learn from this playbook, which includes flatter hierarchies to shorten decisionmaking, decentralization to increase customer responsiveness, and flexible working hours to retain valuable employees throughout their working lives. Techniques such as "intrapreneurship" encourage and reward employees for successful new ideas.

The notion that the government's personnel system needs reform is not new. Over the past decade, many commentators both inside and outside the public service have concluded that government agencies must be given greater flexibility to improve recruitment, training, and career development. But two powerful forces are now making this change urgent. The first is demographics. As our retirement population increases, a growing shortage of skilled labor is forcing government agencies to make better use of their people. The second is computer and information technology, which enables organizations to integrate cheaply and easily with their customers and their suppliers irrespective of geography.

For all the talk about reform, there is a conspicuous lack of new models to serve as templates. The people factor is not a management technique like "total quality management" or "time-based competition." Rather, it is a fundamental value system that focuses on motivating every worker by recognizing his or her contribution to the success of the enterprise. Organizations that embrace this philosophy tailor their personnel systems—how they recruit, train, evaluate, compensate, reward, and promote people—to the individual worker and the specific type of job. Using this approach, federal government agencies can achieve gains in productivity similar to those achieved by the best private sector and military organizations.

Part I of the book explains *why* the personnel system is so badly in need of reform and describes the financial and other costs of inaction. Drawing on a large body of research on the benefits of investing in people, we show that organizations can make substantial gains in effectiveness, productivity, and stock performance when employees are highly motivated and satisfied with their jobs. In part II we turn to *what* needs to be done to achieve these gains. The system we propose is structured around the people-management techniques that have worked best in other organizations and is specifically designed to attract and retain talented professionals in an intensely competitive marketplace. It focuses on training, leadership skills, credentialing of supervisors, best human resources practices, greater flexibility, and performance management. We also propose the establishment of a "core ring," using human resources "passports" to enable some private, nonprofit, and public sector employees to flow back and forth more freely between sectors. Drawing extensively from our own surveys of students and workers, as well as case studies and interviews with government leaders who have been able to transform their organizations, we demonstrate that this vision is both workable and practical in the public sector.

Part III focuses on *how* to implement the new system. We imagine a world in which civil service reform is a high priority to the president, who places the weight of his office behind change. We lay out a roadmap for the various stakeholders in such a process, including details of the infrastructure, the resources, and the specific authorizations that will be essential to ensure success.

We believe that this is the time for change. The personnel system is in a period of uncertainty, transformation, and openness to new ideas. Recent efforts at the Departments of Homeland Security and Defense have drawn attention to the complexities of how to motivate and compensate people. The employee unions, having been largely excluded from the reform process over the past decade, are ready to engage in the discussion. There is a growing consensus that adjustments are necessary especially given the expanding role of government in revitalizing the U.S. economy.

For this book, we collected a number of specific best practices from the federal government, the military, and (in some cases) state, local, and international governments. These practices demonstrate the success that can be achieved in a government environment. The military provides a compelling example of how a government organization can train behavior; in this regard, military personnel managers are far ahead of their civilian counterparts. Although this book focuses on the federal workforce, most of the principles we endorse apply equally to public service in general and would lead to substantial productivity improvements if introduced throughout state and local governments and in multilateral agencies.

Our proposals are based on new research. We conducted two surveys of college juniors and seniors—the target recruits for the next-generation civil service. The results shed new light on their perception of the public sector and the specific changes needed for them to consider a government career. We engaged current government employees in discussions of the situation facing them. We also interviewed dozens of leaders throughout the government and organizations that care about good government. In this process, we sought answers to some key organizational questions: What skills and tools are needed to manage the government and get things done? Where can we find these skills and tools, and how can we adapt them for government? What are the needs and requirements of different stakeholders in this process, and how can they be accommodated? On the basis of the response, we have designed a reform plan that will rejuvenate the public service.

The people factor is a simple concept that has strong empirical support. It can deliver powerful results for the federal government by creating a human resources advantage to attract a new generation of public servants. We believe that it can enhance governance and strengthen our nation into the next millennium.

Acknowledgments

This book would not have been possible without the assistance, encouragement, and inspiration of many people. We are particularly indebted to Jeffrey Neal of the Defense Logistics Agency, who provided us with enormous insight into the federal personnel system and with suggestions for how to make it better, and who took the time to comment on several chapters.

Several people made significant contributions to our research. At the Boston Consulting Group, Peter Strüven and Konrad Wetzker worked with Linda to conduct original studies showing the relationship between investing in people and total shareholder return. Research assistants who provided invaluable assistance in many aspects of our work include Matthew Lindsey, Margaux McDonald, Tony Park, Ryan Raffaelli, and Michael Roarke. Max Stier of the Partnership for Public Service and his excellent staff generously provided comments and assistance. Sallyanne Harper and others at the Government Accountability Office were generous with their time and provided us with important feedback on the manuscript. We also thank Mark Penn, Jonathan Penn, and Yoni Gedan of Penn, Schoen & Berland for their help in formulating and conducting our surveys of college students and private sector workers.

We are grateful to a number of Linda's colleagues at the Harvard Kennedy School for their comments and suggestions, including Mary Jo Bane, Bob Behn, Jack Donahue, David Gergen, Steve Goldsmith, Elaine Kamarck, Steve Kelman, Joe Nye, and Larry Summers. We also thank Tammy Sopp, an outstanding faculty assistant. The Mossavar-Rahmani Center for Business and Government at the Kennedy School provided not only grant funding for our research but also a supportive environment in which to work, study, and write. We especially thank Associate Director Shannon Murphy, who helped us perfect and finalize the manuscript.

We are also indebted to a number of Scott's colleagues at IBM who made significant contributions to the book, including Julie Anderson, Jonathan Bruel, Yolanda Comedy, Michelle Cullen, Suzanne Geigle, Charlyn Isaac, Laurie Skantze, and Solly Thomas. And we appreciate the support of the IBM Global Business Services executive team, who provided unfailing support for the effort, especially Dave Amoriell and John Nyland, who uphold the IBM core value of "innovation that matters to our company and the world."

We are grateful to many former colleagues from the Departments of Treasury and Commerce who helped us to understand the challenges facing the federal workforce. They include Alan Balutis, Tony Fleming, Ron Glaser, Scott Gudes, Suellen Hamby, Carol Hayashida, Dave Holmes, Renee Miller, Carl Moravitz, Ann Murphy, Deborah Tomchek, Kim Walton, Lori Way, and Bob Welch. We also salute Robert Mallett, who served as Deputy Secretary of Commerce during our tenure, and William Daley, who served as Secretary, for their strong, decisive leadership and commitment to public service.

This book would never have been written without the support of Chris Kelaher at Brookings. He believed in this project from the start, inspired us when we flagged, and provided us with excellent suggestions throughout the entire writing process. We also thank our editors at Brookings, Venka Macintyre and especially Janet Walker. Susan Woollen was responsible for the book cover, which captures the link between people and our nation's public service. We thank Phil Murphy for his freelance editorial assistance as well.

We especially wish to thank our families. This book has involved many long hours and nights stolen from them, and we thank them for their patience and understanding. We are grateful to Jonathan Hakim, who edited several chapters of the manuscript, and to Michèle Flournoy for her wise counsel. Both are truly delighted to finally see it in print. Our mothers, Lila Lynn Humphrey and Dolores Coleman Gould, always taught us to see the best in people and to believe in ourselves throughout the research and writing process. We also thank our friends who provided encouragement along the way, including Kurt Campbell, James Adams, Chris Hoenig and Adam and Glynis Gould, Dana Gould and Janet Govostes, and Sharmini Coorey and John Hicklin, who opened their homes for our frequent stays in Cambridge and Washington.

Finally, we thank the nearly 1.9 million men and women of the U.S. federal government, who work every single day to keep America strong and safe.

LINDA J. BILMES and W. SCOTT GOULD
January 2009

Strengthening Public Service

1

A Call to Arms
Why the Federal Workforce Must Become a National Priority

In the time it takes to read this chapter, federal government agencies will have solved multiple crimes, supervised the safe take-offs and landings of hundreds of airplanes, issued an updated national weather forecast, monitored the skies for any sign of enemy attacks, issued visas to tourists around the world, planted trees, rescued struggling ships at sea, paid food stamps to hungry citizens, operated on wounded soldiers, and processed some $50 million in banking transactions.

For the most part, Americans take all this public service for granted. After all, the federal government is the largest single employer in the United States. We devote one-quarter of the national budget to federal government salaries, retirement benefits, and other labor costs, so we expect that things will run well. The only time the federal government attracts much attention is when things go wrong.

But after a half-century of neglect, cracks are beginning to show. The system is coming under increasing strain. In almost every sphere there are backlogs, customer service failures, security lapses, cost overruns, and, in some cases, real disasters such as intelligence mistakes (Iraq), regulatory failures (weak oversight of the financial system), breakdowns in emergency response (Hurricane Katrina), or administrative meltdowns (loss of personal data for thousands of veterans).

The primary reason is that the civil service is trying to cope with an increasingly complex world while hobbled with an inflexible, outdated management structure. It is run by a revolving door of political appointees, many with limited management skills and little interest in long-term efficiency. In short, the federal government is an anachronism in a world where technology enables new and versatile ways of working. It is increasingly unsuited to deliver complex services.[1]

What threatens to turn this slow decay into a real crisis is the looming wave of retirements that in the next decade will strip away most of the federal government's experienced managers. Many of the approximately 1.9 million federal employees who run the government are nearing retirement, yet the political agenda continues to overlook the dire need for civil service reform. The civil service needs a plan that will enable it to attract, train, and retain its fair share of the "best and the brightest" in a competitive labor market. This will not happen until the nation adopts a fresh approach to managing the government's human capital. The government is becoming dangerously overdependent on private contractors to perform core government services. Without action, the government will struggle to maintain the standards of efficiency, honesty, and accountability that every citizen in the world's richest country has a right to expect.

The federal government's personnel system was built in the image of the large centralized manufacturing companies that dominated the U.S. economy during and after World War II. Management had a top-down, command-and-control structure, and the majority of federal government workers were clerks, performing repetitive tasks and processing paperwork. Young people joined at entry levels and expected to remain in the civil service throughout their working lives, doing well-defined jobs and retiring with handsome pensions. The bureaucracy was designed to be slow and deliberative and to resist change. It was a comfortable system, and it worked fairly well for nearly half a century.

But the system is not appropriate for the twenty-first century. Parts of the world that barely knew of one another's existence fifty years ago are now in daily communication—and competition. The U.S. industrial base has shrunk, replaced by technology and service businesses that evolve at a rapid pace. The revolution in computer technology and telecommunications has brought rapid globalization. Advances in genetics and life sciences, the changing global climate, and the threat of terrorism and viral pandemics pose economic, regulatory, ethical, and financial challenges that were unheard of by previous generations of civil servants.

Faced with similar challenges, private sector companies have had to rethink the way they do business. The successful ones have embraced new models and changed the ways they recruit, train, measure, reward, and manage their workforces. In today's knowledge economy, attracting and motivating skilled workers and making them highly productive are crucial to an enterprise's continued success. People

Put simply, the United States is not managing its enormous investment in human capital strategically to deliver the highest possible quality of government for everyone.

are a strategic asset, to be leveraged through careful investment. Companies as diverse as GE, Proctor & Gamble, IBM, and Pfizer have evolved and thrived over many decades by following that course.[2] The GE of today, the world's second-largest global conglomerate, is barely recognizable as the company founded in 1876 by Thomas Edison. The information age has spawned new giants such as Microsoft and Google—growing from nothing to global companies in less than a generation. The irresistible pressure of market forces has pushed industry to change and adapt in order to survive. By contrast, the government systems and structures that served an earlier age are still in place.

The civil service, however, has no mechanism for reforming itself organically—it has to rely on the president and Congress to initiate major change. Not even a cabinet secretary can overhaul the human resources system in a department without congressional approval. But Congress has paid little attention to the widening gap between the demands of increasingly vast and complex government programs and the ability of the government personnel system to deliver them. Put simply, the United States is not managing its enormous investment in human capital *strategically* to deliver the highest possible quality of government for everyone (see box 1-1).

The malfunctioning of the federal government is becoming evident in many spheres. The Iraq War was predicated, in part, on flawed intelligence about weapons of mass destruction. Wounded veterans are waiting years to obtain disability benefits. Hurricane Katrina, the Madoff scandal, rats and vermin at Walter Reed Medical Center, the backlog of half a million

BOX 1-1. What Is Strategic Human Capital?

To understand the term "strategic human capital" used throughout this book, consider the circumstances surrounding "Jim," a forty-nine-year-old federal government employee who processes disability compensation claims for veterans. He has worked for the U.S. Department of Veterans Affairs (VA) for twenty-one years and is now a GS-13. Jim, whose older brother is a Vietnam veteran, believes deeply in the program's mission and works long hours reviewing claim documents, detailed medical records, and military service records for approximately twenty veterans each week.

The VA provides disability benefits to 3.5 million veterans. Its fifty-seven regional VA offices process 800,000 claims a year. With the increased complexity of claims related to the wars in Iraq and Afghanistan, the VA's backlog of unprocessed claims has risen to 400,000 in the past few years. To deal with this backlog, the agency needs to retain experienced employees, hire new ones to increase production, and train everyone to be more efficient.

Jim does the best he can with the tools currently available. However, if Jim were used as a *strategic resource,* he could be spending his days differently. Jim could be seeking new and innovative solutions to expedite claims processing by reaching out to a wide range of fellow government employees, nonprofit veterans service organizations, and vendors in the private sector. Jim could be asking private medical insurance claims companies to donate their time to help him execute claims. He could be asking his superiors to pilot a completely different model for claims approval. However, Jim cannot succeed in this effort unless the VA provides four kinds of support, which are currently missing.

1. Jim needs additional training. He needs to learn about innovations and pilot programs in different parts of the country that successfully increased the throughput of claims and improved the quality of rating decisions. He also needs to know how to assemble, coordinate, and manage the performance of his staff. This requires new soft skills (such as negotiation) and new technical skills for state-of-the-art computer systems.

pending patent applications—the list goes on and on. When these failures come to light, the public service often becomes the political scapegoat. The media and the general public—and sometimes even the president and members of Congress—are quick to blame the government's bureaucrats. But the main problem is not the people. It is that the system is failing, despite the good people in it.

2. Jim needs to be empowered to assume risk and take the initiative by trying new approaches. Currently, the VA uses an assembly-line method of processing claims. Jim should be rewarded if he suggests and implements a new model that improves the delivery of benefits to veterans. He should not be penalized if the new process does not yield improved efficiency. And the agency should trust that his efforts are honorable—that if Jim works with veterans' advocates or the private sector, he is doing so in good faith and not just trying to make a dime on the side.

3. Jim needs to be able to freely establish links with other federal agencies as well as with the private and nonprofit sectors. For example, he might choose to spend six months working with the Department of Defense, the Social Security Administration, the Department of Labor, veterans service organizations, or with insurance companies in the private sector learning new skills. Or he might work with new employees with particular skills to implement new approaches, who could be either new hires or staff on loan from other government agencies, businesses, or nonprofit sectors.

4. Jim needs a modest and reasonable amount of dedicated funding to pay for regularly scheduled training, travel, and the skills development necessary to undertake the first three measures, including any training for his staff.

If policymakers provide Jim with the right tools, create an environment in which he can experiment with new techniques, and fund those efforts, he is much more likely to be able to develop innovative strategies for processing disability compensation claims more quickly and accurately, at a lower cost, and at more convenient locations for U.S. veterans and their families.

This is what we mean by investing in "strategic human capital." Using Jim *strategically* means going far beyond simply paying him more or offering additional benefits. It means leveraging his knowledge, performance, and commitment as a federal government employee and a human being.

In this book, our shorthand for this approach is the "people factor."

Total Spending on Public Service

By any metric, the federal government is a dominant player in the U.S. economy. It alone accounts for some 20 percent of the gross domestic product.[3] In 2007 more than 14 million individuals, including current and retired employees and the military, were paid directly or indirectly by the

TABLE 1-1. **Estimated Number of Persons on Federal Payroll**

Branch	Number
Executive (excluding U.S. Postal Service and Department of Defense)	1,888,055
Postal Service	747,805
Legislative	29,660
Judicial	33,469
Military (active)[a]	1,379,551
Military reserves (active)[a]	71,781
Contractors (estimated)[b]	7.6 million
Grantees (estimated)[b]	2.9 million
Total (actual plus estimated)	14.6 million

Source: Unless otherwise noted, figures are from Office of Personnel Management, "Employment and Trends," September 2007 (www.opm.gov/feddata/html/2007/september/charts.asp).

a. Defenselink, "Department of Defense Budget for Fiscal Year 2009" (February 2008).

b. Paul C. Light, *A Government Ill Executed* (Harvard University Press, May 2008), p. 197.

federal government (table 1-1), with a total labor cost of approximately $800 billion, or about one-quarter of total federal expenditure (table 1-2). On top of the federal budget, pension and health care benefits for retirees are piling up large future liabilities of nearly $5 trillion (table 1-3).

Although labor costs are clearly one of the largest categories of government spending, this factor receives little serious scrutiny. The media print sensational articles about trivial problems (for example, whole newspaper series have been devoted to overpriced hammers and ice cube trays) but seldom ask if the public is getting the best possible value for the trillions of tax dollars spent on personnel. We argue that the federal workforce is no longer able to deliver the highest value on a consistent basis as a result of five major constraints:

1. Increased volume and complexity of government transactions accompanied by rising expectations for quality of service.

2. The legacy of an old-fashioned personnel system not designed to manage human capital strategically or to meet current demands.

3. A lack of leadership.

4. The retirement crunch: a growing loss of expertise resulting from the retirement of experienced public servants.

5. A deep-rooted negative perception among young people about the federal government as an employer that makes it hard to attract "the best and the brightest" to public service.

TABLE 1-2. Total Cost of Personnel
Billions of dollars

Workforce	Cost
Civilian executive (excluding Postal Service)	157.0
Retired civilian[a]	56.1
Contractors[b]	264.0
Postal Service	50.8
Legislative	2.3
Judicial	3.2
Military (active and retired)[c]	158.0
Federal grant–funded[d]	100.0
Total	791.4

Source: Unless otherwise noted, figures are from OPM, "Employment and Trends," September 2007, Table 4 (www.opm.gov/feddata/html/2007/september/table4.asp).
a. OPM, *Fact Book 2006* (federal employee payroll estimates); based on data available for 2005.
b. Based on the Acquisition Solutions estimate that two-thirds of the total $500 billion in government contracts is for service-based contracts, where labor costs account for 80 percent of expenditures.
c. GreenBook (www.defenselink.mil/comptroller/defbudget/fy2009/fy2009_summary_tables_whole.pdf).
d. Light, *A Government Ill Executed.*

1. Increased Volume and Complexity of Government Transactions Accompanied by Rising Expectations for Quality of Service

The complex environment in which the civil service of the twenty-first century operates is characterized by fiscal imbalances, escalating entitlement spending, demographic shifts, technological and scientific changes, threats to homeland security, and constant challenges in education, health care, and the operation of global institutions.[4] In order to operate successfully, federal workers must be able to capture, manage, and share knowledge quickly and effectively. The task is a monumental one: to fix a host of long-standing social problems, protect against new physical and economic threats, and do it all without increasing costs. Government workers will be unable to succeed in this endeavor unless they become far more productive.

To complicate matters, the tools for delivering programs have become more numerous and complex. In an old-fashioned federal program, the system worked top-down. Today, if a Washington-based agency mandated that schools serve lunches to low-income children during summer vacation, local communities would not simply open up their schools and

TABLE 1-3. Federal Employee Benefits Payable
Billions of dollars

Benefits	Civilian	Military	Total
Pensions and accrued benefits	1,386.3	1,028.8	2,415.1
Post-retirement health	311.6	833.8	1,145.4
Veterans' compensation and burial	N/A	1,127.7	1,127.7
Life insurance and accrued	35.9	13.1	49.0
FECA	15.9	8.7	24.6
Liability for other benefits	0.5	6.8	7.3
Total employee and veteran payable	1,750.2	3,018.9	4,769.1

Source: Government Accountability Office, "FY 2007 Financial Report of the United States Government" (www.gao.gov/financial/fy2007/07frusg.pdf), p. 72.

do it. More likely, there would be a discussion of how best to implement the program, perhaps through a network of nonprofit organizations and private contractors in conjunction with local governments. It is not unusual for the federal government to provide matching funds to state and local governments, which may in turn reimburse nonprofit groups for providing meals in local facilities such as community centers, churches, and recreation centers. Senior agency officials might not ask for input on program design from the local federal employee administering the program. But even if they did, local employees would suddenly need a whole new set of skills to do the job well.

Harvard professor Stephen Goldsmith, a former mayor of Indianapolis, points out that such a "networked" delivery model demands new skills of government workers, including agility, creativity, flexibility, and resourcefulness.[5] Today's government employees, he notes, need to be comfortable negotiating with partners and vendors, coordinating the activities of multiple organizations, and facilitating collaboration among the components of the network. They must also understand how to assemble these networks and how to set performance standards for all parties that can then be audited independently.

Shifting security priorities are also driving the need for a new kind of civil servant. "We are in a post 9/11 security environment," says Admiral James Loy, former deputy secretary of homeland security and commandant of the Coast Guard. "We need skills and competencies that never before were part of the civil service system. . . . Now there is a need for agility, adaptability and speed of service. If government is going to gain the capacity to do what needs to be done, we must have these capabilities."[6]

The huge increase in contracting and outsourcing has also changed the basic nature of a federal worker's job, adding a "make-or-buy" dimension to decisionmaking. According to Nobel Laureate economist Ronald Coase, a fundamental reason that firms exist and perform functions internally is to reduce the transaction costs that make it more expensive to buy from an outside vendor.[7] These costs include finding vendors, evaluating them, making contracts, communicating with them, and monitoring their activity and results. In the federal government, the role of private sector contractors has exploded without any robust mechanism for capturing those transaction costs. Consequently, federal employees are responsible for selecting contractors, overseeing them, and bearing all the burden of interacting with them. Yet in many cases this make-or-buy decision is made haphazardly. It is unclear whether the decision to "buy" instead of to make has saved money and produced better outcomes for the taxpayer.

Even the job of procurement has changed. Bob Welch, former procurement executive at the Departments of the Treasury and Commerce and founding partner of Acquisition Solutions, notes that two-thirds of Department of Defense procurement dollars are now spent on services and only one-third on products, creating a major challenge for its employees: "They need to understand how to purchase and manage service contracts, which requires a completely different set of skills than buying products."[8]

During the past five years, the amount of contracting done by the federal government has more than doubled, from $240 billion to $500 billion, in large part because of the Iraq War.[9] But federal workers have not been trained to manage the performance of these contracts. Another layer of responsibility has simply been added to their jobs. The consequence for the taxpayer has been a serious lack of oversight of war contracts. The inspector general for the Defense Department has already referred 28 cases involving millions of dollars in Iraq contracts to criminal investigators. Separately, the Army Criminal Investigation Command has 90 investigations under way related to alleged contract fraud in Iraq, Afghanistan, and Kuwait.[10]

There have been lapses, too, in handling one of the government's key assets, information. The government owns and controls huge quantities of data across the full spectrum of its functions. The task of managing and protecting this information, analyzing it, and using it to improve services is enormous. The federal government has spent hundreds of billions of dollars on new information technologies (ITs). In some respects, this move has transformed government (for example, enabling it to make a wide range of information available to the public online). But in many cases, agencies have simply automated old paper-based processes without fundamentally rethinking them. Moreover, the chronic shortage of skills needed to manage large IT projects among senior civil servants commonly contributes to failed projects, huge cost overruns, and lengthy delays.

More Government Work, Fewer Government Workers

The volume and complexity of federal government transactions have increased dramatically in the past fifty years. In the case of intellectual property—which is vital to U.S. economic competitiveness—patent applications have quintupled from 100,000 a year in 1970 to nearly half a million in 2007.[11] Struggling to cope with this influx, the U.S. Patent and Trademark Office now faces a backlog of close to 1 million patent applications just awaiting action by a patent examiner.[12] Many of the new applications stem from research into genetics, nanotechnology, and other highly specialized fields. Lawyers evaluating these proposals need to understand biochemistry, physics, and biology, as well as patent law.

At the Department of Veterans Affairs (VA), pending disability claims have increased from 150,000 in 2001 to upward of 400,000 in 2008, with waiting lists ranging from six months to two years.[13] And the new claims are more complicated: troops returning from Iraq and Afghanistan file claims for five conditions on average, whereas Vietnam veterans on average cited just three.[14] The picture is similar in almost every area of government activity, in part driven by demographics. The growing size and the aging of the U.S. population have magnified the scale of the administrative burden compared with a generation ago. The increase in the number of airline flights, complexity of the tax system, and growth in environmental, health, and safety regulations, not to mention the number of claims under Medicare and Social Security, have all added further

T A B L E 1 - 4 . Increasing Demands on Government, 1970 to Current

Selected indicators	1970	Current
Annual patent applications[a]	109,359	484,955
Federal prison population[b]	20,038	199,118
Pages of the Federal Register published annually[c]	20,036	78,724
College students[d]	8.6 million	18.0 million
Medicare enrollees[e]	20.0 million	43.0 million
U.S. population[f]	205.0 million	301.0 million
U.S. federal debt[g]	$371 billion	$10.6 trillion
GDP[h]	$1.0 trillion	$14.0 trillion

a. U.S. Patent and Trademark Office, *U.S. Patent Statistics Chart,* calendar years 1963–2007.

b. Ibid.; Pew Charitable Trusts, "One in 100: Behind Bars in America 2008" (as of January1, 2008). This does not include state and local prisons.

c. National Archives, *Annual Federal Register Index, 2006* (www.archives.gov/federal-register/the-federal-register/2006-pages.txt).

d. U.S. Census Bureau, *2008 Statistical Abstract* (www.census.gov/compendia/statab/tables/08s0207.pdf).

e. U.S. Census Bureau, *2008 Statistical Abstract* and *1980 Statistical Abstract;* for 2006, see www.census.gov/compendia/statab/tables/08s0136.pd.

f. U.S. Census Bureau, *2008 Statistical Abstract;* the 2007 figure is a projection.

g. U.S. Treasury Direct; see www.treasurydirect.gov.

h. U.S. Department of Commerce, Bureau of Economic Analysis, Table 1.1.5, "Gross Domestic Product" (www.bea.gov/national/nipaweb/TableView.asp?SelectedTable=5&FirstYear=2005&LastYear=2007&Freq=Qtr).

weight to that burden (see table 1-4). Despite technological advances, the traditional ways of providing services are not working. Admiral James Loy attributes this breakdown to "something like a hardening of the arteries in the current system."

> When I was in the Department of Transportation, I was frustrated with how long it took to process EEO [Equal Employment Opportunity] and civil rights complaints for the Coast Guard and for the entire department. The published standards were six months, but we had backlogs of three, four, and even five years. The system has become overwhelmed by volume. It was designed when the volume was much less, so it has run it course. There is a crying need to renovate the system.[15]

Although the complexity of government has increased, the number of civil servants in the direct employ of the federal government has declined. Over the past twenty years, their number has decreased from nearly 2.2 million to about 1.9 million. Much of the reduction is a result of the "peace dividend" at the end of the cold war, which enabled the civilian military establishment to reduce the number of full-time employees. Because of this decline—coupled with the sharp growth in the U.S. population—the ratio of federal workers to the population as a whole has fallen from 1 per 68 Americans to 1 per 112 Americans.[16]

This decline is largely illusory, however, because of the rapid growth in outsourcing. The fall in the number of *direct* federal employees has been more than offset by the rapid growth in private contractors and an expansion in state government. Once these trends are taken into account, the total number of government workers has actually grown. The number of private contractors is difficult to quantify with precision, but the most recent estimate by scholar Paul Light pegs it at about 7.6 million.[17] The number of state and local government employees has almost doubled since 1970, from 9.7 million to about 18 million today.[18] Many of them work on implementing federally mandated programs. An additional 2 million to 3 million people are performing functions paid for with federal grants. This huge "shadow" workforce has become indispensable to the functioning of the government.[19] But direct federal employees are still the ultimate managers of all the federal government's interests, ranging from security in coastal waterways to poultry inspections. This is a far-flung workforce, with only 15 percent of it based in Washington, D.C., and the remainder stationed throughout the fifty states and the world.[20]

2. The Legacy of an Old-fashioned Personnel System Not Designed to Manage Human Capital Strategically or to Meet Current Demands

To compound its problems, the current civil service system is organized hierarchically and stove-piped by specialty, much like the giant industrial enterprises of the 1950s. It has more in common with the ponderous top-down Soviet bureaucracies of the past century than it has with the companies that dominate today's marketplace. It was not designed to foster creativity or innovation, and in most cases it discourages them. While global competition has forced leading companies to become flatter, leaner, and more productive over the past two decades, the federal government has made an already unwieldy hierarchical system even worse by adding layer upon layer of political appointees and managerial positions.

Much of the system's rigidity is due to the complex rules and regulations designed to ensure "merit" hiring. These date back to the nineteenth century when government workers commonly obtained their positions through patronage. President James Garfield complained that job-seekers were like "vultures lying in wait for a wounded bison." He was prophetic: on July 2, 1881, a mentally unstable job-seeker named Charles Guiteau shot him. The Garfield assassination ultimately led to the reforms of the Pendleton Act of 1883, which is still in effect today. The act requires open competition and hiring based on merit, rather than

While global competition has forced leading companies to become flatter, leaner, and more productive over the past two decades, the federal government has made an already unwieldy hierarchical system even worse by adding layer upon layer of political appointees and managerial positions.

favoritism. But in the intervening years the system has grown so elaborate that few people outside government are able to navigate it on their own.[21]

Arcane Job Categories

Today's federal government is still organized vertically, despite the fact that federal workers need to work horizontally across agencies. In the early 2000s, a study of government performance by the second National Commission on the Public Service (the second Volcker Commission) concluded that this design inhibits the work of agencies and hampers their coordination with one another, with nongovernmental organizations, and with the private sector.[22] Among the problems agencies face are duplication, overlap, and competition for resources, much to the frustration of their employees.

Efforts to address these structural issues, especially since the end of World War II, have proceeded incrementally. They include the Classification Act of 1949, the Federal Wage System introduced in 1972, the Civil Service Reform Act of 1978, and the Federal Employees Pay Comparability Act of 1990, as shown in appendix B. Every recent presidency has tried to address the personnel situation to some extent. These efforts include the National Performance Review led by Vice President Al Gore and the personnel initiatives that President George W. Bush introduced at the Departments of Defense and Homeland Security. (For a longer view of the history of personnel reform in government, see appendix E.)

In the wake of these efforts, certain aspects of government have improved markedly: for example, nineteen of twenty-four cabinet-level departments have achieved clean financial statements as a result of the requirements of the Chief Financial Officers Act of 1990. Congress and taxpayers now have much greater assurance that money is spent where it is supposed to be. However, the reforms also added new layers of job requirements for civil servants—without increasing their pay commensurately or giving them additional training.

Although individual agencies have made great strides in specific areas, many of which are described in part II of this book, progress has been largely at the margin. Half of the federal workforce remains bound by a classification system enacted in 1966 under Title V that is now a major obstacle to effective government.[23]

Under Title V, each government worker is classified into a specific job category.[24] The system of classification is organized around two main occupational groups: professional and trade jobs. These categories are subdivided into occupational families, which are further subdivided into series of related occupations. The federal classification system consists of nearly 60 job families subdivided into more than 600 job series. The 23 families of the professional group are broken down into 418 series, and the 36 families of the trade group are divided into 250 series.[25] Families and series are identified by numerical codes, such as 3727 for Buffing and Polishing.

The pay for these main divisions is set out under the Federal Wage System, which grades jobs according to the kinds of duties, responsibilities, and qualifications required. The pay scale used for the majority of professional personnel is known as the General Schedule (GS) and that for the trade division is the Wage Grade (WG). These letters are added to the numerical codes to indicate the pay scale alongside type of job: for example, WG-7641-Beautician, WG-5034-Dairy Farming, WG-6903-Coal Handling, WG-6941-Bulk Money Handling, and WG-3716-Lead-burning. The Federal Wage System has fifteen nonsupervisory pay grades, fifteen leaders' grades, and numerous other grades. Given the number of individual job classifications in each family and the fact that most job classifications have five or more grade levels, there are more than 2,000 ways to classify a government job.[26]

The system is so complicated and arcane that it frustrates even those who know it best. "Title V makes my head hurt, and I've spent 30 years in federal service," says Claudia Cross, chief human capital officer at the Department of Energy. "No new manager can master it. It's just too complicated."[27] The classification system has effectively trapped government workers in specific jobs that typically follow a narrow path, often keeping them in one job series throughout their careers. Managers are constrained in their ability to hire people with new skills because when a vacancy occurs, it is narrowly defined for a specific job. These strictures, combined with a lack of promotion opportunities once employees reach the journeyman level of their occupation, create resentment in the workforce and make for an extremely rigid organization.

Compensation for GS positions is based on grade and the ten pay levels (steps) within each grade. There is little flexibility, and it is difficult to link pay to performance. The step functions even make it possible to earn less than someone classified two GS levels below. With the pay structure fixed, managers often resort to gaming the system to resolve pay problems. In order to pay people more, they may inflate the duties in a job description to make them appear more substantial. Some also use this tactic to avoid hiring someone (for example, to get around the law that gives preference to veterans).

The lack of flexibility also makes it very difficult to fire, demote, or even deny a pay raise to an individual who is not performing well. This is one of the biggest complaints of federal workers. In surveys by the Office of Personnel Management (OPM), employees in both the federal and private sector said that about 25 percent of the workforce performs below expectations.[28] However, only 9 percent of federal employees said their organizations are competent at disciplining poor performers, while more than two-thirds said that their agencies are "not too good" or "not good at all."[29] By stark contrast, 20 percent in the private sector said their companies are competent at handling poor performers, and fewer than half said their companies are not competent at dealing with them.[30] This single issue—managers' inability to deal effectively with poor performers—is a source of anger and frustration among many government employees.[31]

About 50 percent of federal workers are employed in agencies that have been granted varying exemptions from Title V. But the new systems that have emerged are very similar to the old ones, says Harvard professor Elaine Kamarck, who served as director of the Reinventing Government initiative during the Clinton administration: "The agencies have mostly re-created their old personnel systems. They have not used the flexibilities to make themselves more flexible. This is partly because it is so hard to imagine something you've never seen."[32]

After studying the federal workforce for the past three decades, Paul Light suggests another reason for the stodginess of the current system: "Additional flexibility costs money that is simply not in the budget."[33] Indeed, one of the system's grievous flaws is that the United States invests little or nothing in developing the strategic potential of its workforce. On average, the federal civilian government spends only about 1.9 percent of salaries per year per person on annual training.[34] By contrast, the private sector spends 4 percent on average, and leading firms spend much, much more.[35] This low level of investment in human capital makes the government even more vulnerable to a dramatic loss of competencies as its workers retire.

Where some reform has been attempted, the system has simply become more uneven, not less—as is evident among law enforcement personnel. Of the nation's 106,000 federal law enforcement officers, half are employed by the Department of Defense (DOD) or Department of Homeland Security (DHS).[36] There is wide variation in how such jobs are defined and classified. Some officers carry weapons and can make arrests but are excluded from special pay and pensions provided to other federal law enforcement officers with similar duties. Entry-level pay also varies significantly, and overall federal law enforcement pay lags behind that offered by many state and local governments. This has been a long-standing problem, yet the new flexibility that allows the DOD to offer higher salaries and bonuses to their own law enforcement officers has created greater discrepancies and may lower morale at other agencies.[37]

Addressing personnel problems in isolation may undermine positive aspects of the current system, such as the basic commitment to merit, equity, and fairness. In 2003 the second National Commission on Public Service recommended adopting a government-wide legislative framework for reform so that "the unique status of the federal public service may be retained."[38] The Government Accountability Office (GAO) has urged that human capital reform should "avoid further fragmentation within the civil service, ensure reasonable consistency within the overall civilian workforce, and help maintain a reasonably level playing field among federal agencies when competing for talent."[39]

The experience in state government provides evidence that compensation needs to be roughly uniform. Though highly decentralized in most respects, Texas has a single compensation system to ensure uniformity in what various departments pay employees for similar work. By contrast, Georgia has lacked a central compensation system, which drew complaints of "compensation anarchy" in a 2002 survey.[40] The lesson is that compensation systems must preserve pay equity for equal work across departments (with adjustment for local labor market disparities). What should be avoided is a situation in which procurement officers doing similar work in two different agencies in the same locale are paid differently.

OPM adviser Doris Hausser points out:

> We have some experience with intra-governmental competition, so it would be irresponsible to ignore this possibility. We saw it occur with the banking regulatory agencies, which were able to offer more-competitive salaries and were successful in drawing talent from other agencies. The most recent example was the start-up of TSA [Transportation Security Administration], where the Administrator had significant freedom in the pay area. That created an immediate draw of talented staff. Observers said it would not be a continuing phenomenon, because it was triggered by the start-up of a new agency. But in an analysis of turnover data in law enforcement agencies after the TSA start-up, researchers found that the former Immigration and Naturalization Service experienced a 500 percent increase in separations in 2002. Most of these employees left the Border Patrol to join the TSA. The Secret Service experienced a 10% increase in separations during the same period.[41]

Put simply, variations in salaries for comparable work can create a negative recruiting effect, which in turn creates turnover, particularly when the skills and competencies needed are already in government (that is, when the government constitutes the pool of candidates). Without consistent personnel rules across government, the Department of Defense's Wright-Patterson Air Force Base in Ohio will have the freedom to use occupationally sensitive pay for scientists and engineers, whereas the National Aeronautics and Space Administration (also in Ohio) will not.[42]

Many believe that a government-wide framework will not be flexible or responsive enough to adapt quickly to changes in mission-critical needs. The central questions are: what must be done consistently across government, and what can be left flexible for the individual agencies?[43] Whatever the right balance, there is no obvious way to address these issues in the current environment.

3. Lack of Leadership

Many federal employees attribute the government's management problems to the lack of a clear direction for the future: "We need some competent people with vision leading the organization, not just political hacks," commented one respondent. "Then we need to set forth clear goals and objectives for middle-level workers and managers to make sure the goals and objectives are clear all the way around."[44]

A peculiarity of the federal government is that political appointees who lead it typically have a shorter time horizon than the rest of the federal workforce.

A peculiarity of the federal government is that political appointees who lead it typically have a shorter time horizon than the rest of the federal workforce. In this respect, government differs from both private and nonprofit organizations, where senior managers often come up through the ranks and stay with the organization for years. In local government, most elected and senior appointed officials live in the municipality where they work—many have spent their lifetime there—so they have an interest in what happens beyond the period of their service. In the federal government, the average tenure of a Senate-confirmed political appointee is less than twenty months, compared with four and a half years for a senior executive in the private sector.[45]

This transience contributes to a lack of leadership. It fosters a culture in which it is acceptable to "lead" employees without defining long-term strategic goals. Corporations, museums, universities, and municipal governments expend a good deal of brainpower putting together long-term plans and capital budgets. Planning exercises help managers set goals and priorities, for both the organization and individuals. Career planning, training needs, recruitment, physical office design, performance measurement, and other aspects of human resources are pegged to long-term goals.

The Government Performance and Results Act (GPRA) of 1993 forced federal departments to develop five-year strategic plans and performance metrics, but the process is hollow. Who will be held accountable for a five-year goal if all the top leaders will be gone before then? Indeed, despite an enormous amount of hours spent on them, the plans have had little impact on day-to-day management. Only 39 percent of federal employees believe the effort to measure government results has been even *somewhat* successful.[46] The Performance Assessment Rating Tool (PART) program has also tried to establish clear targets for each government agency. But despite the strong backing of President George W. Bush, it has not proved possible to link budget allocations to the achievement of PART goals or obtain reliable performance data to put into the tool. In other words, the program lacks teeth. Without financial incentives, it is difficult for managers to galvanize and lead their employees toward achieving PART goals.

The personnel reform undertaken by the Departments of Defense and Homeland Security was supposed to rejuvenate the agencies by removing Title V restrictions, linking pay more closely to performance, and allowing greater flexibility in certain hiring and staffing practices. But this reform effort was destined to fall short of its goal because it concentrated on *fixing a "problem."* The only way for the government to achieve high performance is to adopt a proactive human capital strategy. In other words, it needs to focus on the *benefits* that could accrue from a high-performing workforce, not simply on the shortcomings of the status quo. This requires leaders who can envision a high-performing workforce of the future.

4. The Retirement Crunch

If, as French philosopher Auguste Comte reputedly said, "demography is destiny," then the time for a restructuring of the civil service is now.[47] Nearly 90 percent of senior government executives, as well as nearly half of all other federal workers, can retire by 2010.[48] The first wave of baby boomers became eligible for retirement in 2007. But the average age in the federal workforce is increasing at twice the rate of the private sector. In

F I G U R E   1-1. Percentage of Employees Aged Forty-Five or Older

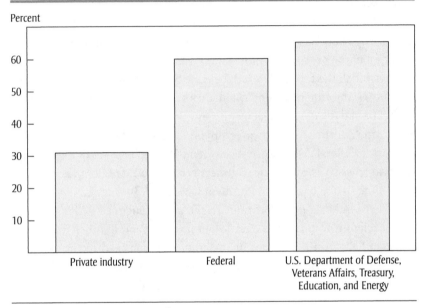

Source: Partnership for Public Service and OPM.

private industry, 31 percent of the workforce is older than forty-five. But 60 percent of federal employees are above that age.[49] At the Departments of Defense, Veterans Affairs, Energy, Education, and the Treasury, approximately 65 percent are over the age of forty-five (figure 1-1).[50]

The federal government's 7,000 top executives—individuals who run the government, control budgets, and write rules and regulations affecting millions of people—have an average age of fifty-two and have served in government for an average of seventeen years.[51] This group forms the core knowledge base of the U.S. government. In 2000, 28 percent of these executives were eligible to retire; today 45 percent can retire on a full pension, with another 45 percent able to retire early if they choose.[52] If *all* those who are already eligible to retire decided to do so tomorrow, then some 6,100 of the 7,000 most senior managers and technical experts would walk out the door.

This exodus constitutes an enormous brain drain. Sixty-three percent of the senior executives have a postgraduate degree. One-fifth are scientists or engineers.[53] Some specialist areas will be especially hard hit:

within four years, 97 percent of administrative law judges, 87 percent of Social Security examiners, and 40 percent of Homeland Security analysts will be able to retire.[54] The impact of such a retirement wave cannot be underestimated, particularly in agencies requiring longer durations to properly train new employees (see box 1-2). According to the nonpartisan Partnership for Public Service, these retirements threaten the functional viability of the U.S. government:

> The loss of experienced personnel is one of the surest ways to undercut an organization's effectiveness. When this loss occurs rapidly and is concentrated in critical positions, the results can be devastating. The departure of top-level employees at the Federal Emergency Management Agency (FEMA) is often cited as a key reason why it struggled to respond effectively to Hurricane Katrina. The coming wave of baby boomer retirements, combined with other turnover, threatens to dramatically diminish the Federal Government's effectiveness in meeting urgent public needs.[55]

In Washington, D.C., the GAO, the OPM, inspectors general, and numerous government commissions and nongovernmental organizations have been warning for several years that a debilitating wave of retirements is in the offing. It has not materialized so far, largely because many public servants delayed retirement after September 11, 2001. Consequently, fewer than projected have actually retired each year for the past several years. However, the demographics guarantee that a large cohort of government workers will retire from the civil service fairly soon.

Most employees who joined the federal workforce before 1984 are eligible for generous retirement benefits. The Civil Service Retirement System (CSRS) provides them with an old-fashioned "defined-benefit" pension. They can retire at age fifty-five after thirty years of federal service and receive a pension of close to 60 percent of their highest three years of compensation, as well as health insurance, life insurance, and survivor benefits.[56] Employees who serve for longer than thirty years are eligible for even higher percentages of their salary, up to a maximum of 80 percent for forty-one years, eleven months. Pension payments are adjusted annually to compensate for inflation. This pension plan is exceptionally valuable given that improved medical care has lengthened the expected life span of retirees.[57]

BOX 1-2. Air Traffic Controllers

The situation in air traffic control illustrates the government's challenges. Clearly, the public values the experience and maturity of the current air traffic workforce. But over the next ten years 73 percent of the nation's 15,000 air traffic controllers will become eligible to retire. The Federal Aviation Administration (FAA) expects to lose 11,000 experienced controllers within the decade. In the same period, the volume of air traffic is projected to increase by 27 percent.[1]

The solution would appear to be obvious: recruit and train new controllers. But it is not so simple. Not only must the agency hire 12,500 controllers in the next ten years in order to have enough recruits in the pipeline to meet its needs, but the training alone takes three to five years, which is as long as a medical residency. The recruits must become adept at dealing with a variety of complex situations, such as weather emergencies and peak flow traffic. The agency can only handle a certain number of on-the-job trainees at a time. Even by increasing its use of high-tech simulators—which cannot substitute entirely for real-world exposure—the agency can train only about 2,000 controllers a year.

Essentially, the FAA needs to figure out how to replace its entire workforce with highly skilled professionals—while at the same time safeguarding public safety and coping with increased air travel. It must therefore find ways to recruit top-caliber candidates more quickly, without long delays in the hiring process itself. It must also invest in training, especially in state-of-the-art, customized technology for simulating air traffic control. All this requires mentoring, performance evaluation, feedback, supervision, and an ability to weed out poor performers early on. Therefore the FAA must do everything in its power to retain existing employees, taking into consideration that they are older and may require different kinds of work schedules.

---

1. Russ Chew, chief operating officer of the FAA Air Traffic Organization, speaking at the Air Traffic Control Association's annual conference, November 2, 2006.

Federal employees have numerous retirement options. Instead of taking full retirement after twenty-five years, they can leave at age sixty with twenty years of service, or at age sixty-two with five years of service, and receive lower percentage annuities, but with full health care benefits.[58] Or they can go to work elsewhere without forfeiting any benefits. Because most government executives have skills and deep knowledge of their subject areas, they are attractive recruits for private sector firms. Often these "second careers" offer additional benefits and part-time, flexible hours. So early retirement is a real option—a lifestyle choice—for many long-term federal workers. The average retirement age in the federal government is fifty-eight.[59] Sooner or later, everyone who is eligible for federal retirement will take advantage of the retirement benefits he or she has earned.

Just below the senior executives is a group of about 300,000 federal employees in civil service grades 13–15. These are the nation's middle managers—the ranks from which senior executives are typically drawn. Positions at this level include military analysts, marine biologists, lawyers, engineers, auditors, trade specialists, economists, agricultural experts, statisticians, diplomats, patent examiners, and experts in many fields. Unfortunately, the retirement pattern for this group will be similar to that of the senior executives, compounding the looming exodus of senior-level talent. Regardless of the precise speed with which they depart, the inescapable conclusion is that virtually the entire generation of public service–minded individuals who joined the federal government in the 1960s and 1970s and who occupy pivotal positions will shortly be leaving. Assuming that federal workers retire at about the average retirement age of sixty-two, one should expect a loss of close to 50 percent of the most experienced government workers within the coming decade.

Financial Consequences of the Expected Retirements

The retirement issue has huge consequences for public finances, not to mention a large impact on succession planning and the operational capacity of government programs. We project that personnel costs will rise to more than $1.3 trillion annually by 2015.[60] If retirement rates were to increase by 10 percent, the cost would reach $1.4 trillion.[61]

The surge in costs is a direct result of the generous benefits provided under the CSRS plan, which was in place until 1985 (when it was replaced by the Federal Employees Retirement System, FERS).[62] Government retirees will, on average, be receiving about 60 percent of their highest three years of compensation plus health insurance benefits, life insurance, and payments to their survivors when they die. Therefore even if retirement stays at the current rate of 3.9 percent, the total amount of spending on people costs will increase sharply.

These expenditures plus the rising cost of U.S. entitlement programs and interest payments on the national debt will further strain the federal budget and put federal labor costs under increased scrutiny.[63] If the workforce is treated merely as a cost and not as an asset that requires ongoing investment, then budget constraints will continue to put downward pressure on both the number of employees and future compensation, compounding the difficulties of attracting and retaining the skilled workers needed to replace the retirees. The end result will likely be even greater outsourcing of government functions without considering the long-term wisdom of doing so.

> *If the workforce is treated merely as a cost and not as an asset that requires ongoing investment, then budget constraints will continue to put downward pressure on both the number of employees and future compensation, compounding the difficulties of attracting and retaining the skilled workers needed to replace the retirees.*

Who Will Replace the Retiring Civil Servants?

The near freeze on hiring in the 1990s, combined with the loss of many young people to private sector jobs during those boom years, contributes to an acute shortage of candidates within government to replace those nearing retirement. The 1990s downsizing was accomplished primarily through reductions in the civilian defense workforce at the end of the cold war. It shrank the non-postal executive branch workforce by 18 percent through a combination of buyouts, layoffs, and significantly reduced hiring.[64] As a result, the federal government lost a disproportionate number of younger, recently hired employees, who were eliminated under a "last-hired, first-fired" policy. Because most turnover of new employees occurs during the first two years of employment, the government hiring freeze further reduced the number of younger employees as a percentage of the total population as young entrants who left the government were not replaced.[65]

This "Generation X" age group is much smaller than the baby boomer cohort in the general population.[66] It is also the first generation of Americans with widespread knowledge of computer technology. Consequently, the federal government competes head-on with the private sector in a "war for talent" to employ its members. The manpower shortage in this age bracket has made it difficult for managers to assign staff to projects. In a recent study, 59 percent of current federal workers said that they rarely, or only sometimes, have enough employees to complete their jobs properly. Among senior executives, the proportion rose to two-thirds.[67]

Nicholas Eberstadt, a leading demographer at the American Enterprise Institute, compares this skewed age profile to "the postwar situation in East Germany in the early 1960s—what you have is a curious-looking curve with a high percentage of older people and a scarcity of young people from the next generation. This happened in Germany because the birth rate was so low during the 1940s."[68] It is worth remembering that one reason for the downfall of communist economies in the Eastern Bloc countries was their low birth rates and the consequent lack of well-trained younger managers prepared to run government enterprises.

The Crisis in Hiring

The private sector is paying considerable attention to what the Boston Consulting Group (BCG) calls "demographic risk," which is "the potential loss of productivity and capacity that a company will experience as its work force ages and retires." To deal with these challenges, BCG recommends that organizations develop succession plans, groom and train internal candidates, and recruit aggressively from outside. BCG also advises its clients to use innovative ways to manage productivity and motivation in an aging workforce—for example, by providing on-site medical care and preventive health care, enhancing workplace design, and linking compensation more to performance and less to longevity.[69]

The federal government's demographic problems are compounded by the fact that most agencies do little workforce planning or go about it incorrectly. Successful organizations, including nonprofits, focus on strategic human capital workforce planning. Typically, they map their internal skills portfolio against projected needs and then try to fill the gaps through targeted recruiting, training, rotational assignments, and promotions. But federal managers who engage in succession planning risk being accused of "preselection" (that is, rigging the selection process). Careful planning is blocked by the legal requirement for open competition for vacancies. Laws designed to safeguard the fairness of hiring have the perverse effect of prohibiting the government from doing everything possible to ensure the continuity of service to the public.

Not only is it an uphill battle to hire talented young entry-level recruits, but agencies have difficulty hiring experienced workers in mid-career from outside the government. As discussed in part II of this book, a number of federal agencies have made progress in shortening their hiring cycles, improving the quality of recruiting materials, and matching hires to their strategic skill needs. But overall, the government is still light-years behind the best hiring practices in the private sector.

The Hiring System: "Slow, but Expensive"

The federal government hires about 250,000 employees each year, and this number will increase as the pace of retirement accelerates. But the process is slow and cumbersome. As Jeffrey Neal, who has worked in senior positions in the human resources departments of the U.S. Navy, the Department of Commerce, and Defense Logistics Agency, has quipped, "We're very slow, but at least we're expensive."[70] Most agencies hire in response to job vacancies within stove-piped job classifications. They seldom perform detailed workforce planning and assessment of what skills they will need to hire or prepare to make the best strategic use of their employees.

The hiring process is frustrating for both the job-seeker and the hiring manager. Applying for a federal job can be a daunting proposition, particularly for recent college graduates or workers interested in moving from the private sector. The system bears little resemblance to anything outside government. A large hurdle is to identify federal job vacancies in the first place. Then the applicant must determine which of numerous parallel applications processes—based on veterans status, grade point average in college, disability status, or eligibility for one of dozens of special hiring programs (such as former Peace Corps volunteers)—is appropriate. There are even more channels, such as the "merit promotion" program aimed primarily at current or former federal employees (but in some cases open to others as well), that make the system even more opaque.

The hiring system has been deficient in helping agencies recruit talented workers in midcareer. Half of the posted jobs are not open to applicants from outside the government.[71] The job description may be written in a way that requires knowledge of specific laws, rules, and regulations (as opposed to the ability to learn them) and direct experience of government projects. Many midcareer applicants have little idea of how to navigate through the maze of federal employment regulations. All this places midcareer applicants at an unwarranted disadvantage.

In 2001 only 15 percent of the 68,000-plus midmanagement hires (GS-12 to GS-15 levels) were from outside the government.[72] Since then the government has made a concerted effort to attract more talent from this cohort. There has been some progress: the number of midmanagement hires from outside the government increased to 26 percent in fiscal 2006. However, even when outside applicants are successful, they are given little help in integrating to their new work environment. Government agencies typically bring in a new person only after his or her predecessor has already left—consequently giving little opportunity to "learn the ropes." Hiring managers thus become caught in a vicious cycle of recruiting existing government employees who can "hit the ground running," precluding the entry of newcomers who might bring ideas, expertise, and skills from the outside.

Even entry-level positions have cumbersome requirements. Job announcements, which may run four to six pages of single-spaced type for a position paying $46,000 to $59,000, are filled with jargon, acronyms, and unexplained requirements such as "eligibility under 5 CFR 330.60(b)." The "How to Apply" section alone consists of well over 1,000 words. Standard résumés are often rejected in favor of something approaching a graduate school application. Applicants may even be asked to demonstrate proficiency in obsolete software such as WordPerfect or Lotus 1-2-3. (See appendix D.)[73]

By design, essential information needed to prepare an application is withheld from the job-seeker. Most agencies consider the "crediting plan" used to evaluate the applicant's experience confidential, so applicants have no sense of what information is critical to the application process. Thus federal job-seekers routinely submit lengthy applications that describe everything the reviewers might possibly be looking for.

Not surprisingly, the process discourages qualified individuals from applying. Two-thirds of college students agree with the statement "It is difficult to locate and apply for a job with the federal government."[74] The process is also extremely slow. With only a handful of exceptions, the government takes three months or more to make a hiring decision.[75] This is *double* the time that leading companies take for a job offer at the entry level and nearly three times what college students say they can afford to wait for a government job before taking another offer. When asked, 20 percent said their maximum was two weeks or less, 48 percent said four weeks, and 21 percent could wait up to two months. By the time the government's offer was in the mail, only 4 percent of these students would still be available, and the most attractive candidates would almost certainly have taken other jobs.

Two-thirds of college students agree with the statement "It is difficult to locate and apply for a job with the federal government."

Graduate students are similarly discouraged from applying for government jobs. The flagship program to bring in new talent at this level—the Presidential Management Fellows (PMF) program—hires only about 500 graduate students a year. Only 6,000 students have joined the government since the program's inception in 1977.[76] The program is so highly selective that the majority of applicants from Harvard's Kennedy School, Syracuse University, and other top public policy schools fail to get accepted.[77] Though armed with a master's degree in public policy and trained in economics, statistics, budgeting, and international affairs, most are unable to get a job in the U.S. government, except in a handful of agencies such as the GAO and the Office of Management and Budget (OMB).

Kennedy School students echo these complaints, and others: it is difficult to identify jobs, the application process is long and cumbersome (applicants cannot apply online to many jobs), the hiring criteria are unclear, and it takes far too long to receive a decision. If they are asked to attend a job interview, they must pay out of their own pockets to travel to Washington. Then, should they receive an offer, security background checks can take up to a year (box 1-3). How many students, saddled with loans and fresh out of school, can afford to wait a year to start a government job?[78]

Not surprisingly, federal employees themselves are highly critical of the hiring system. Only 19 percent say their agencies do a good job of recruiting qualified applicants, whereas one-third say that their organizations are "not too good" or "not good at all."[79]

B O X 1 - 3 . Talent the Government Turned Away

Brendan Dallas, a smart and enthusiastic U.S. citizen with experience living and working in Turkmenistan, seemed the perfect candidate for government service. Before earning his master's degree in public policy from the Kennedy School at Harvard University, Dallas was the country director for the American Councils for International Education in Ashgabat, Turkmenistan. In that role, he worked to introduce programs such as the Edmund Muskie Graduate Fellows Program and the Future Leaders Exchange Program for high school students in collaboration with the U.S. embassy.

Dallas excelled at the Kennedy School, winning high scholastic honors and working as a volunteer to help the local town of Somerville, Massachusetts, improve its budgeting. During the summer of 2004, he worked for the U.S. Agency for International Development (USAID). He loved it, and the agency wanted to hire him. They discussed the possibility of a full-time job after graduation, and he was eager to accept such an offer. During the following school year, Dallas wrote his master's thesis on USAID and was invited to fly down to Washington and present it to the administrator of USAID in person.

In the spring of 2005, Dallas received a call from a security official in charge of processing his security clearance. This was confusing because he had not yet received a formal job offer from USAID. "My only thought," he recalled, "was that maybe the job had come through and the security office was just way ahead of the curve." In fact, the security office was calling in reference to clearance for his 2004 summer internship. Rather than being ahead of the curve, the system was so backlogged that it had not registered that he completed his internship more than six months before its call.

Unfortunately for Brendan, the security office was not the only part of USAID that was overwhelmed. Despite constant contact and discussions, the office that wanted to hire him could not get the necessary approval from human resources for another position. The best it could work out was a temporary job with a contractor that supported the USAID office where he had worked. This contractor had previously facilitated his summer internship and was happy to offer him a spot—but it was only a six-month position with no extension guarantee, no benefits, and a salary less than what he made before graduate school.

Brendan recalled later, "The terms were definitely disappointing, but despite the salary, I was very tempted to say yes, just to get my foot in the door. But in

(continued)

BOX 1-3 (*continued*)

the end, I had to say no. In hindsight, it was the right decision because the con-tractor unexpectedly lost its extension with USAID after three months. At the same time, USAID went through some budget issues and severely reduced the number of people it was hiring. Taking the risk to get my foot in the door would most likely have meant starting from scratch three months later."

In September 2005, after waiting without pay for four months after gradua-tion for USAID to make a formal offer, he made the difficult decision to accept a private sector job he had been offered at Acquisition Solutions, Inc.

I really wanted to work at USAID. I turned down many jobs in the private sector that would have paid more, but I care about public service and the mission of USAID. Luckily, my current job is great: they provide me with training and care about me as a person, and I feel a strong commitment here. The irony of it is that in my current job, I spend a lot of time helping the federal government look at solutions to what many call a workforce crisis because the baby boomers are about to retire and Generations X & Y are largely choosing to work elsewhere. It makes you wonder how the federal government can and will function if someone like me, who really wants to work for the government, gets stuck in the hiring system.

Source: Brendan Dallas was a student of Linda Bilmes while at Harvard. This anecdote reflects their personal conversations. In 2008 Dallas finally joined USAID.

5. Deeply Rooted Negative Perceptions of Government Employment among Young People

Perhaps the most formidable challenge facing the federal government is recruiting the next generation of talent to replace the one that is retiring. Our research shows that college students are ambivalent toward the federal government. Although they believe the federal government does important work, they also feel that the qualities they value most highly in a job are absent in the government. Moreover, there are numerous practical impediments that prevent them from considering a government career.

To understand college students' perceptions of the federal government, we conducted extensive research into this recruitment group. We surveyed a total of 1,400 college juniors and seniors at four-year colleges—looking at two groups, the first in 2002 and the second in 2005–06—to determine their attitudes toward working for the government. We investigated undergraduates rather than graduate students because they represent the full spectrum of academic disciplines and personal backgrounds of interest to the government. Although this kind of survey measures only the *perception*s of young people (who may have limited information about the government), it does provide a statistically accurate picture of how undergraduates view the idea of joining the federal workforce.[80]

Overall, our college students expressed a favorable opinion of the federal government. Six out of ten said the government does important, meaningful work. Nearly half think that what happens in government affects their daily lives. But the majority surveyed would not consider working for the federal government because they perceive it as an "uncaring" employer with little concern for individual employees that does not let them rise to their full potential. In general, the federal government lags well behind both private and nonprofit organizations as a potential employer, with the Department of Homeland Security perceived in a particularly poor light.

Only one-third of college respondents said they would even consider government employment. Many expressed reservations about the lack of training, the length of time it takes to get hired, and the difficulty of locating job opportunities. Students with scientific and technical skills were even less willing to consider government employment. In general, 68 percent of students rated the federal government somewhat favorably as an employer, but this was lower than the favorability for leading private companies and state and local government and was on par with the military, which is facing its most difficult recruiting environments in decades (see table 1-5). Students rated federal employees *more* favorably than investment bankers, lawyers, the military, journalists, and state and local employees but *less* favorably than doctors, teachers, public safety workers, and nonprofit employees (table 1-6).

Government Ranks Poorly on Attributes That Students Find Important

Our survey tested how students viewed the government on specific job criteria that are important to them. We asked students to rank thirty-

TABLE 1-5. Student Attitudes toward Employers

Employer	Percent rating "highly or somewhat favorable"
GE	89
Google	88
Red Cross	81
Marriott	73
State and local government[a]	71[a]
Boeing	70
Military	68
Federal government	68
Department of Homeland Security	55
Wal-Mart	50

Source: Survey of 1,400 college juniors and seniors, 2002 and 2006, conducted for Linda Bilmes and W. Scott Gould by Penn, Schoen and Berland Associates.

a. State and local government employers were viewed less favorably in 2006 than in 2002. In 2006, 75 percent were considered somewhat or highly favorable, compared with 71 percent in 2002.

three specific employment attributes such as "strong pension plan," "casual and fun work environment," "rewards and encourages ethical conduct," and "ability to try new things and think outside the box." We then asked whether this attribute applied more to the government or to

TABLE 1-6. Student Attitudes toward Professions

Profession	Percent rating "very or somewhat favorable"
Teacher	94
Nonprofit employee	89
Doctor	88
Public safety	85
Management consultant	70
Federal government	70
Military	68
State/local government	65
Investment banker	62
Lawyer	55
Journalist	49

Source: See table 1-5.

TABLE 1-7. Student Perception of Valued Job/Employer Attributes
Percent

Attribute	Very important	Applies more to private industry	Applies more to government
Cares about its employees	48	49	8
Opportunity to go high	44	47	10
Work/family balance	44	36	16
Secure future	39	14	55
Co-workers you respect	38	27	4
Free from discrimination	35	17	32
Challenging and interesting work	35	31	13

Source: See table 1-5.

private companies. Next, we asked them to compare the government and the nonprofit sector using these same criteria. We also tested their reaction to specific potential reforms to the government personnel system.

Student responses indicate that the most important attributes drawing them to work for an organization are (in order of importance):

1. The organization really cares about its employees.

2. Employees can go as high in the organization as their talents will take them.

3. The organization respects a balance between work and family life.

4. The organization has a secure and solid future.

5. Coworkers can be respected and admired.

6. Absence of discrimination.

7. The work is challenging.

One-third or more of the sample said that each of these attributes was "extremely important" in their choice of where to work. But for five out of their seven top job criteria—including all of the top three—the students scored the private sector higher than the public sector (table 1-7).

Students said the government offers better job security, a stronger pension plan, and a discrimination-free environment. But in most respects that matter to them, they considered the private sector a better employer. This suggests there is a large gap between what prospective applicants want and what they think the government offers. This can be seen clearly

F I G U R E   1-2. Job Attributes Rated as Important by College Students, Government versus the Private Sector

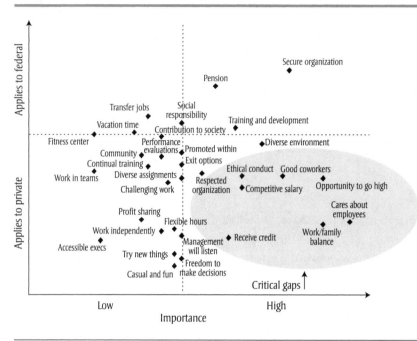

Source: See table 1-5.

in figure 1-2, where the circled gray area shows the difference between what students want and what they identify as advantages of working in the private sector. Students also rated the nonprofit sector higher than the government sector on a variety of attributes, including making a difference and helping the community.

Our results suggest that students prefer to work in the private or nonprofit sectors because they think they will find more of what they want in a job there: a caring employer, a good balance between work and family life, the opportunity to rise to the top of the organization, and smart and capable colleagues. Students believe the private and nonprofit sectors offer greater diversity and higher ethical standards, and greater credit for their contributions. The only important criterion on which the government clearly scores better is job security.

Perhaps not surprisingly for young people, money is a secondary factor in their job selection. Only one in three students says that "competitive salary" is extremely important in choosing an employer, while less than a quarter say that an uncompetitive salary is preventing them from working for the federal government. Student responses were fairly consistent in both the 2002 and 2005–06 surveys, indicating that the attitudes toward government appear to be strongly held and may be difficult to change.

Our findings are consistent with other recent studies, such as those conducted by the Partnership for Public Service (PPS). The PPS survey showed that only 21 percent of mathematics, engineering, and computer science students are "very interested in working for the federal government."[81] Yet, as PPS noted, the federal government is in great need of recruits in engineering and the sciences.

PPS also found that students considering government careers tend to be those with weaker academic records. In the PPS study, 23 percent of students were potentially interested in working for the government, but this group consisted of fewer honors students than average-to-poor students: 25 percent of "B" and "C" students were interested in working for the government, compared with only 20 percent of the "A" students.[82] In line with our findings, student respondents to the PPS study indicated that nonprofit work is the better way to perform public service. Just 19 percent considered government work to be "completely" public service, whereas 30 percent equated nonprofit work with public service and 81 percent with volunteer work.

In another survey of more than 2,000 college students, Paul Light found that students view "public service" as service to others: using phrases like "helping the less fortunate," "helping the community," or "doing your part." When asked to rate specific careers, 58 percent said that working for a nonprofit agency was a form of public service, compared with only 28 percent who said the same about working for government. This was similar to the 23 percent who counted working for a business that serves the government as public service.[83]

Another of PPS's findings is that students pick up some of their negative attitudes toward government service from the media. Of the two-thirds not considering a government career, more than 50 percent agree that "media and politicians project such a negative image of the federal government that I am less likely to work there."[84]

As noted earlier, the students in our survey cited a number of structural problems associated with getting a government job. These included the difficulty of finding out what jobs were available, the difficulty of applying and conducting the application process online, the fact that applications seemed to disappear into a "black hole" because the students seldom received letters of confirmation from the agency, and above all, the length of time required to secure a job offer and to go through security background checking. In all of these situations, students responded that their interest in working for the federal government would rise if the logistical problems were fixed. (For an example of a federal job vacancy announcement, see appendix D.)

Despite a few noble experiments here and there, the federal government's current personnel system remains largely out of date and unequal to the technological and demographic challenges of the twenty-first century. With its unwieldy structure and hiring practices, the system has a long way to go in matching the attractions of employment at Google or GE. A good barometer of the level of these problems can be found in the attitudes of college students. Young people appreciate the importance of the government and, under the right circumstances, about one-third of respondents to surveys would consider working for it. But if it is to hire and keep the best young minds, the government needs to change the way it hires people, and above all the way it treats its workforce.

A New Call to Public Service

Public service is struggling with an explosion in demand and complexity, a lack of leadership, a lack of involvement and attention to skill development, and difficulty in attracting a new generation of talent to replace the one about to retire. The only good news is that the situation is so dire that it will force the country to collectively wake up to the problem. With the old model no longer suitable, what should a new twenty-first-century workforce look like? We envisage a slightly smaller, more prestigious civil service that enjoys wide respect and confidence from the public. This would be a workforce that meets Paul Light's five "tests" of a healthy public service:

—Motivated by the public good, not security or a stable paycheck.

—Recruited from the top of the labor market, not the bottom.

—Given the tools to do its job well.

—Rewarded for a job well done, not for just showing up day after day.

—Trusted by the people it serves.[85]

Restoring the public service to health is an uphill task, but it is well within the power of the nation to accomplish it.

While there are many successful models for driving performance, the one that seems most applicable to the government is the "people factor" strategy. This approach has driven America's most dynamic industries, including those in the technology, information, entertainment, health care, and scientific sectors. As we explain in chapter 2, there is now a substantial body of research to confirm that high returns accrue to firms that are willing to make a serious investment in their workforce.

2

The Power of Strategic Human Capital

Lessons from the Private Sector

There is compelling evidence from the private sector that companies do better—in stock market performance, customer satisfaction, and innovation—when they invest strongly in their workforce. Employees of such "enlightened employers" report much higher levels of job satisfaction and loyalty to their organizations. The established correlation between the level of investment in human capital and organizational performance has profound implications for the federal workforce.

This chapter provides empirical evidence for this correlation drawn from the experience of high-performing organizations that adopted human-capital management techniques to manage and motivate their employees. This "people factor" approach has produced significant, sustained improvement in the financial performance of private sector organizations even during economic downturns. Chapter 3 provides evidence that this approach can work well in government.

Companies have long used human resources policies to gain competitive advantage. In the 1880s, John D. Rockefeller pioneered the linking of a manager's pay to company performance. Rockefeller gave shares (and loans to buy them) to his senior managers. "I would have every man a capitalist," he once remarked. In 1914 Henry Ford broke from his fellow industrialists and doubled the average wages of his assembly-line workers.

Claiming that better-motivated workers made him more money—even at twice the wage—Ford said the pay raise was "the finest cost-cutting move we ever made."[1]

The private sector has devoted substantial resources to people issues over the past thirty years because such investments produce tangible returns. A growing body of research confirms this strong positive link between enlightened employment practices and financial performance. In a landmark 1996 analysis of bank teller performance in separate but comparable branches of a major bank, John Delery and Harold Doty were able to predict 11 percent of stock price variation purely on the basis of the human resources strategies used in the hiring and training of bank tellers.[2] The same year, Theresa Welbourne and Alice Andrews published an analysis of the five-year survival rate of 136 companies that made initial public offerings in 1988. In their study, the companies that emphasized the importance of their people and offered rewards to everyone—not just senior management—survived at a much higher rate than those that did not.[3] Since then, several studies have firmly established the link between organizational performance and investment in human capital. This research has not only established a linkage between the people factor and performance but has also revealed a strong *consensus* about which specific factors help organizations to achieve better results.

Boston Consulting Group GmbH: Enlightened Employers

Research conducted over eight years at the Boston Consulting Group (BCG) by Linda Bilmes, Peter Strüven, and Konrad Wetzker has shown that some of the most successful companies in Germany and the United States are also among the world's most enlightened employers.[4] The authors had set out to study the characteristics of high-performing companies, not to examine human resources. But they stumbled on a surprising trait: all of the top-performing companies had adopted unusually progressive policies toward their employees.

The initial sample consisted of two sets of companies: forty-eight in Germany from ten industrial sectors and thirty-six in the United States from six sectors. To ensure a meaningful comparison, the sectors chosen had to contain a substantial number of publicly traded companies producing similar goods and services.[5] Stockholder return was analyzed over an eight-year period (1989–97) in the United States and a nine-year period (1987–96) in Germany. The research was updated in 2002–03.

The companies were compared along two dimensions: performance in the financial capital markets and human capital characteristics. Relative stock performance was measured by total shareholder return (TSR), which indicates the actual cash value (share price increases + dividends) of an investment.[6] Measuring how a company leverages its employees is a more subjective exercise than calculating TSR, because the necessary information is less readily available, more difficult to collect, and less comparable across firms. To arrive at a set of criteria that could be compared across firms for evaluating how companies treat employees, the authors developed a "people scorecard" by examining high-performing firms and cataloging their activities (see figure 2-1). They then used the scorecard as a yardstick for measuring investment in human capital across industries.

The People Scorecard

Companies that put the "people factor" principle into practice were found to have two distinct characteristics. First, they paid exceptional attention to traditional human resources issues such as recruitment, performance evaluation and feedback, training, and career development. Second, they promoted "intrapreneurship"—that is, they offered workers a degree of autonomy in decisionmaking and scope for individual initiative, reinforced by a reward system.[7] Companies with the highest financial returns provided both traditional human resources (HR) benefits and intrapreneurship. The stock market returns of these companies were three times higher than those of their competitors. Firms that provided only traditional HR benefits (without combining them with intrapreneurship) enjoyed only average returns.

The people scorecard offers a yardstick to rate organizations on specific attributes such as investment in training and education, job security, corporate recognition of the importance of human resources, the quality and size of the traditional human resources package, promotion policies (such as opportunities within an organization), flexibility of work (content of work and hours), flexibility of the organizational structure, lateral

F I G U R E   2-1. The People Factor Scorecard

Human resource criteria		Intrapreneurship criteria	
Staff training and education • Expenditures/days per employee • Career-long training opportunities • Employee-driven curricula	☐	*Flexibility of work structure* • Flexibility in structuring work content • Flexible hours/scheduling	☐
Employer loyalty • Layoffs compared with industry • Strong outplacement efforts	☐	*Organizational structure* • Fewer levels of hierarchy • Prevalence of team structures • Decentralized decisionmaking	☐
Corporate recognition of employees • Breadth, frequency, and consistency	☐	*Versatility of employees* • Lateral transfers within company • Cross-functional exposure and training	☐
Quality of HR policies • Recruiting incentives • Generous benefits • Detailed performance evaluations and feedback • Promotion from within/career development	☐	*Entrepreneurial opportunities* • Recognition of innovation and contribution: awards, bonuses, etc. • Profit-sharing opportunities at business, team unit, or product level • Linkage of compensation to individual performance	☐
Job satisfaction indicators • Employee sick days taken • Employee turnover	☐		
Human resource score	☐	*Intrapreneurship score*	☐

and developmental training opportunities for employees, and recognition and rewards for individual, team, and organizational performance. The scorecard consists of two parts: one part measures traditional HR benefits, the other intrapreneurship. Each criterion was based on the methods of managing and rewarding the workforce at the companies with the highest stock performance in each sector. Although no company was equally outstanding on every characteristic, virtually all companies that were financially successful had very high scores—in relation to their industry peers—on each criterion.

The people scorecard evaluated traditional employee focus in terms of four main benefits:

—Training: expenditure per employee on training, continuing levels of training, training for supervisors and managers.

—Job security: the number of layoffs in relation to the industry average and outplacement efforts to relocate employees who were made redundant.

—Extent to which the corporate philosophy recognizes the contribution of employees and the role of human resources as a strategic partner (as reflected in mission statements, organizational structure, corporate strategic plans, and publications).

—Quality of human resources policies, including recruitment, compensation, benefits, performance evaluations and feedback, career development, mentoring, promotion opportunities, and accessibility of personnel data.

Two additional factors were taken into account to provide a basic "health check" on employee morale, job satisfaction, and attitudes toward the firm:

—Total number of sick-leave days per employee versus the industry average.

—Annual employee job turnover versus the industry average.

The most significant difference between the best-performing companies and the average performers occurred in the area of intrapreneurship. The principles behind this concept—such as flexibility, trust in the judgment of the employee, a culture that supports new ideas and tolerates mistakes, and financial rewards for performance—are easy to observe in "intrapreneurial" companies but difficult to quantify.

Drawing on interviews with companies that foster such an environment, we developed four "proxy" criteria to measure the extent to which companies encouraged this culture of intrapreneurship:

—Flexibility along two dimensions: flexible working hours and arrangements (such as teleworking, job sharing, flextime, paid and unpaid sabbaticals, and "mini-sabbaticals" and work and family flexibilities) and flexibility in structuring work content and assignments.[8]

—Support for the individual within the organizational structure: levels of hierarchy, decentralization of decisionmaking, alignment of incentive structures, and independence of work units.

—Versatility of employees: the opportunity for employees to learn new skills, transfer laterally, and participate in cross-functional teams; and the speed with which the firm can retrain and redeploy workers to meet changing business needs.

—Compensation and financial risk-sharing: the extent to which an employee's compensation is linked to performance as an individual and part of a team, division, region, and company; and incentives, bonuses, prizes, recognition, and rewards linked to performance, innovation, and contribution.

The authors interviewed employees from each company, including managing directors, human resources directors, and financial officers. The authors also conducted roundtable discussions with groups of employees who described what it was like to work in their company. Additional information was drawn from published and unpublished materials related to the companies, including their annual reports, employee newsletters, corporate mission statements, company brochures, recruiting and training materials, and benefits packages. The authors then ranked the human capital practices on the nine people scorecard categories (on a scale of 1 to 10), comparing them with the practices of other firms in the same industry, and produced scorecards for each company, integrating hard data (such as the annual training expenditure per employee and the number of layers of hierarchy in a firm) with the softer data (such as corporate recognition of employees). Each firm was then ranked against the others in its industry cluster and compared with its relative total shareholder return (TSR) for the period.

Financial data for the companies were tallied over periods of one, four, and eight years. *The companies that scored highest on the people scorecard were consistently more successful than the other companies in their industry peer group.* In the eight-year study, those that scored highest had an annual average TSR of 27 percent, compared with 8 percent for the lowest-scoring companies. In each industry sector, the highest-scoring company had a TSR well above the industry average and—in two-thirds of the cases—had the best TSR in its sector. Companies with the worst financial performance always scored lowest or second lowest on the people scorecard. A similar pattern was evident in the four-year study. The relationship between investment in human capital and financial performance can be seen in figures 2-2 and 2-3.

Companies with the highest TSRs focused to an enormous degree on the strategic role of human capital. They treated human capital as a critical

F I G U R E   2-2. TSR of U.S. Companies with Highest versus Lowest People Score

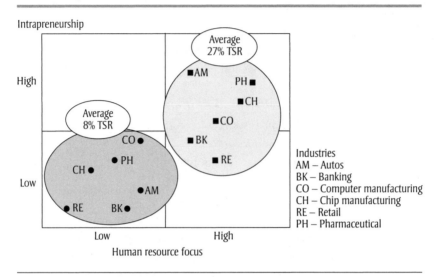

Source: Peter Strüven, Konrad Wetzker, and Linda Bilmes, *Gebt uns das Risiko Zurück: Strategien für mehr Arbeit* (Munich: Carl Hanser Verlag, 1998).

Note: S&P 500 increased 18.7% P.A. in same period (1989–96). Middle cluster (not pictured) had average TSR of 21%.

source of competitive advantage, alongside traditional business priorities such as sales, distribution channels, marketing, costs, suppliers, branding, and financing. This manifested itself in two ways:

—First, *in all cases,* companies with the highest TSRs invested more in training, provided higher salaries and benefits, devoted more attention to recruiting and performance evaluations, and promoted high performers to senior positions more frequently than the industry average.

—Second, companies with the best TSRs provided far greater opportunities for intrapreneurship. This was true across industries. In low-technology industries such as construction, the best companies invested significantly in training their personnel. For example, Bilfinger|Berger, a highly successful German construction and engineering firm with 50,000 employees worldwide, developed a strategy based on intensive training of its workers in a variety of technical skills, sales skills, and languages.[9] This enabled the firm to win contracts across a greater range of project types and in more European countries than its competitors who tried to

F I G U R E   2-3. TSR of German Companies with Highest versus Lowest People Score

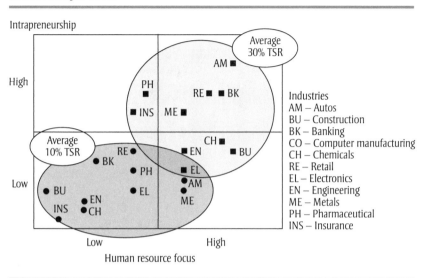

Source: Peter Strüven, Konrad Wetzker, and Linda Bilmes, *Gebt uns das Risiko Zurück: Strategien für mehr Arbeit* (Munich: Carl Hanser Verlag, 1998).
Note: RTSR 1989–96.

compete merely on price. The firm was founded in 1880, and this has been a guiding philosophy ever since. By investing more heavily in its workforce during economic downturns, the company rose from the eighth-largest to the third-largest construction firm in Germany.

In service industries (such as insurance, retailing, and banking) and in technology firms, the highest-performing organizations had impressive strategies for creating intrapreneurship, such as policies that enabled employees to initiate partnerships, to "spin out" successful units within the organization, and to benefit financially from taking risks and instigating new services. For example, at Chiron, the pharmaceutical research company based in Emeryville, California, employees were allowed to initiate partnerships with a handshake. "Instead of losing half a year to draw up legal documents for a venture that might not work out, we wanted our scientists to have the freedom to explore concepts with others around the world. There was plenty of time to formalize the arrangements later on, if needed," according to Rajen Dalal, the company's then vice president.[10] Partly as a result of this intrapreneurial strategy, Chiron discovered the hepatitis C virus and a cure for it and became a leading manufacturer of antiviral vaccines worldwide.

A strategy of intensive training of its 50,000 workers in a variety of technical skills and languages during economic downturns enabled a German firm to win contracts across a wider range of projects than its competitors, who competed merely on price. With this people strategy, the company rose from the eighth-largest to become the third-largest construction firm in Germany.

The companies that invested in a people factor strategy did not simply provide *more benefits*; they had an *entirely different framework* for thinking about human capital. From the chairs of the companies to the line managers, they devoted a great deal of thought and attention to recruiting, educating, retaining, and motivating their employees.

One additional characteristic of these firms—noted but not catalogued by the authors—was their strong leadership. Many of the companies were family-run businesses whose founders had a long-standing commitment to their employees. The publicly quoted firms in the sample also enjoyed strong leadership that put in place a people-centric strategy.

Better Financial Performance Linked to Higher Job Satisfaction

The strong link between investment in people and financial performance raised a classic chicken-and-egg question: were the companies performing better as a result of their investment in human capital, or do successful companies simply invest more in their people?

To examine this question, the BCG authors conducted a survey of 2,000 workers in the United States and Germany.[11] The questionnaire probed whether employees who worked in enlightened companies felt more satisfied with their jobs and more loyal to their companies than those who did not receive such a high level of human capital investment. It was designed to test the hypothesis that people perform better if they are more satisfied, or more loyal, to their organization. Employees were asked to rate twenty-six specific job attributes on the people scorecard in terms of their own experience.[12] These attributes were expressed in statements such as "I have done more than one kind of job in my company,"

"My pay is linked to the company's performance," and "I have received thorough training in all new technologies my company uses." Participants were then asked to rate the importance of these attributes to their satisfaction as an employee. Separately, the responses were cross-tabulated to determine the extent to which overall job satisfaction and loyalty to the employer correlated with the job experiences of the employees.

The survey results indicated that even in the private sector the majority of employees are not receiving a high level of people factor benefits. For example, 83 percent of U.S. respondents said that "working in teams" was very important to them, but only 39 percent said that this described their own work experience. Seventy-one percent rated "influencing decisions that affect me" very important, but only 34 percent reported that they could do so.

However, those working for companies that provide a high level of these people attributes were *significantly* more satisfied with their work and more loyal to their employers. Between 50 and 60 percent of those employees were very satisfied with their jobs—a much higher figure than the median job satisfaction level of 34 percent (figure 2-4). This relationship was evident in both the U.S. and the European companies.

Employees who claimed strong loyalty to their companies were also much more likely to experience high-quality human resources. For example, 70 percent of employees who strongly agreed that "my company makes it easy for me to put my own ideas into practice" were highly loyal to their employers, compared with a median loyalty level of 46 percent (figure 2-5).

The people surveyed wanted to receive credit for their ideas, to be recognized financially for their contribution to the firm, to receive training and feedback on their performance, and to work in a team-based, nonhierarchical, and caring atmosphere. Similarly, government employees and potential recruits who have been surveyed appear motivated by reasonably good pay and interesting work, combined with more intangible things, such as an employer who cares about them and gives them recognition for their ideas.[13]

The attributes that contributed most significantly to the satisfaction and loyalty of employees in our survey included training and performance

F I G U R E   2-4. Investing in the People Factor Increases Job Satisfaction

Overall, 34 percent of corporate employees are "strongly satisfied" with their jobs. However, satisfaction was much higher among those who agreed with these statements.

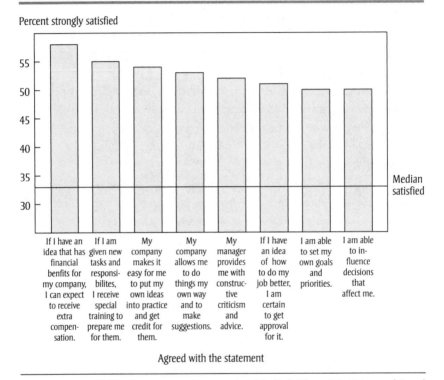

Source: Surveys of 2,250 private sector employees, conducted for Linda Bilmes, Peter Strüven, and Konrad Wetzker and for Linda Bilmes and W. Scott Gould by Penn, Schoen and Berland Associates.

evaluations, as well as the less tangible things related to autonomy and supervision for the employee. As table 2-1 (page 52) shows, those who were very satisfied with their employer experienced the highest degree of the attributes tested. For example, 48 percent of those "very satisfied" with their jobs said they had "freedom to make my own decisions within my job area." By contrast, among those dissatisfied with their jobs, only 23 percent enjoyed this freedom. This pattern is evident across the range of attributes shown in table 2-1.

F I G U R E   2-5.   Investing in the People Factor Increases Loyalty to the Employer

Overall, 46 percent of corporate employees claim to be "strongly loyal" to their companies. However, loyalty was much higher among those who agreed with the following statements.

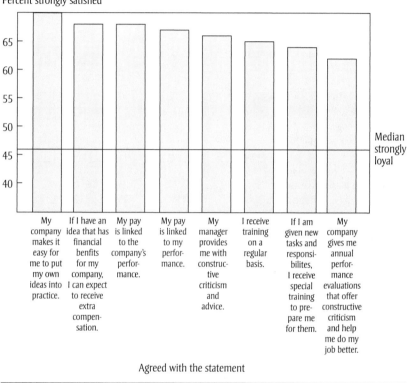

Source: See figure 2-4.

Although the BCG work demonstrated a clear relationship between investment in human capital, financial performance, job satisfaction, and loyalty to the employer, it was unable to prove that financial performance would improve solely by investing in human capital. Since then, however, a growing body of literature has confirmed the positive implications of people investment for organizational and financial performance, as described next.

TABLE 2-1. Job Satisfaction among U.S. Employees versus Degree of Attribute Provided[a]

Percent

Attribute	Dissatisfied[a]	Not very satisfied	Satisfied	Very satisfied
I have freedom to make my own decisions and do things my way within my job area.	23	25	43	48
I am able to influence decisions that affect me.	23	16	34	48
My company makes it easy for me to put my own ideas into practice.	9	15	31	47
If I request it, I can transfer to another part of the company to learn a new skill.	15	28	29	38
I have received thorough training to use all new technology.	21	19	31	48
My pay is linked to my performance (I receive a bonus if my team or I do especially well).	9	15	24	33
My company allows me to do things my own way and to make suggestions.	20	24	36	58
I receive training on a regular basis.	8	25	35	44
My company gives me annual performance evaluations that offer constructive criticism and help me do my job better.	17	21	39	50
Promotion opportunities are clearly spelled out so I know what I need to do in order to be promoted.	16	29	30	47
I feel free to give feedback and suggestions to the boss.	40	46	62	74
My manager gives me constructive criticism and advice on an ongoing basis.	8	18	35	45

Source: See figure 2-4.

a. How to read this table: For example, in the first row, 23 percent of respondents rated as "dissatisfied" said they had "freedom to make my own decisions and do things my way within my job area." By contrast, 48 percent of respondents who rated themselves "very satisfied" said they experienced this freedom.

Watson Wyatt Study: Benefits of Investing in Human Capital

Watson Wyatt, a global human resources consulting firm, has been studying the relationship between financial performance and human capital since 1998. In three seminal studies, the company has found strong evidence that superior human resources practices lead to higher shareholder value.[14] The first study, conducted in 1999, surveyed 400 publicly traded companies in the United States and Canada with a minimum of $100 million in revenues. It identified thirty human resources practices that were associated with a 30 percent increase in market value in the companies studied. Expanding this analysis to European companies in 2000, Watson Wyatt found nineteen human resources practices associated with a 26 percent increase in market value. A year later, the company examined 500 additional North American companies, this time including larger companies with average annual sales of $4.7 billion and more than $8 billion in market value.

Overall, Watson Wyatt found that companies with a higher "human capital index" (HCI) score—a score based on their human resources practices, including pay, people development, communications, and staffing—turned out to have higher shareholder value. The highest HCI scores correlated with an average 64 percent return to shareholders over five years, medium scores with an average 39 percent return, and the lowest scores with only a 21 percent return.

Watson Wyatt found that practices such as an increase in total rewards and accountability, creation of a collegial and flexible workplace, recruiting and retention excellence, strong communications, and excellent use of HR technologies led to expected increases in market value. When they quantified the market impact in relation to the improvement in each practice, they found it was highest in the category of "total rewards and accountability" and equal to a 16.5 percent increase

> *W*atson Wyatt found that organizations that fill positions quickly (in about two weeks) outperformed those that take longer (around seven weeks) by 48 percentage points.

in market value. This category includes a wide range of benefits: health care, defined contribution and benefit plans, pay linked to business strategy, employee choice of benefits, company desire to help poor performers improve, paying employees above market rates, promoting competent employees, and terminating poor performers.

Advances in the category of "creating a flexible and collegial workplace" (which included factors such as supporting flextime and job sharing and trusting in senior leadership) led to a 9 percent increase in market share. This was closely followed by an 8 percent increase in companies with excellent recruiting and retention policies and a 7 percent potential improvement for those with excellent communications skills, easy access to technology, and a propensity to share goals and plans with employees.

Perhaps most important, the study helped resolve the question of whether positive financial results are the by-product of, or the precursor to, better human resources practices. When Watson Wyatt compared two different correlations for fifty-one companies that had participated in the 1999 and 2001 surveys, it found that such practices *lead* to higher financial performance—not the other way around.[15] Watson Wyatt's research also confirms BCG's findings that the approach of "people-focused" companies is fundamentally different from that of other firms: "The best performing companies did not simply have better-funded [human resources] programs, they had entirely different programs than the poorly performing companies."

In its 2005 report, the company again demonstrated that superior human capital practices generate a higher shareholder return and that the positive linkage holds constant regardless of economic and stock market conditions.[16] The report has direct implications for the federal government, particularly with respect to recruiting. Watson Wyatt found that organizations that fill positions quickly (in about two weeks) outperformed those that take longer (around seven weeks) by 48 percentage points. The three-year shareholder return for companies with quick hiring was 59 percent, compared with only 11 percent for the slower companies. The average hiring time in the federal government is eighty-two days—which is nearly twice as slow as the *slow* companies in the Watson Wyatt study. The firm also reported these findings:

—Companies with the highest financial returns fill about half their nonentry-level vacancies internally.

—The highest-performing organizations make substantial distinctions in pay on the basis of performance.

—Firms that had maintained their training budgets during recessions and downturns had a three-year financial return of 54 percent, compared with a 10 percent return for firms that had cut their training budgets.

Pfeffer-O'Reilly: Strong Leadership with Focus on HR Investment

Another leading researcher on this topic, Jeffrey Pfeffer at Stanford Business School, notes that some of the nation's most successful and creative companies deliberately adopted a strategy that rests on developing human capital.[17] Pfeffer and his colleague Charles O'Reilly have argued that the much-publicized war for talent is making it all the more important for organizations to invest in human capital from top to bottom.[18] They point out that "only 10 percent of the organization will be in the top 10 percent" no matter what is done to recruit the best and brightest. Therefore organizations must make it "possible for regular folks to perform as if they were in the top 10 percent."[19]

To learn how highly successful firms in a variety of industries have energized their employees, Pfeffer and O'Reilly studied a number of them—including Southwest Airlines, Men's Wearhouse, New United Motor Manufacturing, and Cisco Systems. They discovered that the firms shared a key characteristic: strong leadership that is intent on treating people well and investing in them. These firms also have many of the attributes described on the people scorecard, including excellent traditional benefits and a high degree of autonomy, scope for creativity, and problem solving by employees. As the authors noted, the difference between a people company and an ordinary one can be intuited:

> Certainly you have worked at, or at least seen, companies that are filled with smart, motivated, hard-working, decent people who nevertheless don't perform very well because the company doesn't let them shine and doesn't really capitalize on their talent and motivation. Maybe you have even worked at such a place yourself and could describe, in agonizing detail, all the myriad things that happened that prevented you and your colleagues from doing your best for the business. What could those places accomplish if they just stopped undermining the performance of their people? And you've seen other places where somehow things just hum, even though the people don't, at first glance, seem to be particularly smarter, nicer or harder-working. Maybe you've even seen companies that have gone from being the first kind of place, where talent is wasted, to the second, where the potential of the company and its people is more fully realized.[20]

Like Pfeffer and O'Reilly, we believe that organizations that "hum" differ greatly from lackluster organizations in both their leadership philosophy and specific practices. Hence it is not sufficient to simply adopt best human resources policies: the most successful organizations also create an environment of intrapreneurship. This has profound implications for government. It is not enough to simply tweak the HR system; the public sector needs to foster a different culture and environment in order to flourish.

Becker and Others: Quantifying Gains through Human Capital Investment

Taking the research one step further, HR experts Brian Becker of Concordia University and Mark Huselid of Rutgers University have helped quantify and measure the extent to which human capital investments produce financial gains. They have shown that a change of one standard deviation in an index of innovative human resources management practices produces increases of $20,000 to $40,000 in stock market value *per employee*.[21] Among the companies Huselid studied, those that were one standard deviation higher in their use of high-performance work practices enjoyed more than $27,000 in increased sales per employee, $18,000 in increased market capitalization, and $3,800 in increased profits, as well as less employee turnover.[22]

Becker and Huselid's research with Dave Ulrich of the University of Michigan proposed a methodology for measuring investment in human resources and its effect on the bottom line. Drawing from a study of 3,000 companies, they identified the differences between the companies with high- and low-quality human resources management (for some examples, see table 2-2).

The body of research by BCG, Pfeffer, Becker and his colleagues, Watson Wyatt, and others reveals fundamental differences between firms that choose to focus on their workforces and those that do not—differences that are not the result of firm size, industry, or age. As Becker states,

> Firms with high-performance work systems adopt HR management practices very different from those adopted by firms with low-performance work systems. They devote considerably more resources to recruiting and selection, they train with much greater vigor, they do a lot more performance management and tie compensation to it, they use teams to a much greater extent, they have roughly double the number of HR professionals per employee, and they are less likely to be unionized. Indeed,

TABLE 2-2. Comparison of Low- and High-Quality Human Resources Management in Best and Worst Companies

Human resources practice	Bottom 10 percent of companies	Top 10 percent of companies
Hours of training for new employees	35.0	116.8
Annual hours of training for experienced employees	13.4	72.0
Percent in a formal HR plan, including recruitment, development, and succession	4.8	46.7
Percent receiving regular performance appraisal	41.3	95.2
Percent whose merit increase or incentive pay is tied to performance	23.4	87.3
Percent routinely working in a self-managed, cross-functional or project team	10.6	42.3
Number of employees per HR professional	253.9	139.5
On a scale of 1 to 5, the extent to which		
Executive leadership team is visionary	3.0	4.3
Top management shows commitment to, and leadership in, knowledge sharing	2.9	4.1
Average employee understands how his or her job contributes to the firm's success	2.8	4.0

Source: Brian E. Becker, Mark A. Huselid, and Dave Ulrich, *The HR Scorecard* (Harvard Business School Press, 2001).

the most striking attribute of these comparisons is not any one HR management practice—it is not recruiting or training or compensation. Rather, the differences are much more comprehensive—and systemic.[23]

The same points appear over and over again in the many studies on human capital: the need for leadership, training, performance management, excellence in HR benefits, and flexible work and organizational structures. Table 2-3 outlines the similarities among the people practices found to yield gains in the studies cited.

Why Isn't the People Factor Used Universally?

Evidence compiled by the Boston Consulting Group and Watson Wyatt over a period of fifteen years clearly indicates that companies perform much better when they invest a great deal in people. Yet few organizations do it. As Strüven, Wetzker, and Bilmes discovered, most CEOs are

TABLE 2-3. Comparison of Requirements for Strategic Human Capital Success

Criteria	Strüven, Wetzker, Bilmes	Watson Wyatt	Pfeffer	Huselid and others
Training and education	X	X	X	X
Job security	X		X	
Quality of human resources practices (performance appraisals, pay/benefits, skills assessment, career development)	X	X	X	X
Leadership		X	X	X
Work flexibility	X	X	X	X
Organizational structure (low hierarchy, teams)	X	X	X	X
Versatile workforce	X	X	X	X
Rewards and recognition tied to performance	X	X	X	X
Communications		X	X	X

content to focus on sales, marketing, finance, distribution channels, brand development, advertising, manufacturing, accounting, pricing, technology, market penetration, customer relationships—in short, everything else—before considering their own employees as a source of sustained competitive advantage.

Becker and his colleagues claim that this is the result of a difference between "leading" and "lagging" indicators: when a company decides to invest in human capital, there is a lag between cause and effect. Changes in HR may have a great impact, but it is less obvious than that of more direct short-term actions (such as cutting costs). Since the HR effect is difficult to identify and measure, CEOs tend to ignore it in their attempts to improve performance.

> Problems in financial performance get everyone's attention, but no one thinks about how HR can help. Nevertheless, because HR drivers are so foundational, small changes in how they're managed gather momentum as they work their way through the strategy implementation process. For example, at Sears, a mere 4 percent increase in employee satisfaction reverberated through the profit chain, eventually lifting market capitalization by nearly $250 million.[24]

Another impediment to widespread adoption of the people factor is that until recently it was hard to measure the link between performance and investment in human capital. Nowhere is this attitude more pronounced than in government. "In the Department of Defense, the attitude is that a dollar spent on technology is an *investment*, whereas a dollar spent on people is an *expense*," says Jeffrey Neal, chief human capital officer at the Defense Logistics Agency (DLA). "I tell people, 'We have a billion-dollar asset—the only asset we have—the 22,000 people that work for us. We absolutely positively need to invest in it.'"[25]

Although the academic literature has only recently focused on ways of measuring this relationship, some of the world's best companies have been working on this type of calculation for a long time. In the 1950s, General Electric developed an "employee relations index" based on eight indicators of employee behaviors such as absenteeism, grievances, work stoppages, and terminations.[26] Many companies conduct employee attitude surveys and attempt to link them to organizational performance. The range of techniques that have been tried includes HR auditing, HR management by objectives, and competitive benchmarking. Becker and his colleagues also offer suggestions for designing a company-specific "HR scorecard" that would enable organizations to better align their HR practices with their strategy.[27]

A detailed process for measuring return on HR investment proposed by Jack Phillips, Ron Stone, and Patricia Phillips monetizes the benefits of specific HR programs such as those designed to reduce turnover rates or lower the number of grievances filed. These are then compared with the actual cost of the programs.[28]

Another approach has been to incorporate the measurement of human capital into the "balanced scorecard."[29] First developed by Robert Kaplan and David Norton in 1992, the balanced scorecard methodology swept the business world and has been successfully adapted for use by nonprofit and governmental organizations. In essence, it creates a "dashboard" that allows managers to integrate financial and nonfinancial metrics in managing an organization. According to Norton, the scorecard's weakest link is its inability to measure human resources; however, recent work by Huselid, Becker, and Richard Beatty has provided a system for measuring the quality of people systems within the framework of the balanced scorecard.[30] This method holds substantial promise for use in the government.

Conclusions

According to state-of-the-art thinking, organizations that invest in their employees perform better and have more contented and dedicated work-forces. There is a clear correlation between investment in employees and corporate performance. The relationship is bidirectional: successful com-panies do invest more in their people, and companies that invest in their people become more successful. Most high-performing organizations have developed best practices in human resources management—practices that have largely passed government by.

We identified two federal agencies that have been able to adopt the full-fledged people factor approach: the Defense Logistics Agency (DLA) and the Government Accountability Office (GAO). Until recently, neither agency would have scored very highly on anybody's people scorecard. Yet, between 2000 and 2006, the DLA improved its performance and morale dramatically—while simultaneously reducing costs—by focusing on its people. This transformation (see chapter 3) has been largely due to a huge investment in training and strong leadership from the top. The GAO has worked to transform itself almost beyond recognition, and in doing so has saved taxpayers hundreds of millions of dollars. Under the leadership of David Walker, the GAO made strategic human capital the cornerstone of the agency. While this process has been facilitated by a series of increasing flexibilities granted by Congress, it has also become a self-fulfilling prophecy; the best and brightest young people have flocked to join the agency because of its "people factor" culture.

What the GAO and DLA have in common—despite vast differences in their mission and types of employees—is that both *invested in people* to revitalize their organizations and boosted their levels of performance higher than even they themselves anticipated. In many respects, the two offer a good model for other federal departments, most of which bear striking similarities to the DLA and GAO prior to their reforms. It is time for the rest of the government to catch up.

3

The People Factor
in Government

The people factor approach to management has produced financial benefits in the private sector by making every worker feel valued and by recognizing his or her contribution to the success of the enterprise. Organizations that adopt this strategy tailor their management systems—the way they recruit, train, evaluate, compensate, reward, lead, and promote employees—to the individual worker and the specific type of job.

Our research sought to answer several related questions about the people factor:

First, does this model of management work equally well in governmental organizations? Given the many differences between for-profit and nonprofit organizations, we can intuit that the model needs some adaptation in order to be used successfully in the nonprofit world. Therefore it is instructive to look at organizations that have applied similar formulas to see if the people-centric philosophy appears to work whether or not the organization is a for-profit enterprise.

Second, can the impact of the model be measured? In other words, is there a way to judge whether a "people focus" produces the same amount of improvement in the public sector as in for-profit organizations, where performance is easier to measure?

Third, what would be the impact of making public sector organizations perform at the highest possible level? If the public sector made a significant investment in its workforce and adopted a modified version of a "people-focused" model, how can one project whether the federal government would produce concrete benefits for the taxpayer in terms of productivity, performance, cost efficiency, reduction of waste and errors, and intangible benefits such as courtesy and ethical practices?

Fourth, would the government become a more appealing employer to young people if it were a better place to work? In other words, would college students be more eager to accept a job with the federal government if it adopted some of the features that students valued most highly (such as making job offers more quickly and allowing employees to move between sectors during their careers)? We used the student survey data to learn about the attitudes and preferences of those the government wishes to hire.

We explored the first and second questions using employee surveys and case studies. We compared our survey of private sector employees with studies of motivation and job satisfaction in the government. We then examined two government organizations that have adopted a "people-focused" management system, evaluating them as we did private sector firms, by using the people scorecard to measure their level of human capital investment before they had implemented the philosophy and five years after adopting it. We also measured the performance of these government organizations.

Low Level of Government Investment in Human Capital

Even a cursory review of government agencies suggests that they treat their employees in ways that are very different from—sometimes nearly the opposite of—the people-focused model. Of course, departments and agencies vary in their management style, and some government offices have already introduced a people-focused culture. But on average, the typical government agency concentrates on its mission; it devotes little time and budget to training, mentoring, monitoring, and developing its workforce (see table 3-1). Employees carry out the mission according to certain rules and procedures, performing essentially fixed assignments for fixed pay. By contrast, leading people factor companies believe they can

TABLE 3-1. **People-Focused Company Compared with Typical U.S. Government Agency**

People-focused company	Typical government agency
• Flexible.	• Inflexible.
• Generous HR benefits; highly flexible; often include wide range of benefits.	• HR benefits inflexible; not competitive in some occupations.
• Frequent training and skills development for all levels, especially managers; large departments and budgets dedicated to training.	• Little training; sporadic; inconsistent across agencies, occupations, and levels; low training budgets.
• Pay linked to performance and benchmarked to competitors; often includes stock options, bonuses linked to firmwide performance.	• Most pay fixed to classification system; limited experience with setting criteria for performance-based pay; no financial benefits if the agency performs well; bonuses often not related to performance.
• Additional recognition for achievement; promotions and perks usually linked to achievement.	• Few meaningful avenues of credit and recognition.
• Innovation and risk-taking rewarded; acceptance that sometimes a new idea will not work.	• Innovation and risk-taking discouraged; low tolerance for mistakes.
• Flat organizational structure.	• Extremely hierarchical in most agencies.
• Detailed performance evaluation, with training for evaluators; long time-consuming process in which managers are required to do it properly.	• Perfunctory performance evaluations in many agencies; little training of managers/ evaluators.
• System accommodates individual needs and variety.	• One size fits all; limited variety.
• Company philosophy: caring about employees makes good business sense, and satisfied employees produce higher revenues.	• Culture focused on mission, not employees.
• Versatile workforce; many employees trained in multiple jobs.	• Narrow job classification; stove-piped workforce.
• Career development aligned with long-term strategic planning; employee training and assessment linked to firm's long-term plans.	• Little career development; decoupled from strategic plans; employees' priorities often shift with change in administrations.

achieve their corporate goals more effectively if they invest a great deal in their employees and allow them some leeway in deciding how the mission is to be accomplished.

Efforts to Achieve Human Capital Improvements

Companies that have used a "people strategy" to achieve high performance have made an investment over a long period of time. They have invested management time, focus, energy, money, and political acumen to figure out—sometimes by trial and error—how to recruit, train, deploy, and motivate a workforce to achieve their strategy. Their tool kit covers a wide range of actions, from reconfiguring workspace to experimenting with different models to balance work and family life.

Successive administrations and individuals in virtually every government agency have made numerous efforts to improve the quality of people management. There is no question that many agencies have taken these efforts seriously and tried to fix specific problems. Scattered throughout government are success stories that have led to better performance. These are described in part II of this book. But apart from pockets of reform here and there, true reform of the civil service has been elusive. (See our testimony regarding the Working for America Act at www.brookings.edu/~/media/Files/Press.Books/2009/peoplefactor/appendixes.pdf.)

The statutory reforms introduced at the Departments of Defense and Homeland Security were the most significant such attempt in recent years. They provided sweeping opportunities to change the way employees are compensated, categorized, motivated, and organized. But the reforms became bogged down, not only because of technical flaws, but also because they were promoted as an "HR fix," rather than as a *fundamental shift* in how the government views the people who do its work.

One of the challenges in studying investment in human capital is that many organizations claim to make people their highest priority, yet few succeed. Although most companies pay lip service to their employees, on close examination they seldom place employees at the core of their operation. Few companies embrace the people factor philosophy fully—despite the well-documented benefits of doing so. Likewise, most government organizations say that their employees are their most important asset, but few really treat them as such.

Two agencies that have brought fundamental change to their workforce are the Defense Logistics Agency (DLA) and the Government Accountability Office (GAO). In recent years, the GAO and DLA have instigated the kind of total transformation that we advocate. Both agencies have been led by visionary leaders who revamped their human resources systems and created a more entrepreneurial atmosphere. In both cases, the return on taxpayer investment has risen dramatically since they began their transformations.

Defense Logistics Agency

The Defense Logistics Agency (DLA), headquartered at Fort Belvoir, Virginia, is a branch of the Department of Defense (DOD) that provides logistical support to the U.S. military. It has 21,000 civilian employees (plus 600 military employees) operating in forty-eight states and twenty-eight overseas locations. The workforce includes a large number of technical and blue-collar workers and is highly unionized. The DLA is funded through customer fees, not by congressional appropriation.

The DLA is a massive organization. It procures 100 percent of the food, fuel, medical supplies, clothing, and construction equipment for the U.S. military; provides 95 percent of the repair parts for more than 1,000 weapons systems; and disposes of hazardous materials.[1] It also sells supplies to 124 other countries. The agency provides a wide range of logistical, technical, and acquisition services, including materiel management, warehousing and distribution, procurement, and reutilization of surplus supplies. This is a complex process that involves purchasing the items, storing them, managing their inventory, transporting and delivering them all over the world, and then billing the DLA's customers for its services.

In fiscal 2006, the agency handled sales and services worth $35 billion, an amount that has been growing by 15 percent a year since 2001.[2] *Every day*, DLA employees must process (on average) 54,000 requisitions and close to 8,200 contracts in twenty-six distribution depots.[3] The DLA stocks, stores, and delivers a staggering list of 5.2 million individual items—everything from body armor to dental supplies, from jet fuel to fresh fruits and vegetables.[4] (By comparison, a typical Wal-Mart Superstore handles about 100,000 items.)[5] If the DLA were a Fortune 500 company, it would be about number 50, alongside Intel, Walt Disney, and Nextel.

From 2001 to 2007, the DLA was led by Vice Admiral Keith Lippert, former commander of Navy Supply Systems. Under his leadership, the agency more than doubled its volume of business, from $17 billion to $35 billion (table 3-2). At the same time, it cut operating costs from 25 percent to 14 percent of sales and reduced back orders by 29 percent.[6] Even taking economies of scale into account, DLA cost-cutting has saved taxpayers about $4 billion. Equally striking, customer satisfaction has

TABLE 3-2. DLA Performance, 2001 and 2006

Performance statistic	2001	2006
Sales	$17 billion	$35 billion
Number of employees	23,000	20,805
Cost as percent of sales	25%	14%
Back orders, aviation, land, and maritime	400,000	275,000
Percent customer satisfaction (very satisfied or satisfied)	n.a.	89
Days to hire a new employee	111	54
Cost per personnel transaction	$936	$669
Ranking on PPS "best places to work"	Middle third	Top third

Sources: Interviews with Jeff Neal and DLA; and PPS, "Best Places to Work in the Federal Government."
n.a. Not available, because customer satisfaction was not tracked in 2001.

reached an all-time high. Eighty-nine percent of the DLA's customers in the U.S. military report they are "satisfied" or "very satisfied," and only 1 percent say they are "dissatisfied."[7]

Employee job satisfaction has risen as well, and job turnover has declined, dropping to as low as 2 percent in many locations. According to the Partnership for Public Service (PPS) annual "Best Places to Work in the Federal Government" survey, the DLA's rating in this regard increased 18.9 percent from 2003 to 2006 and was significantly higher than the DOD average.[8] It improved across eight of ten areas, including training/development, teamwork, work/life balance, performance-based rewards and advancement, family-friendly culture/benefits, effective leadership, and employee skills/mission match.

This remarkable performance is due primarily to the DLA's relentless focus on human capital. "What we discovered," according to Jeffrey Neal, director of the agency's human resources, "is that customer satisfaction and employee satisfaction are two sides of the same coin. Our employees derive a great deal of satisfaction from providing excellent service to our customers. So what we have done, essentially, is give them the tools, training, and flexibility so they can be responsive to our customers."[9]

An Agency with an Unusual Background

The DLA was set up in 1962 as the Defense Supply Agency (DSA) under Secretary of Defense Robert McNamara.[10] Its mission was to purchase, store, and distribute all the "consumable" items used by the military. These ranged from helicopter blades to medical supplies to breakfast cereals.[11] The DSA was also made responsible for managing the Federal Supply Catalog and for disposing of surplus military materiel.[12] McNamara's objective was to realize savings both in the price of items (by purchasing them in larger volumes) and in efficiency (by reducing overlap and inefficiency among the four services). The agency has supported every major war and contingency operation of the past four decades, including those in Vietnam, Bosnia, Kosovo, the Persian Gulf (in 1991), and Iraq and Afghanistan (currently). It also supports the U.S. military and other nations in humanitarian missions.

> "*C*ustomer satisfaction and employee satisfaction are two sides of the same coin. Our employees derive a great deal of satisfaction from providing excellent service to our customers. So what we have done, essentially, is give them the tools, training, and flexibility so they can be responsive to our customers." —Jeffrey Neal, DLA

Over the years, the DSA absorbed numerous additional duties. It became responsible for the purchase and distribution of all food and fuel supplies for the military and then for the disposal of surplus military materiel overseas, as well as at home. In addition, the Defense Contract Administration Services, which managed most DOD contracts after they had been awarded, was reorganized under the DSA umbrella. In 1977 the DSA was renamed the Defense Logistics Agency. By 1990 it had grown into a huge organization, with a budget of $13 billion and more than 62,000 employees with about 60 percent on the supply-and-distribution side.

In 1992 the DOD changed the way it funded the DLA.[13] Instead of receiving an appropriation, the agency had to recover the costs of its headquarters operation as well as of the buying, storing, and distribution of its goods through the sale of the items. Under the new system, all the money was appropriated to the users, who would then buy their goods from the DLA. "The new system," according to then DLA general counsel Karl Kabeiseman, "focused you on the customer very quickly."[14]

By 2001, however, the DLA was facing numerous challenges. Under the new system, it was forced to operate more like a business. Its customers could purchase many items elsewhere if they did not like the prices the DLA charged or the service it provided. By this time, the Defense Contract Management Agency (with its 13,000 employees) had been removed from the DLA, but that still left more than 24,000 employees at DLA supply centers and distribution depots. According to a PPS study, "During the 1990s, DLA did slip. The organization's decentralized structure contributed to higher costs and created growing concern that customers would demonstrate their dissatisfaction by shopping elsewhere."[15] The agency also faced high employee turnover, a growing backlog of orders, and a high cost of operations as a percentage of its sales.

People Reform at DLA

In 2001 the DLA embarked on a radical program to transform itself. No part of the organization was untouched: it introduced global stock positioning, reorganized its warehouses, and created a single point of entry for data processing. In particular, the agency began a massive business systems modernization project to replace dozens of legacy systems, many designed in the 1960s, with modern commercial off-the-shelf software and hardware to improve order filling, planning, procurements, financial tracking, and inventory management. The agency had tried on five previous occasions to replace its outdated systems. The sixth attempt—led by then DLA director Vice Admiral Keith Lippert—marked the first time it succeeded. The successful effort has been recognized in numerous awards.[16]

To bring about this business transformation, Admiral Lippert adopted an explicit people factor strategy. This would prove to be the primary mechanism for improving DLA's supplier and customer relationships. The strategy consisted of two main elements. First, the agency increased the responsibility and influence of the HR function, asking it to design ways to link employee performance to the agency's mission. Second, the DLA established a number of specific initiatives to provide training, education, feedback, evaluation, performance management, and recognition of employee contributions. This had to be accomplished within an agency that was highly unionized, geographically dispersed, and operating under Title V. When Vice Admiral Lippert retired in 2007, the new director, Army Lieutenant General Robert Dail, explicitly endorsed continuance of the agency's people-focused strategy, making leadership one of four focus areas. According to the Partnership for Public Service (PPS):

At the heart of the change was a whole new way of managing people. To successfully change the performance of 21,000 people requires world-class human capital practices and a first-class human resources function. The Human Resources Office served as a catalyst and model for change within DLA. Prior to the transformation effort, the HR function suffered from all the same symptoms as the rest of the organization. It was fragmented and not effectively focused on customer service and cost effectiveness. The activities of HR were devoted to transaction activities and not in meeting the strategic business needs of the organization.[17]

HR Function Split into Two Divisions: Strategy and Operations

Companies that have used a people strategy to drive change are known to elevate the HR function to the top of the organization, giving it a central role in the strategic decisions of the firm. The DLA hired Jeffrey Neal, a visionary HR professional, to be a full strategic partner in the reshaping of the agency. Neal brought with him a wide range of experience in personnel and technology, having served as both deputy director of HR and deputy chief information officer at the U.S. Department of Commerce, in addition to previous HR experience in the U.S. Navy. He immediately recognized that the DLA would need to focus on several strategic human capital problems, including planning for workforce retirements, retraining employees to use new technology, developing leadership skills, and creating a more customer-focused culture.[18]

Neal devised an innovative approach to running the HR function. To separate the strategic needs from the day-to-day requirements of processing HR needs, he organized the HR office into two divisions: one to serve as a "think tank" to handle strategic planning and new initiatives, the other to handle operational services and transactions. The strategic planning team was able to step back from day-to-day operations to focus on critical areas such as workforce planning, skills acquisition, and cultural transformation within existing personnel law. The operational team was subdivided into two further groups: one focused on staffing, classification, and information technology, and the other focused on labor and employee relations.

The empowered HR team quickly introduced improvements throughout the organization, making it more efficient, innovative, and strategic:

—*Hiring.* By automating the merit promotion program, the DLA was able to reduce the time it needed to fill vacant positions from 111 days to 54 days.

—*Innovation.* It developed a new concept, the "electronic official personnel folder," an automated system that allows employees, supervisors, and HR personnel to access personnel records easily and within existing privacy laws. The Office of Personnel Management (OPM) subsequently asked the DLA's vendor to offer the same service government-wide.

—*Streamlined HR transactions.* The agency consolidated HR operations from seven to two centers, thereby achieving significant gains in efficiency and cost reductions. This effort reduced full-time-equivalent (FTE) HR staff by 28.5 percent with minimal reductions in force (RIFs). It also reduced annual HR transaction costs per employee from $936 to $669.[19]

Under the direct guidance of Jeffrey Neal, the strategy group looked for the best workplace practices in both the public and private sectors to introduce to DLA. The result was a "workforce transformation to alter every facet of the environment."[20] It defined this as a "portfolio of strategic initiatives addressing critical human resources issues facing the Agency . . . designed to make DLA a more customer-focused, world-class, employer of choice."[21] The workforce transformation encompassed every facet of human capital development, including skills development, workforce planning, teleworking, work/family balance, efforts to become a "model workplace," performance appraisals, management, and recognition. And it consisted of a vast array of initiatives implemented vigorously:[22]

—*Competency assessment and management tool (CAMT).* DLA introduced this tool to ensure that the agency has the right skills mix. It enables the agency to identify the required competencies in a specific job series, assess employee and supervisor skills, and analyze whether there is a gap.

—*Enterprise leader development program (ELDP).* The agency launched a program to develop leadership skills throughout the agency, both among current leaders and those who may be promoted into leadership positions in the future. It provides individually tailored training for different levels of supervisors, using tools such as feedback, videotaping, and education. A Partnership for Public Service study highlights the agency's ELDP as a model for the federal government.

—*Climate survey.* DLA designed its own tool to measure the morale and job satisfaction of employees. It also measured metrics related to the strategic plan and balanced scorecard that it had put in place.

—*Culture survey.* One of the agency's most innovative initiatives was a survey based on the Denison Culture Survey.[23] It provides a baseline assessment of current cultural strengths and weaknesses based on 1,000 high-performing organizations. Its purpose is to shed light on the role of cultural elements in supporting or hindering an organization's performance in areas such as sales/revenue growth, market share, quality, innovation, and employee satisfaction. The results are then used to develop individual leaders who can support and sustain the desired benchmarked culture. On the basis of the four cultural traits found to have a significant impact on performance, the DLA organized a group of "culture champions" to address culture issues in the agency.

—*Multisource feedback (MSF).* To provide each DLA supervisor with comprehensive and anonymous feedback, the agency introduced a questionnaire for obtaining "360-degree feedback" from peers, employees, and supervisors.

—*New performance appraisals.* The DLA implemented a completely new performance management system that sets clear expectations, provides managerial support, and links individual performance to the organization's mission and strategic goals. To this end, it shifts the focus of the performance appraisal from a single event (the annual rating) to an ongoing year-round process. In addition, performance appraisal was reshaped so that it would be viewed as a positive experience for the supervisor and the employee and be linked to concrete steps that would help the employee develop new skills and thus achieve more.

—*Web-based exit survey.* DLA set up an automated exit survey to collect information on employee reasons for leaving the agency. This feedback is used to develop strategies to make the DLA an "employer of first choice" and to improve employee retention.

—*Workforce shaping plan.* The agency adopted an agency-wide plan for developing employees with the needed competencies, and it links up with the curriculum plan for training.

—*Model workplace standards.* A common feature of companies that score high on the "best places to work" surveys is attention to the quality of the workspace. Unique in this regard, the DLA has instituted a program to set standards; to improve "cube etiquette," air and water quality, and ergonomic design of space; and to provide lactation rooms for mothers who are nursing, and meditation rooms for quiet thinking or prayer.

—*Executive development plan.* The agency created a training program to groom high-potential employees for leadership positions, and to provide them with specific development plans and opportunities.

—*"Ninth House."* The DLA began an e-learning training program from the Ninth House Network to help senior employees build their business and communication skills. The program offers seven modules with interactive instruction from world-class instructors. This is available to all senior employees.

> "*I*t is impossible to manage if you don't deal with the problem of poor performers. They are demotivating to other employees. You can train, coach, or put them in a job that is more suited to them. But at the end of the day, if those things don't work, you need to get them gone. The unions are essential to make this happen."
> —*Jeffrey Neal*

Labor Relations

In contrast to the adversarial relationship that existed between the DOD and employee unions during the development of the National Security Personnel System (NSPS), the relationship between the DLA and its unions has been constructive, and the unions have been key facilitators of the agency's human capital reforms.[24] More than 75 percent of its workforce belongs to a union, and about 15,000 employees are members of the American Federation of Government Employees (AFGE), which was opposed to NSPS at the DOD.

The HR department conducts quarterly meetings with union officials, each lasting three days. "Basically, we share a lot of information," says Neal. "We keep our lines of communication open, even when we don't agree. We have built a relationship that is based on trust. When there is basic trust, there is basic common ground."[25] This relationship has provided an environment in which DLA has been able to restructure its workforce, close field offices, downsize the depot workforce, grant more flexibility to individual managers, require training for large segments of the workforce, and improve its handling of poor performers. "It is impossible to manage if you don't deal with the problem of poor performers. They are demotivating to other employees. You can train, coach, or put them in a job that is more suited to them. But at the end of the day, if those things don't work, you need to get them gone. The unions are essential to make this happen."

Rating on the People Scorecard

We evaluated the DLA on the same criteria that we used to measure investment in human capital in the private sector. The scores are based on our analysis, research, and interviews with DLA employees. On this yardstick, the DLA has significantly improved its score on each criterion and would now rank as a high-performing people factor organization (see table 3-3).

According to Jeffrey Neal, "the so-called 'soft' skills are really the hard skills. They are part of the ethical requirement of being a good supervisor." The DLA's ability to master the "softer" management skills has enabled the agency to make significant progress toward achieving excellence in human resources in all dimensions.

Training

Before the transformation, the agency provided little training to its employees. This was where Admiral Lippert and Jeffrey Neal saw the greatest potential for change. Both men had backgrounds in the military, which invests heavily in training. They invested in a multitude of state-of-the art training programs covering leadership and supervisory skills, commercial supply and inventory management, business systems modernization, and other subjects for the DLA.

The cornerstone of the transformation effort was the leadership training, which consisted of a five-tier program for all those with the potential to become supervisors (tier 1), current supervisors (tier 2), managers (tiers 3 and 4), and senior executives (tier 5). The tier-2 training, for example, is a two-year program comprised of classroom education, field experience, coaching, and training in the "soft skills" (such as disciplining poor

TABLE 3-3. DLA's People Factor Scorecard, Human Resources, 2001 and 2006[a]

Human resource criteria	2001		2006	
	System	Score	System	Score
Staff training and education	Small amount of poor quality training, not linked to strategic objectives	3	Training for GS-9, -11, -12s in commercial supply; training for business systems modernization, leadership, supervision, coaching; continuous learning	8
Employer loyalty	"We used to give new people a pile of forms, copied crooked"	4–5	Downsized by aggressively outplacing; model workplace; free fitness centers; provides good-quality information to new hires	9
Corporate recognition of employees	Average	5	Greater focus on results-oriented recognition; greater recognition within agency that "we have 21,000 assets who walk home at night"	7–8
Quality of HR policies	Slow, expensive, inefficient; hiring takes 114 days	2	Efficient hiring (56 days); excellent service focused on benefits to agency; detailed performance appraisal system; career guidance and development	10
Job satisfaction	Low	4	Survey of job satisfaction every 18 months; benchmark against best organizations (Denison survey); entrance and exit surveys; satisfaction higher on all 12 factors tested	7–8
Other indicators	High turnover	5	Turnover reduced to 2 percent	8
Human resource score		23.5		50

Source: See table 3-2.
a. Scale: 1 (low) to 10 (high).

performers and providing feedback). The tier-3 training for managers includes role playing in giving performance feedback, using videotapes and a coach. Neal says, "The coach advises them how to do it better. Giving feedback is the hardest thing to do, but it's part of the ethical requirement of being a supervisor. If I can't tell you why you're not doing a good job, then I'm not doing a good job."

The DLA spends about $25 million a year for employee training. Leadership training programs cost less than $1 million a year. This cost is offset by the savings achieved, which includes $6 million annual direct savings in the HR function and an estimated $4 billion in savings passed on to customers, which in turn has boosted sales.

Training dollars are still a battle. The agency spent $700 million on its business systems modernization during 2001–07, says Neal, but only 2 percent of that went into training for the people who use it: "I have to fight for every dollar of training budget, even here."

Employer Loyalty

Part of the reform effort has been to demonstrate a commitment to employees, a critical factor in recruiting talent. In our college survey, students considered "caring about the individual" as the most important attribute of employers and rated the government poorly in that regard when compared with the private sector. The DLA has made significant progress here.

"We used to give new people a pile of forms, copied crooked," Neal says. "Today, new hires receive good-quality information in a canvas briefcase with the DLA seal, with a copy of our Strategic Plan and Balanced Scorecard." Furthermore, as noted in table 3-2, the DLA downsized from 23,000 to about 21,000 with a minimum number of RIFs. For those who were laid off, the agency used outplacement programs to help them find new jobs. The agency has also made significant progress in providing employee amenities such as free fitness centers, accredited childcare centers, and clean, environmentally attractive workspaces.

Corporate Recognition

Like most agencies in the Defense Department, the DLA had a strong sense of mission and used the normal methods of recognizing employee performance. But under the new system, recognition is more directly linked to specific results tied to the strategy. "We are a collection of 21,000 assets who walk home at night," says Neal. "The new recognition policy better reflects this basic fact."

HR Policies

The DLA transformation has focused to a large extent on raising the status and role of the HR department and changing HR policies. Neal has promoted his reforms as "business initiatives," because "people things are regarded as squishy, touchy-feely things." In addition to separating HR into strategic and operational groups, Neal focused on reducing the time to hire. "We hire 1,000–1,500 employees every year. This used to take months. Now, from the recruiting visit to offer-in-hand, it takes fifty-four days." Many job descriptions throughout the organization have been rewritten to more accurately capture the skills and competencies the DLA requires.

Among its other major HR accomplishments, the agency reformed its performance appraisal system, launched a 600-person internship program, and made significant improvements in benefits related to the work/family balance and the workplace. It has also devoted a large amount of time and effort to working with union representatives throughout the HR reforms. Although its salary structures and benefits remain under the constraints of the civil service system, the cooperation and communication between the DLA and its unions suggest that both would be able to reach agreement on these larger issues as well, if the agency were granted further flexibilities.

Job Satisfaction

While many organizations monitor job satisfaction, the DLA has gone several steps further in its numerous surveys to measure its progress in this area. To facilitate teleworking for employees who desire it, for example, the agency did not simply ask how many people participated in telework, but instead designed a survey to provide more accurate indication of bottlenecks that impede the use of teleworking. Another innovation has been the use of entrance surveys "to find out why people want to work for us" and exit surveys "to find out why they left." All of the resulting information is digested by the strategic unit of the HR department and used as the basis to design new initiatives.

Intrapreneurship

DLA made significant progress not only in the HR characteristics of the organization, where HR scores increased more than 200 percent during the six-year period, but also in the level of intrapreneurship. Intrapreneurship is an expression of the ability and authority employees have to innovate within an established organization. It can be gauged by several

TABLE 3-4.   DLA's People Factor Scorecard, Intrapreneurship 2000 and 2006[a]

Intrapreneurship criteria	2000		2006	
	System	*Score*	*System*	*Score*
Flexibility of work structure	"30-year-old homegrown system ready to collapse"	3	Reengineered business process; written new job descriptions; training for all jobs	7
Organizational structure	Legacy	3	Common metrics and guidelines	6–7
Versatility of employees	Average	5	More specialization because of business modernization; over time can unspecialize them	5
Entrepreneurial opportunities	Average to good	5	Leadership training required; need to demonstrate proficiency before taking any kind of supervisory job	9
Intrapraneurship score		22		33.5

Source: See table 3-2.
a. Scale: 1 (low) to 10 (high).

measures. Here we measured flexibility of work structure, organizational structure, versatility of employees, entrepreneurial opportunities, and leadership. As table 3-4 shows, DLA's reforms in this area produced a less dramatic but still significant increase of 50 percent over six years. Efforts to improve intrapreneurship were hindered by the lack of statutory flexibility. But given its role as a government agency within the military, the DLA cannot be expected to transform itself across all the intrapreneurship criteria.

The DLA also introduced two other important changes: it made work more flexible, and it restructured the organization into a more streamlined and transparent entity. Despite the constraints of the government's job classification system, the agency was able to redefine numerous job positions to bring them in line with its strategic needs.

DLA Summary

The DLA improved its performance across most people factor dimensions by adopting an aggressive people-focused strategy. This required the agency to invest heavily in training and to reengineer or redesign processes that were not working (such as the hiring process). Above all, the effort required strong leadership from the top. Admiral Lippert made a number of difficult decisions, such as closing some of the field offices and vesting greater authority in the human resources department. But his steadfast commitment to change, and his support for Jeffrey Neal and his team, enabled the organization to reach new levels of performance.

This is not to say that the DLA faces no problems. Despite its overall success, the agency has been investigated by its inspector general for allegedly overpaying for certain items, including ice cube trays. This incident was widely reported in the media and led to a congressional hearing in which Admiral Lippert was forced to explain why a DLA refrigerator cost more than one from Best Buy—the latter being theatrically rolled into the hearing room as an exhibit.[26]

We deplore an environment in which even an agency that has delivered radically better results for the taxpayer is lambasted for a small number of mistakes. This tendency, as noted by Harvard professor Steve Kelman, poses a significant risk to better management of the public sector. Concerning the general efforts to improve public management in recent years, Kelman says:

> Media coverage of public-sector management is no different from what it was before the performance turn occurred: it continues to be dominated by the same themes traditionally characterizing it—corruption, dishonesty, and "waste, fraud and abuse." . . . [O]ne may see the persistence of performance improvement efforts among public management practitioners as a tribute to the mission identification and public spirit of career public employees, because there has been precious little encouragement from the political environment in which government agencies exist.[27]

What the DLA story demonstrates even more clearly is that the principle of focusing on people to improve performance can work extremely well in the public sector. The ingredients for success appear to be the same as in the private sector: strong leadership, an HR department empowered to play a strategic role in the organization, investment in training, a focus on managing performance and methods of dealing with poor performers, and viewing employees as a precious strategic asset. However, there is no evidence from the case study that DLA has received the recognition— either within the DOD or in the government community—that it deserves.

Government Accountability Office

The GAO has undertaken human capital reform perhaps more vigorously and openly than any other federal agency. At the other end of the government spectrum from the DLA, the GAO is a small, elite workforce of about 3,200 individuals, two-thirds of whom have postgraduate degrees. The GAO produces financial and performance evaluations (of the various agencies and activities of the government) for the U.S. Congress. Eighty percent of its budget goes to people.[28]

Unlike most political appointees, the head of the GAO, the U.S. comptroller general, has a fifteen-year term. David Walker served for ten years from November 1998 to March 2008. He was a leading spokesperson for human capital reform in the federal government. Early in his tenure, he made a public commitment to help the GAO become a "model agency" that practices what it preaches about investing in people. Clearly, the GAO needs to excel at recruiting, managing, and training a knowledge-based workforce to fulfill its mission; however, the GAO has gone far beyond the basic commitment to its employees in an effort to use its workforce strategically.

This strategy has produced extraordinary results over the past seven years, with a 93 percent increase in financial value (in terms of recommendations implemented across government).[29] The GAO has also become one of the most quoted organizations in America, and it has transformed its hiring and recruiting into leading practice in the federal government. Students applying for entry-level positions at the GAO and other departments regularly point out that they *received a job offer* from GAO before they were even *contacted for an interview* by other departments.

Background

The GAO was created in 1921 to help Congress investigate how budget money was being spent. Initially comprised of mostly clerks and accountants, it examined vouchers and conducted financial audits. During the

1960s, its role expanded to include more program evaluations, and it began to hire a wider range of experts in many fields. From its inception until 1980, the GAO operated under the same civil service laws as executive branch agencies.

The GAO Personnel Act of 1980 exempted the agency from some aspects of Title V. In particular, the GAO was given more flexibility in appointing, classifying, promoting, and assigning work to employees. It also gained independence from the Office of Personnel Management and was able to establish pay-for-performance systems for some of its employees.

Despite this increased flexibility, the GAO went through a difficult period in the 1990s. Because of budget cutbacks, it was forced to downsize its workforce by 40 percent. It did this by suspending new hires, closing field offices, and ordering RIFs that disproportionately affected more recently hired staff. By 1998 the GAO's workforce was demographically skewed—much as many federal agencies are today—with very few younger employees and more than one-third of the workers nearing retirement.[30] The workforce had become unbalanced in employee experience, level, and skills, leaving it demoralized and uncertain of the future.

In addition, structural challenges were mounting. The organization was hierarchical, stove-piped, and segmented into groups that did not always work together smoothly. Employees were assigned to specific subject areas, with little cross-fertilization of people or ideas. In addition, some members of Congress had begun to question its impartiality.[31]

Strategic Human Capital

When David Walker was appointed in 1998, he decided to address human capital as a top priority. Before becoming comptroller general, Walker had been a partner and global managing director of the human capital services practice at Arthur Andersen LLP (1989–98). A certified public accountant by training, Walker also had high-level government experience, having served as a public trustee for Social Security and Medicare (1990–95), assistant secretary of labor for Pension and Welfare Benefit Programs (1987–89), and acting executive director of the Pension Benefit Guaranty Corporation (1985).

This unique background had made Walker a true believer in the importance of the people factor. His ambition was bold: not only to make the GAO a high-quality, well-respected government agency but also to turn it into a showcase of excellence that would be an inspiration for the rest of government. His logic was that the GAO needed to be ahead of the pack to have credibility when it made recommendations to other agencies.

Walker's roadmap, established shortly after he took over, was a comprehensive strategic plan with four major strategic goals:

Provide timely, quality service to the Congress and the Federal Government to . . .

1. Address current and emerging challenges to the well-being and financial security of the American people.

2. Respond to changing security threats and the challenges of global interdependence.

3. Help transform the Federal Government's role and how it does business to meet 21st century challenges.

4. Maximize the value of GAO by being a model federal agency and a world-class professional services organization.[32]

"Goal 4," as it is called, was a very unusual objective, in that it unabashedly set an internal goal of making better use of people and treating them better to do a more effective job at achieving the first three goals.

HR Reform

The GAO people reforms have much in common with the DLA effort: strong leadership, a strategic focus, the use of leading-edge technology to help leverage the workforce, and training, training, training. However, Congress has given the GAO a series of flexibilities that have enabled it to go even further.

The GAO has drawn virtually the entire organization into the human capital effort. This included a great deal of personal effort by Walker and the chief administrative and financial officer, Sallyanne Harper. Walker set the tone in his public comments: "When you're running a professional services organization—and I consider GAO to be a professional services organization—you're only as good as your people. Your value walks out the door every day, and you hope it comes back tomorrow."[33] Harper has operationalized this vision through a relentless program of planning, communicating, and implementing changes and then monitoring results.

One cannot underestimate the power of a strong top-down commitment to this issue. In the view of Chris Mihm, the GAO's managing director for strategic issues, Walker made a compelling case for these changes:

> I think that in government, you need a burning platform. David [Walker] did a good job of explaining why we *must* do this. The urgency was clear. Those affected are not just feds. With the blended workforce—temps, contractors, NGOs—they are all involved. In the 1980s and 1990s, the business case for flexibilities in HR practices would be based on poor performance. Now, the business case is: we are high-performing and can be even higher-performing.[34]

Early on, Walker persuaded Congress to enact the GAO Personnel Flexibilities Act of 2000, which gave the agency the flexibility to offer voluntary early retirement and separation incentives, establish senior technical positions with pay and benefits equivalent to the senior executive service, modify its RIF rules to give greater weight to performance rather than length of service, and allow the agency to renew certain short-term appointments. This helped the GAO begin to reshape its workforce. To make the GAO more efficient and effective and less siloed, Harper says,

> We closed some field offices, flattened the organization, and reduced layers. We revised the performance management system—made it more transparent and competency-based. Our staff validated the competencies and we held training for the staff and managers on the new performance management system. And at the agency level, we focused on what we were measuring—the financial benefits and the nonfinancial benefits, as well as client service, the number of our recommendations implemented, and our employees' feedback.[35]

The agency has focused on recruiting, training, and aligning its workforce with the strategic needs of the organization. All significant human capital and other agency efforts are linked directly to the strategic plan. According to the GAO's own documents, "Under strategic goal 4, we establish performance goals focused on each of our objectives and management challenges, track our progress in completing the key efforts for those performance goals quarterly, and report each year on our progress toward meeting the performance goals."[36]

The GAO creates a "line of sight" between employee performance and agency goals. After the senior leadership team agrees on the agency's strategic goals, these goals are cascaded down to individual organizations. Each supervisor or "designated performance manager" establishes expectations for his or her staff that are derived from the unit's goals. The competency-based standards used to evaluate performance link to the strategic plan, core values, and professional standards and protocols. The employee is then evaluated and compensated by comparing his or her performance against the appraisal standards.

> "*When* you're running a professional services organization—and I consider GAO to be a professional services organization—you're only as good as your people. Your value walks out the door every day, and you hope it comes back tomorrow." —David Walker

Instead of giving employees overall ratings, the GAO assesses each competency in terms of four levels of performance: "acts as role model," "exceed expectations," "meets expectations," and "performs below expectations." For the purposes of compensation, numerical values are assigned to each rating level and an appraisal average computed for each employee. This average is directly converted to an amount of performance-based compensation. Employees who are rated below expectations on any competency are not eligible for pay increases.

Entry-level employees undergo a two-year developmental program. They are assigned an adviser, complete designated training courses, and typically rotate between different units within the GAO. Every six months, the performance and progress of development staff are reviewed, and employees are eligible for pay adjustments. This performance framework is similar to the one used by leading management consulting firms and other competitive service organizations.

Key GAO innovations have included the following:

—The GAO's *Public/Private Sector Executive Exchange Program,* modeled after the federal government's Information Technology Exchange

Program, allows up to thirty private sector employees to spend some time at the GAO, and fifteen of its own staff to receive specialized training in the private sector. The private sector executives must have backgrounds in accounting, auditing, finance, information technology, and other specialties. They work on GAO projects from three months to a year.

—Designated performance managers are *trained to conduct strategic performance evaluations.*

—Employees are able *to appeal performance appraisal decisions* and other adverse actions if they disagree with them.

—*Two-way communication and transparency are encouraged.* A key component is the Employee Advisory Council, an elected body comprised of employees from various groups, which meets monthly by itself and quarterly with the GAO's Executive Committee.

—*Performance appraisal standards have been revised.* New standards have eliminated the "grade inflation" that allowed most ratings to be in the "outstanding" category. Now the average ratings are much more realistic and less concentrated at one level.

—The agency's *reengineered recruiting process* is now a leading practice in government recruiting at top colleges and universities. In recent years, the GAO has brought in about 300 hires, many concentrated at the entry level. At the end of 2006, more than a third of its workforce had been at the agency less than five years.[37]

—*An Educators' Advisory Council* helps advise the GAO about student needs. It is comprised of deans and heads of schools where GAO recruits candidates in the fields of accounting, public policy, economics, and statistics. This is a two-way relationship. Council members listen to GAO's needs, but they also provide input on the demographics of their upcoming classes.

—*Training has been increased* for supervisors and managers, executive candidates about to enter the senior executive service (SES), and midlevel managers. The latter are the analysts in charge of most projects, and their development is essential to the agency's success. The GAO designed thirteen new competency-building courses, created a new adjunct faculty program to expand the range of education available to employees, and provided the courses at three regional learning hubs, instead of only at headquarters.

TABLE 3-5. GAO's People Factor Scorecard, Human Resources, 2000 and 2006[a]

Human resource criteria	2000		2006	
	System	Score	System	Score
Staff training and education	Minimal, no significant requirements	5	Employees required to attend 80 hours of training over 2-year period	9
Employer loyalty	No system for addressing poor performance	6	GAO assists entry-level hires who are not meeting performance requirements, has a GAO career center to help them find other jobs, allows them to do special projects while looking	10
Corporate recognition of employees	Below average for government	4	Awards to individuals, team leaders; full focus on people as strategic human capital	10
Quality of HR policies	Below average for government	4	Pay-banding, clear definition of performance requirements, best hiring system in federal government, best performance evaluation system; benefit package includes student loan repayment	10
Job satisfaction indicators	Average	6	Retains > 90 percent of hires; 74.3 percent overall satisfied with their jobs	9
Human resource score	Average organization	25	Best use of strategic human capital	47

Source: Interviews with David Walker, Sallyanne Harper, and other GAO employees.
a. Scale: 1 (low) to 10 (high).

Using the people scorecard to evaluate the GAO's performance in human resources and intrapreneurship, we found a significant change across all criteria over the six years from 2000 to 2006 (see tables 3-5 and 3-6). The key characteristics of the transformation are the same as those at the DLA and the leading private sector firms: strong, visionary leadership; a strong manager to implement the vision; a focus on training, performance measurement, flexibility, and monitoring of job satisfaction; and a clear system for handling poor performers.

TABLE 3-6. GAO's People Factor Scorecard, Intrapreneurship, 2000 and 2006[a]

Intrapreneurship criteria	2000		2006	
	System	Score	System	Score
Flexibility of work structure	Inflexible	4	Expanded opportunities for telecommuting and flextime; work structure reorganized by teams	9
Organizational structure	Hierarchical, 6–7 levels	6	Reduced hierarchy, closed field offices, team-oriented; now 4–5 layers from top to bottom	10
Versatility of employees	Static, very little opportunity for lateral movement	5	Lateral movement best in government; professional development program rotates analysts; exchange program with private sector executives	8
Entrepreneurial opportunities	Compensation not linked to performance	4	Compensation and performance linked	8
Leadership	Not available	4	Leadership from Walker and senior team; employee/manager steering committee	10
Intrapreneurship score		22		45

Source: See table 3-5.
a. Scale: 1 (low) to 10 (high).

The GAO's new culture of intrapreneurship is making the work environment more flexible and more team-based. Now trained in several areas, employees are more versatile. The hierarchy has been slashed from six or seven levels to an average of four. Pay is more closely linked to performance; not quite as directly as in the private sector, but more than in most government organizations. Walker says the GAO was able to do this because it invested a great deal in training managers to ensure that professional judgment is applied in performance evaluations. The GAO has implemented a process for appealing appraisal decisions that holds managers accountable for standards and improves fairness for employees.

Market-Based Compensation

The GAO is among the first government agencies to introduce market-based compensation, the trickiest subject that Walker tackled. Under GAO's old "pay-band system," employees with significantly less responsibility (nonsupervisory analysts) and possibly lower performance could make more money than persons with significantly more responsibility (for example, assistant directors) and possibly better performance. The changes were intended to make the system more equitable. "At our middle level, we had a big problem," says Walker. "For the engagement leaders in the organization—senior supervisory-level people whose work bears higher risk—and Ph.D. economists and other specialists, and attorneys, we could afford to pay more. But for those who were not leaders, we were paying too much—so many were at the upper end of the salary range." The GAO therefore restructured its middle-level band, working with a compensation consultant to establish new market-based ranges, implemented in January 2006. "The changes have been controversial," Walker noted, "as some employees were found to be overpaid in relation to the new market-based ranges. With the new system, not everyone will be a winner, but the old system was not fair and needed to be fixed. And this is an essential step in an era of deficits and tighter budgets."[38]

Walker also pointed out that the old system needed to be corrected because under the General Schedule (GS) system, every employee can reach the top of the pay range: "In the GS system, 85 percent of pay increases are automatic. Then there is the cost-of-living adjustment (COLA), which even unacceptable performers get. So about two-thirds of pay increases are automatic."[39]

The implementation of this sweeping reform was done, characteristically, through a massive amount of communication from the GAO leadership to its employees. Walker announced the changes in a televised presentation to all employees. Before that, Harper had spent months with her team, laying the groundwork, explaining the rationale, and building an understanding, if not enthusiasm, for the reforms: "We have been able to make sweeping changes because there is a strong trust that is established. Everyone here is focused on achieving our strategic goals, and the only question is how to best do it."[40]

Performance since 2001

The GAO has developed a rigorous methodology for measuring its own performance. The principal financial criterion tracked annually is "net financial benefits." This is defined as how many dollars have either been (a) saved by the federal government or (b) recommended for better use in light of GAO reports and testimonies. Financial benefits are calculated as the measurable monetary impact of implementing the GAO's recommendations. This impact may derive from the reduction of annual operating costs or the costs of multiyear projects. It may also include increases in revenues obtained through changes in the tax code, the introduction of user fees, or the sale of government assets. The value of the financial benefits is estimated by outside agencies such as the Congressional Budget Office or the Joint Committee on Taxation.

The GAO itself does not have the authority to implement the changes suggested in its reports and testimony, and not every recommendation is acted upon. Therefore when identifying the benefits accrued, the GAO includes only those recommendations that Congress or the relevant federal agency has fully or substantially implemented within the past two fiscal years as a clear result of GAO efforts.[41] (Of course, the identification and measurement of financial benefits does not necessarily translate directly to reduced expenditures government-wide because Congress or the agency may redirect the savings to other projects.)

Over the past six years, the value of the GAO's financial benefits has increased by about 93.2 percent, from $26.4 billion to $51.0 billion (table 3-7). In the same time period, nonfinancial benefits increased by 68 percent. A more conservative calculation would take into account the underlying growth in discretionary federal spending, which increased by 56 percent during the same period.[42] GAO financial benefits, other things being equal, could have been expected to grow at the same rate—or from $26.4 billion to $41.3 billion. Using this calculation, pure productivity increases added an impressive $9.7 billion in additional savings over and above underlying spending growth.[43]

Another measure of performance used by the GAO is "benefits per dollar spent." On this measure, the GAO returned $105 for every dollar spent in operations in 2006. Measured by return per dollar spent (subtracting the investment that GAO has made in its employees), the GAO

TABLE 3-7. GAO's Financial and Nonfinancial Benefits, 2001–06

Fiscal year	Financial benefits (billions of dollars)	Number of nonfinancial benefits	Cost of operations (millions of dollars)	Financial benefit per dollar spent (percent)
2001	26.4	799	413.1	69
2002	37.7	906	453.0	88
2003	35.4	1,043	471.1	78
2004	44.0	1,197	490.1	95
2005	39.6	1,409	505.8	83
2006	51.0	1,342	511.5	105
Net change since 2001	93.2%	68.0%	23.8%	56.0%

Source: GAO Performance and Accountability Reports, 2007.

has seen a nearly 56 percent average increase since 2001, when major human capital reform efforts began. (This return is shown in table 3-7.)

These improvements in GAO's performance are a direct result of management transformation efforts, of which human capital improvement is a large component. Indeed, David Walker has attributed nearly 80 percent of the increase in financial and nonfinancial benefits since 2001 to improvements in human capital.[44]

The GAO also tracks a series of "people measures" to monitor its internal performance on meeting hiring, retention, training, and organizational targets. This balanced scorecard approach helps to keep the organization focused on its quantitative and qualitative goals (see table 3-8).

Taxpayer Gains

If 80 percent of the agency's improvement is due to the workforce transformation, the people-focused strategy has generated $7 billion or more in financial benefits for the taxpayer. To achieve these gains, the GAO spent about $23 million annually on its workforce, which represents between 4 and 5 percent of its annual budget. This is highly consistent with best practice in the private sector, where leading companies tend to spend approximately 4 percent on training and related employee investments. This extraordinary return on investment gives but a tiny glimpse of the potential savings for the entire U.S. government if it were to adopt similar people practices.

TABLE 3-8. Summary of Actual Annual Measures and Targets from GAO Balanced Scorecard, 2002–07

Percent unless otherwise indicated

Performance measure	2002	2003	2004	2005	2006 target	2006 result	Met/ not met	2007 target
Results								
Financial benefits (billions of dollars)	37.7	35.4	44.0	39.6	39.0	51.0	Met	40.0
Nonfinancial benefits (number implemented)	906	1,043	1,197	1,409	1,050	1,342	Met	1,100
Past recommendations implemented	79	82	83	85	80	82	Met	80
New products with recommendations	53	55	63	63	60	65	Met	60
Client								
Testimonies (number)	216	189	217	179	210	240	Met	185
Timeliness[a]	n.a.	n.a.	89	90	98	92	Not met	95
People								
New hire rate	96	98	98	94	97	94	Not met	95
Acceptance rate	81	72	72	71	75	70	Not met	72
Retention rate								
With retirements	91	92	90	90	90	90	Met	90
Without retirements	97	96	95	94	94	94	Met	94
Staff development	71	67	70	72	74	76	Met	75
Staff utilization	67	71	72	75	75	75	Met	78
Leadership	75	78	79	80	80	79	Not met	80
Organizational climate	67	71	74	76	75	73	Not met	76
Internal operations								
Help get job done	n.a.	4.0	4.0	4.1	4.0	n.a.	n.a.	4.0
Quality of work life	n.a.	3.9	4.0	4.0	4.0	n.a.	n.a.	4.0

Source: GAO Performance and Accountability Highlights, 2006.

a. Since fiscal 2004, GAO has collected data from its client feedback survey on the quality and timeliness of its products, and in fiscal 2006 it began to use the independent feedback from this survey as a basis for determining its timeliness.

n.a. Not available.

GAO Summary

One of the reasons for the GAO's success has been that Congress was willing to give it a great deal more flexibility than it has granted the rest of government. In 2004 Congress enacted a second package of reforms that permitted the agency to introduce an exchange program with the private sector, to set the amount of its annual pay adjustment rather than apply the same standard used for the rest of the federal government, to withhold pay increases from employees who are not performing at a satisfactory level, to provide greater flexibility in the reimbursement of relocation expenses, and to provide twenty days of annual leave for mid-career hires.

The GAO would point out, however, that it was already far enough along in its personnel reform program to know what to ask for. Walker has advocated that all government organizations should be in step with the GAO—but not until they demonstrate that they have a strong performance management system in place, ensure necessary safeguards of key employee rights and appeals, and have the management skills to run the new system. The GAO is advocating these as "certification requirements."

Indeed, many of the legal challenges that have stymied implementation of the human capital reforms at the DOD and Department of Homeland Security stem from labor issues and relations, such as flaws in the appeals process. Since there were no unions in the GAO at the time of this transformation, it did not face such issues.[45]

The main lesson from the GAO experience is that investing in the government workforce is likely to improve government performance—potentially by an order of magnitude. To unlock that value as people-focused organizations in the private sector did, the GAO needed to invest some 4 to 5 percent of its annual budget in training, communications, appeals, performance feedback, leadership development, and other people-centered efforts. This fundamental conclusion—that the government needs to spend resources on its workforce in order to produce concrete gains for the taxpayer—is the foundation of the recommendations put forth in part II of the book.

The People Factor Dividend in Government

In our research, the companies that scored highest on people factor attributes enjoyed, on average, a 27 percent higher financial return than the lowest-scoring firms (which would be equivalent to the score of most government agencies). Watson Wyatt found a range of 26–30 percent gains in its surveys. Productivity gains at the DLA were in the neighborhood of 20 percent. The GAO improved its productivity by 56 percent.

The across-the-board improvements in these organizations suggest that the government as a whole would almost certainly achieve some gain by making a concerted investment in its workforce. To estimate the possible gain to the federal government, we based our estimates on three main sources of improvements:

—Productivity increases through better operational and managerial practices.

—Cost savings from reduction in waste, fraud, and duplication.

—Cost savings from better design, supervision, and accountability for results from contracts.

The projected productivity increases derive from achieving the missions of government more effectively—for example, by collecting more taxes and fees with the same amount of resource inputs, and having fewer appeals of benefits claims related to errors. They would also accrue from using technology more effectively for back-office and other tasks, as the DLA showed. Just as industries vary in the amount of benefits they can achieve, government agencies can expect some variance as well. In addition, the government could significantly multiply its potential savings if it made reforms in budgeting and accounting. But significant improvements in productivity can be achieved simply by using people more strategically, focusing rigorously on achieving the goals and outcomes that have already been defined in the Government Performance and Results Act and Performance Assessment Training Tool, and training the workforce to have the right skills.

McKinsey & Company, the global management consulting firm, has recently examined this issue. It concluded that potential productivity gains in the government would be on the order of $100 billion to $300 billion over ten years. The McKinsey study projects this by comparing the productivity gains of the private sector, which averaged 1.5 percent per year from 1987 to 1995 and 3.0 percent per year thereafter, to the productivity gains of the government, which have been essentially flat since 1987.[46] McKinsey estimates that if the U.S. government could increase productivity by just 5 percent over a decade, this would translate into $100 billion in economic gains, while a 15 percent productivity increase would produce $300 billion in gains:

Our [McKinsey's] 15% figure envisions a scenario in which government services are able to achieve the same productivity growth rates as private sector services did in the period between 1987 and 2001. Many have argued that the public sector will never match the productivity gains of the private sector but we are not convinced. Our 5% figure takes account of the doubters, making the modest assumption that government services are only able to achieve half the productivity performance of comparable private sector services.[47]

It is difficult to estimate the amount of potential savings from detecting and preventing waste, fraud, inefficiency, and duplication as a result of better personnel practices. Without doubt, the total amount of waste is huge: the Defense Department's own inspector general has cited some $15 billion in expenditures for the Iraq war that cannot be accounted for at all.[48] However, those savings cannot be realized without better financial accountability at the Pentagon.

Even so, the GAO, the inspector general, and other government watchdogs have repeatedly drawn attention to areas where waste and duplication can be prevented. In a detailed analysis in 2003, the Heritage Foundation estimated that the potential government-wide saving is equal to 1 percent of federal expenditures, or about $190 billion at that time.[49] Even if one agrees with only 25 percent of those recommendations and assumes they could be accrued gradually over five to ten years, those savings would equal $75 billion from today's budget. If coupled with budget and financial reforms in the Defense Department, those savings could easily reach $150 billion over the next decade.

There is other fertile ground for cost savings from improving the ability of federal managers to design and manage outsourcing and to hold down contractors fees (see box 3-1). This is an area in which most government employees are woefully unprepared, so they lack the skills and the confidence to rein in spending. To manage contracts effectively, they need not only to partner with the contractor better (to develop clearer requirements and more effective solutions to problems) but also to limit the requirements and length of engagement of the contract. More effective program management once contracts have been awarded would result in fewer change orders, which are a major source of cost overruns

BOX 3-1. How to Manage Consulting Costs

The monthly fees charged by consultants are driven by the composition of the team in terms of seniority (for example, how many hours of the senior partner's time are included) and by the "deliverables" agreed to in the design of the project. If the government manager can control these aspects of the assignment, he or she can significantly reduce the total cost.

Suppose that "Jim" at the Department of Veterans Affairs has received training in this skill. He could insist that the management team working with him include more mid-level consultants and fewer hours of the senior partner. He could also choose not to be given written reports on what his office already does. Anyone who has ever hired a management consultant has had this experience: the client pays for the consultant to "get up to speed" and for an expensive deck of PowerPoint slides that seldom get looked at again.

Instead, Jim could specify that he only needs assistance with, for example, the redesign of the veterans' claims process. He does not need to pay for a full-blown presentation on what that process currently looks like because he already knows it. (This is difficult, because the senior partner at the firm will argue compellingly that the project needs to be placed within context.) But Jim could restrict the scope of the project. This would reduce the length of the assignment by at least four weeks. Therefore by changing the composition of the team and specifying more precisely what is and is not needed, Jim can save almost 30 percent on the contract:

	Before	After
Monthly team	$150,000	$130,000
Length	6 months	5 months
Total contract cost	$900,000	$650,000

for large procurements. If such gains could shave even 2 percent off the total cost of service contracting throughout the government, that would yield $6.6 billion in annual savings; and a 5 percent reduction would yield savings of $16.5 billion. The cumulative effect of productivity increases through better operational and managerial practices, cost savings from reduction in waste, fraud, and duplication, and cost savings from better design, supervision, and accountability for results from contracts over a ten-year period are shown in table 3-9.

T A B L E 3 - 9 . Potential Government Gains over Ten Years from Investing in the Federal Workforce

Billions of dollars

Gain	Low range	High range
Productivity	100	300
Reduction of waste, fraud, duplication	75	150
Contract management	66	165
Total	241	615

Some productivity gains can be quantified, but many equally significant gains are hard to quantify. It is difficult to put a price tag on homeland security, but there is no question that investing in public service
enhances it. For example: twenty-four hours a day, seven days a week, the
global movement system—comprised of people, cargo, conveyances,
money, and information—shuttles goods and services, capital and labor,
and bits and bytes across the United States and around the world. The
global movement system keeps the economy moving. And government
personnel play a critical role in making it work. Therefore investment in
the people who regulate, operate, and protect these systems is likely to
produce a more efficient, secure, and resilient system for the country.
Moreover, since these systems are largely owned by the private sector
and their users are mostly companies and the general public, the positive
economic effects of a better system are shared by many.

Implications of People Reforms for Recruiting

The level of people-focused investment at the DLA and GAO may shed
some light on the earlier question: would the government become an
employer of choice among top college graduates if it adopted a more
people-focused philosophy? The answer from students is overwhelmingly yes.[50]

To measure student response to specific reforms, we first established a
base scenario in which they were asked: "If you were offered a full-time
job that was identical in job description, compensation package, and
location at the U.S. federal government and at a private company, which

offer would you accept?" In this base case, 50 percent said they would work for the government, and 50 percent preferred private industry. Of course, the surveys showed that many students are deterred from government by the length of time it takes to secure a job offer, the complexity of applications requirements, and other structural problems. But this question was designed to isolate the concept of "working for the government" from the logistical hurdles.

We tested several basic reforms—many of them currently implemented at the DLA and GAO—to measure their impact on student enthusiasm for a government job. For example, students said that if they could apply for a government job by "using a standard résumé instead of filling out government forms," then they were 25 percent more likely to choose the government job over the identical private sector job. Similarly, if the current human resources benefits system was replaced with one that offers "cafeteria-style" benefits, students were 28 percent more likely to opt for the government job.[51]

The two overwhelmingly popular reforms (even among those who had been negative toward the government initially) were making it easier to move back and forth between sectors and reducing the number of political appointees. Easy mobility between sectors is a key driver of student attitudes. Today, most college students expect to have a greater number and variety of jobs during the course of their careers than did previous genera-

Student respondents were almost 50 percent more likely to join the government if it was "easier to go back and forth between government and the private sector."

tions. The survey confirmed this expectation. Student respondents were almost 50 percent more likely to join the government if it was "easier to go back and forth between government and the private sector." Ninety percent who were considering a government job said they would choose it if this "ease of mobility" prevailed. Even students not considering government work were twice as likely to join government if mobility with the nonprofit and private sectors were possible.

All the changes that made the government more flexible, more accessible, less hierarchical, and more prestigious and that provided more skills, more training, and better benefits made more students more likely to work for it. If all of the proposed reforms were adopted, nearly three out of four students said they would work for the government rather than private industry if they were offered an identical position.

Conclusions

The two examples discussed in this chapter—the large unionized DLA workforce and the elite Title V–exempt GAO workforce—are powerful reminders that all people will work better and aim higher in an environment where they can reach their full potential. We estimate that U.S. taxpayers would save hundreds of billions of dollars over the next decade if the government made this kind of serious investment in its workforce. We now turn to the elements of a plan that would raise the entire federal government to this higher level of performance.

PART

Investing in
Public Service

4

Leadership in
the Public Sector

The many hundreds of books about the "art" of leadership emphasize qualities such as vision, optimism, self-confidence, persistence, charisma, and originality. These traits are the mark of good leaders in the public as well as the private realm, but there are fewer such leaders in government. However, effective leadership will be essential to the success of a major change effort[1]—especially one that requires transforming organizational cultures.[2]

Government poses many unusual leadership challenges, in terms of sheer scale and influence. For example, the secretary of commerce is responsible not only for 40,000 permanent employees but also for the nearly 1 *million* temporary workers who are hired to conduct the decennial census. Few private sector leaders (apart from chief executive officers of the world's largest corporations) have to deal with an organization of this size. Senior political appointees may also become de facto leaders and spokespersons for large constituencies outside government. The secretary of veterans affairs, for example, effectively takes on an influential role for the 24 million U.S. veterans and their families.

Equally daunting, government leaders are required to manage networked organizations that seldom resemble the traditional hierarchical bureaucracy. Networks are notoriously difficult to lead, especially in government, where organizational, management, and personnel systems were originally designed to operate within a hierarchical, not networked, model. The leader of a network that involves state and local governments may find herself not just in one fishbowl, but in a veritable pet shop full of fish tanks—being scrutinized by local and state media and constituencies, citizen watchdog groups, and nongovernmental organizations. Leaders of networked structures in government must address a new set of basic questions. Few organizations, even in the private sector, exist to serve as useful models.

The leader of a network that involves state and local governments may find herself not just in one fishbowl, but in a veritable pet shop full of fish tanks—being scrutinized by local and state media and constituencies, citizen watchdog groups, and nongovernmental organizations.

There are at least eight distinct ways in which the challenges for public sector leadership are unique:

1. *Dispersed decision rights.* The power to make critical decisions is in the hands of both the executive branch and Congress. Among congressional leaders, authorizers as well as appropriators have significant power over agency activities and spending. The courts also guide and constrain the activities of the congressional and executive branches. Within the agencies themselves, leadership responsibility is divided between political appointees hired to carry out the president's priorities, senior civil servants with extensive experience in the agency, regional or program managers, and others. Compared with the leadership structure of a private sector company, typically led by an autonomous management team and board of directors, the individual leaders within the government wield less power and thus have less freedom to implement their vision. The chief executive of a Fortune 500 company has far more control over hiring, firing, resource allocation, and strategy in his or her organization than does the secretary of a cabinet agency.

2. *Compulsory performance requirements.* While a company may decide to abandon a specific line of business (for example, because it is not profitable or because it does not fit well with the firm's portfolio), government agencies do not have that option. They are required to serve all their constituents in an equitable fashion. In the same way that running a public school is different from running a private school, government leaders

cannot pick and choose the people they serve. In effect, most government services are monopolies. So customers have little choice. The result is that government leaders serve an extremely diverse range of constituencies.

3. *Constant scrutiny.* To complicate matters, government leaders must function in an environment of almost constant scrutiny and second-guessing. Their decisions and effectiveness are continuously scrutinized by stakeholders and the media at every stage of virtually every issue. Complex decisions are worked out under the public gaze. Preliminary ideas and analysis often leak throughout the deliberative process. In the private sector, leaders have far greater discretion. They rely on the best data that they can obtain but may also employ gut instinct to deal with uncertain or ambiguous situations that nevertheless require immediate action. Ultimately, they are held accountable for results. By contrast, government leaders are often judged on purely political grounds, with the focus on their intentions and short-term outcomes of long-term changes.

4. *Ambiguous performance objectives and measures.* For many government activities, it is especially difficult to reach a consensus about what constitutes success and then to monitor and measure progress toward it. Finding metrics to accurately and clearly measure and communicate performance can be very difficult. If desired results are at all ambiguous, it is it more difficult for leaders to be held accountable for results in their own agencies. This in turn makes it harder for them to manage within their own organizations.

5. *Poor information.* Agencies lack the information systems needed to effectively manage complex organizations. Successful private sector managers who have entered government service—from Paul O'Neill, who became secretary of the Treasury after serving as chair of Alcoa, to Charles Rossotti, who led the transformation of the Internal Revenue Service (IRS) after a long and successful tenure at American Management Systems—consider this deficiency one of the larger obstacles for government leaders.[3]

Effective decisionmaking is also hampered by the panoply of restrictions on the disclosure of information. In the national security realm, the system of classifying secret materials prohibits sharing information with the public and those within the organization who lack the requisite clearance level. The decision on what information to classify, and to what extent, is often highly subjective. Privacy and confidentiality laws further restrict the use of information to inform stakeholders of the need for change. In sum, a lack of information and restrictions on sharing some of it make it hard for leaders to explain their actions to employees and to the public at large.

6. *Conflicting direction.* In some ways, Congress functions like a board of directors. But congressional oversight is highly fragmented with multiple committees, each providing conflicting guidance and demanding customized reports that are extremely time-consuming to prepare. The Department of Homeland Security (DHS) famously has over seventy committees to which its secretary must report. Officials in the executive branch must respond to congressional inquiries regardless of the merits of the inquiry. Unlike corporate managers, government leaders are seldom able to use operating efficiency and financial results to measure their progress. Instead, various members of Congress may judge government leaders on entirely different criteria.

7. *Multiple stakeholders.* The stakeholder network in government is broad and filled with asymmetries of power such that a single player can bring the entire reform process to a stop.[4] Political leaders are frequently responsible for proposing new policy ideas that support the president's agenda. Career civil servants then refine and translate these policy ideas into coherent regulatory frameworks and manage the day-to-day operations of the government's massive agencies. Congressional leaders apply the power of the purse by reviewing and approving agency budgets. Employee leaders—that is, the myriad supervisors and managers who actually deliver products and services to the nation's citizens—control the quality and efficiency of government services. Leaders of groups outside government (such as unions, think tanks, advocacy groups, and corporations) bring new ideas, concerns, and expertise to Congress and the executive branch for their consideration.

8. *Lack of alignment between stakeholders.* Political leaders and career civil service leaders think very differently about how to get things done. Political leaders have a short-term time horizon and are frequently ill informed about the mechanics of their agency. Career civil service executives have a very long-term time horizon, and they are more concerned about operational implications and service delivery on the ground—

effects that often take many years to emerge. This tension between career and political leadership can provide useful checks and balances in the system, but it can also be an impediment to change. One of the challenges for political leaders is to harness the support and expertise of the career staff and listen to their advice about what it will take to make a change stick. For career leaders, the challenge is to provide leadership and continuity to the agency and to motivate the staff and help them adapt to sudden changes in political direction and style.

The Need for Leaders Who Can Transform Government

Increasing the leadership quotient in government will be essential to making the transformational changes we are proposing. When discussing personnel reform in our research, one message we heard repeatedly was that organizational leaders must be openly engaged in and supportive of reform. "If the top person is not committed, it won't happen," many remarked.[5] Greg Rothwell,

> *"The leaders we attract have to get it that people are important. A bad system won't hurt you as much as bad leaders." —Greg Rothwell*

former acquisitions chief at the Department of Homeland Security, added: "The leaders we attract have to get it that people are important. A bad system won't hurt you as much as bad leaders."[6]

Successful political leaders understand that transformative change in government is necessary for dealing with the special characteristics of the public sector. James MacGregor Burns, who first introduced the concept of transformational leadership in a political context (in contrast to transactional leadership), has explained it as follows:

> Transforming leadership . . . occurs when one or more persons engage with others in such a way that leaders and followers raise one another to higher levels of motivation and morality. Their purposes, which might have started out as separate but related, as in the case of transactional leadership, become fused. Power bases are linked not as counterweights but as mutual support for common purpose. Transforming leadership ultimately becomes moral in that it raises the level of human conduct and ethical aspiration of both leader and led, and thus it has a transforming effect on both.[7]

Transformational leaders offer a purpose that transcends short-term goals and focuses on higher-order intrinsic needs.[8] An example of such leadership is the reorganization of the IRS under former IRS commissioner Charles Rossotti. Following a set of public hearings at which the IRS came under fire for harassing and penalizing ordinary, honest taxpayers, Rossotti was selected for the job precisely because he had a reputation for transformative leadership as CEO of the 9,000-employee AMS company. He also had knowledge of the federal government from his service decades earlier in the Kennedy-Johnson administrations.

Rossotti undertook a massive reorganization of the IRS, to make it more customer-friendly. The objective was to change a culture that was suspicious of the outside world into one that would view taxpayers as basically honest (just confused by the tax system, and wanting help to figure out what exactly they owe). He recognized that if the agency could get "knowledgeable insiders to lead the design of the new organization, we could not only make more reliable decisions, but also begin to break down the skepticism and resistance from everyone else."[9] Rossotti employed his persona as a highly successful business leader, motivated the IRS executive team, provided a set of clear arguments for change, and spent time mentoring and developing senior IRS staff. He inspired the career civil service team to identify with his goals and work to implement reform. The effort was not without its setbacks, of course, in part because of technology failures. But overall, the agency transformation was successful, thanks in large measure to Rossotti's leadership.

The Need for Leaders Who Can Serve the Public

Leaders who view themselves as public servants exhibit several useful qualities that make them more effective in the reform of government. First, they are visibly committed to the organization's mission. Those who enter government service still do so because they want to make a difference, believe that the government can play an important role in people's lives, and think the public has a right to expect its leaders to embody that commitment. This is consistent with the findings of a study of the career plans of graduating students of the Harvard Kennedy School, who felt the most enticing aspect of public sector work is the possibility of "making a difference"—especially in a policy area of interest.[10]

A second characteristic is a strong moral compass—placing a value on fairness and diversity in the workplace. When we asked current managers and executives what elements of the current civil service system should be retained, everyone we interviewed (and every report from the Government Accountability Office [GAO] and other institutions) pointed to the merit principles listed in appendix F, which are designed to promote fairness and to minimize the impact of unfair bias on personnel decisions. Studies show that employees remain committed to those leaders who exhibit fairness in decisionmaking, even when the outcomes go against their personal interest.[11]

Studies show that employees remain committed to those leaders who exhibit fairness in decisionmaking, even when the outcomes go against their personal interest.

A third characteristic is a high level of dedication over a period of time. Managing a major organizational change can consume a leader's entire time and attention. As David Walker, former U.S. comptroller general and head of the GAO, has pointed out, transformations take five years or more to implement and to reap the anticipated benefits.[12] Leaders should be prepared to devote enough hours over several years to manage a transition from start to finish.

Key Transformative Roles for Leaders

Primary responsibility for implementing personnel reform in the public sector will fall to department and agency executives—the people who make decisions that directly affect the direction of an agency and how it is managed. This leadership group has two tiers: the limited-term political leaders who are appointed in each new administration, and the federal government's senior civil servants.

Most political appointees are selected on the basis of their willingness to bring about key policy outcomes for the administration. They are rarely chosen for their proven skills at managing large organizations or major organizational changes. Often they are accused of focusing on crisis management and quick successes. In addition, the tenure of most leaders in the U.S. government is shorter than that of the employees they lead. If, as David Walker suggests, "cultural transformation is a seven-year effort," few political appointees are willing to take on the management challenges associated with such changes, knowing that they are unlikely to be serving in their positions long enough to see the benefits of the changes.[13]

Reporting to the political leaders in government is another tier of leaders, who are equally if not more critical as agents of change. Senior civil servants—the federal employees who run operational and mission support activities on a day-to-day basis—must step up to the considerable challenges of change.

Civil servants in government must play a much stronger role in change leadership. This is especially challenging because senior civil servants are expected to fill the leadership gap whenever political leadership is absent, which has, over time, created a culture oriented toward stabilizing their organizations rather than changing them.

A study of the Internal Revenue Service (IRS) transformation describes resistance among members of its senior executive service to changes initiated by executives hired from outside the government.[14] In contrast, a study of personnel reforms in several state governments noted that all state agency personnel directors who had experienced the transformation of their civil service system said they would never want to go back to the old rigid system.[15]

Another troublesome issue is that some senior civil servants may not want to manage people at all. Many view human capital management tasks as largely tangential to the real work of their agencies, which is all about the mission and their key programs. But if there is to be any hope of persuading staff that personnel reform will contribute to the success of their agencies, the first step will be to convince their senior and middle managers of this. Operational managers from the senior executive service level down to line supervisors must come to believe that there is a real link between human capital reform and accomplishing the mission. When these managers are involved in developing the strategic human capital plans and when they are held accountable for addressing people issues, they will begin to see how human capital management contributes to, or detracts from, achieving strategic objectives (see box 4-1).

BOX 4-1. DOE's NNSA Engages Senior Management in Planning Its Transformation

When Congress established the National Nuclear Security Administration (NNSA) in 2000, the new administration within the Department of Energy (DOE) confronted the challenge of integrating and downsizing its support offices in multiple field locations. This was necessary in order to allocate a larger portion of its funding to key nuclear security programs. As its leaders began the difficult job of analyzing the agency's staffing needs and reshaping its federal workforce, they chose to involve front-line managers and employees openly rather than make the decisions in secrecy. When headquarters announced that field managers would have the authority to make necessary changes and would be held accountable for their decisions, the field managers embraced this greater degree of control. In less than three years, eight field offices were consolidated into three, and more than 300 employees were reassigned. Most employees felt satisfied with the way this reform was handled, and the agency received only six complaints. This case illustrates the benefits of engaging operating managers in planning and implementing personnel reforms. The managers take on leadership roles instead of off-loading the tough decisions to an impersonal personnel resources function at headquarters.

Source: Michael Kane, former NNSA associate administrator, interview with authors, December 1, 2005.

Employee Leaders

Every organization has a cadre of respected employees whose insights into the events and issues in the organization are listened to by their colleagues. These opinion leaders are often long-time employees whose technical expertise or organizational savvy is admired, but who may not have formal leadership positions in their organizations. Their influence on employee attitudes can be considerable.[16] Staff members rely on these colleagues and co-workers—their immediate circle of trusted sources—to help them interpret the often-ambiguous events during a major organizational change.

As employees try to make sense of changes around them, these informal opinion leaders are important because they can explain what planned changes are likely to mean to specific occupational groups.[17] They serve a valuable purpose because when employees have the opportunity to discuss with knowledgeable, trusted sources how the changes are likely to affect them, their anxiety is reduced, and the likelihood that they will adopt the change improves. (We will say more about how to engage these employee leaders in part III, "Enacting Public Service Reform.")

Former IRS commissioner Charles Rossotti understood the need for, and the value of, the involvement of grassroots change leaders when he undertook a massive reorganization of the IRS: "If we could get . . . knowledgeable insiders to lead the design of the new organization, we could not only make more reliable decisions, but also begin to break down the skepticism and resistance from everyone else."[18] Rossotti looked for people who had two qualities: they had to understand in detail how things worked, and they had to want to be part of designing the new IRS. This combination of practical know-how plus the ability to think strategically is vital for internal change leaders.

The government will need to enlist leaders with a variety of backgrounds and skills. Such leaders can be drawn from many backgrounds. They might be experienced hires who joined the government after working in more volatile environments (such as high-tech industry) or who were in the military, where each person must be able to lead if and when the need arises. Or they might already be working in a government agency without having gone up through the ranks, as candidates for management usually do. Our point here is simply that government must expand its search to nontraditional places for the next cadre of leaders.

Legislative Branch Leaders

In the private sector, a leader can often implement major personnel changes unilaterally, as long as he or she retains the overall backing of the board of directors. These changes may be reversed or modified later on, but the leader has the power to experiment. In the government, every major personnel change requires the support of many stakeholders, including members of key congressional oversight committees. Unfortunately, many members of Congress remain woefully undereducated about the topic of personnel reform. As one committee staffer noted, "Personnel reform is a complex issue and has usually not been a high priority in Congress, where there is substantial apathy about this issue. Very few people in Congress focus on the federal workforce."[19]

Those in Congress who have taken an interest in this issue have worked hard to educate their colleagues. In recent years, congressional committees have held dozens of hearings on personnel issues in which experts have testified about reform priorities. A few members have emerged as leaders on this issue because of the high percentage of government employees in their districts or their committee assignments (for example, Senators Daniel Akaka of Hawaii and George V. Voinovich of Ohio and Representatives Thomas Davis of Virginia, Eleanor Holmes Norton of Washington, D.C., and Chris Van Hollen of Maryland). Other members have taken on this issue because they understood the impact of personnel management on organizational performance *before they got to Congress*. These members have been influenced by their previous experience in organizations in both the private and the public sectors.

The leadership role played by key members of Congress and their staffs is an important one. Some members have been effective political partners to their executive branch counterparts, making needed modifications to bills so that key reforms have the weight of law behind them. Charles Rossotti took advantage of another important source of change leadership in his quest to reform the IRS. His story of the IRS transformation describes the important role played by Senator Bob Kerrey, who co-chaired the National Committee on Restructuring the IRS, and Senator William Roth, former chair of the Senate Finance Committee, which oversees the IRS. Roth's relentless pursuit of a reform agenda for the IRS was essential to achieving the changes that were implemented during Rossotti's tenure.

Members of Congress can also bring reforms to a standstill if they think an agency's actions cannot be defended. Whatever their point of view on the issue, members must use their public positions to become educated and to educate others about the need for, and impact of, specific reforms. As spokespersons on the issue, they must have a solid grasp of the operational realities of the current system and the benefits (and costs) of new system features.

Leaders outside Government

Interested groups outside of government can and do influence change in government. In the case of personnel reform, leaders from these nongovernmental organizations (NGOs) have provided useful input and commentary on the proposals under consideration by Congress and the administration. Unions and associations representing federal employees, the Partnership for Public Service, the Council for Excellence in Government, the National Academy of Public Administration, and various think tanks are among the NGOs that have contributed to the dialogue by conducting research on topics related to personnel reform. In addition, subject matter experts in academia and in consultancies have shared their insights through congressional hearings and various publications. The role of interested groups and individuals is to raise issues that need to be debated publicly and to provide greater depth of perspective on topics of national interest.

Unions are an especially powerful force in the public sector. Since they represent approximately 22 percent of all government employees, it is crucial to build trust with union leaders before, during, and after organizational change.[20] This is fundamental to success. Government employee unions have opposed the new personnel rules proposed for the Department of Homeland Security (DHS) and the Department of Defense (DOD) and have successfully argued in court that both sets of rules violate existing collective bargaining agreements.[21] This outcome might have been prevented if unions had been included in the original design of these reforms. For reforms to move forward, union leaders must be brought into the discussions early on.

Stakeholders should approach reform as willing collaborators. All stakeholders must be open to revising the procedures for collective bargaining and resolving conflicts and must be committed to the prohibition of certain banned personnel practices. And in the face of disputes, stakeholders need to support an appeals process that is fair, fast, and final.[22]

The Role of the People Factor in Change Leadership

What, then, must these diverse group leaders *do* in order to effect the changes we describe in part I? How should they lead? First, they must be comfortable managing change. They must be coalition builders and be able to instill confidence in those they lead. Leaders must sustain the best traditions of public service by showing their commitment to the mission and their commitment to fairness and public integrity.

Research on change initiatives in the private sector consistently shows that effective leadership is essential to the success of major change efforts.[23] Studies of organizational *culture* change—a concept usually associated with significant organizational reform efforts—also find that leaders play a critical role in forming and transforming organizational cultures.[24]

Furthermore, the research on change leadership points to *people management* as the critical component of successful change programs. After decades of study of corporate mergers and acquisitions, rightsizing, continuous quality improvement, reengineering, and whole industry transformations, there is now a solid body of knowledge about

Personnel reforms are fragile and will need relentless tending by those who lead.

how to manage organizational change and how to help organization members make the basic psychological transitions that all people must make when they experience change.[25] These studies consistently cite the managing-the-people side of change as a critical success factor (and common sense suggests that it is vital).

Private sector executives called on to lead change usually know the organization well, or if they have come in from outside, they were hired for their skills and experience as turnaround executives. In contrast, public sector reforms are led by a mix of politicians, political appointees, long-term government executives, labor leaders, and even nongovernmental organizations. New members of Congress and new political appointees often have limited knowledge of the civil service system, and sometimes they have minimal experience with the agencies they oversee. In short, the organizational leaders of public sector change are generally not well prepared to take on a major organizational transformation. Arguably, government leaders are in far greater need of training and coaching than many of their private and nonprofit sector counterparts. Few have the requisite mastery of change tactics that comes from personal experience, and even fewer are lucky enough to inherit a cadre of senior civil servants with this background.

Successful leaders understand that organizational change is a "process that requires awareness and close leadership attention."[26] In short, even the most dedicated and hard-working leaders often find that managing a major organizational change consumes all of their time and attention. Is it any wonder that "most organizations don't have committed leaders in [the human capital] area?"[27] If transformations take five years or longer to implement and to reap the anticipated benefits, leaders accepting these assignments must have real staying power. In addition, implementation plans should include how the baton will be passed when the inevitable leadership changes occur in the organization. Personnel reforms are fragile and will need constant and unrelenting tending by those who lead.

Summary

The simple message of this chapter is that it is not possible to reinvigorate public service without strong leadership. To date, such leadership has been largely absent from civilian government. It is difficult to find inspirational leaders who are willing to take on the challenges of the public sector, and then they are often placed in near-impossible situations once they agree to serve. The success of the plan outlined in the following chapters will require leaders (at many levels) to step forward to receive training, and to provide direction to the reform effort.

5

Why Organizational Structure Is Important

The structure of an organization—whether a small company or a vast government agency—ultimately consists of a set of relationships between people and between their work units. The structure signals the power, prestige, and privilege associated with various positions. It also divides workers into groups with common interests and motivations (such as management and staff, or hourly workers and salaried workers).[1] Thus structure has a profound influence on the way people work and how they feel about their jobs. Its influence is particularly evident in the motivation, behavior, and performance of workers in a hierarchy.

To add to the complexity, workers tend to resist change. Therefore restructuring requires dedicated time and focus from the top of the organization. Lessons from both the public and private sector show that it takes a long period of sustained effort to reorganize successfully. Moreover, a change in organizational structure on its own, without an associated investment in worker training, is likely to degrade efficiency through internal turmoil and higher costs rather than achieve the desired results.

By contrast, a structure that focuses on people allows tasks to be accomplished more easily. Workers can thus become more productive and innovative. Few organizations in government have a structure that is focused around helping the employees serve customers, such as veterans,

Medicare recipients, and small business owners seeking loans effectively. This chapter examines several organizational models that might be employed in government to improve workforce performance.

Improving Efficiency, Agility, and Adaptability

The past two decades have witnessed a wave of organizational change in the private and nonprofit sectors. Organizations have reengineered their management processes, eliminating redundancy in business operations and simplifying overall structure to improve decisionmaking. These improvements have included reducing the number of layers of management and streamlining operations. And there have been many calls to apply this approach to government.

But despite past attempts at "de-layering," government agencies remain hierarchical organizations. In cases where supervisors have become team leaders, for example, they still do the same work.[2] As Paul Light reports, government workers "who are buried under layer-upon-layer of supervision can hardly feel confident that they are personally contributing to their organization's mission. At a time when the flow of information has become the issue of the day, Americans can hardly be reassured that so many federal employees see so many layers between the top and bottom of their agencies."[3] Light found federal employees twice as likely to voice this complaint as workers from other sectors.[4] In addition, the federal government was less likely to offer the kind of challenging work that attracts the top of the labor market or to provide tools to succeed. Such layering, says Light, needs to be replaced by a structure "in which talented employees can see the impact of their work every day."[5]

Streamlining can have both positive and negative effects. Despite the benefits of simplified processes, some business operations require horizontal redundancy to ensure reliability. For example, the emergency 911 system needs to have primary circuits as well as back-up circuits to ensure that emergency calls can always reach their destination. The value of vertical redundancy in preventing bad decisions by employing multiple levels of review has been overcome by the need for more rapid response to customer service and emerging market demands. Flatter organizational structures help speed up decisionmaking because individuals closer to the work and more familiar with the issues can act without unnecessary layers of approval.

To this end, agencies could reduce their levels of hierarchy, decentralize decisionmaking, use team-based structures, and reduce the number of job categories.[6] Paul Volcker has stressed the need to reduce the large layer of junior political appointees in order to put program managers closer to policy leaders.[7] On many fronts, we find agreement that too many layers in government are a barrier to peak performance.

De-layering would improve performance even *more* if staff members were given more flexibility to accomplish their work. As shown in chapter 2, this change also leads to greater job satisfaction. Government agencies traditionally rely on tight control and authority to ensure compliance and structure in the workplace. However, many agencies are now finding that providing employees with more flexibility and autonomy, if coupled with effective monitoring and safeguards, can improve employee morale, stimulate innovation, and improve overall performance.

One common measure of the number of layers in an organization is the manager-to-staff ratio. A ratio of 1:4 shows that managers have a small span of managerial control. In a large organization, this ratio would necessitate many management layers to control the entire workforce. A ratio of one manager to twelve staff reflects a system with greater span of control for managers and greater autonomy for employees. Such a ratio implies fewer hierarchical layers to manage the entire workforce.

Organizations with narrower spans of control are prone to certain maladies. Their managers tend to micromanage subordinates, which can lower morale; personnel and overhead costs tend to be higher because of the many layers of management and the extra staff needed to support managers; and communication is slower because it takes longer for guidance to flow down the chain of command and for ideas to move up. Organizations with a broad span of control usually have a flatter and less hierarchical structure.[8]

From an employee's point of view, the benefits of increasing the manager's span of control can be significant. Communications up and down the hierarchy are more direct and move faster. Managers tend to delegate more authority to lower levels when spans of control are broadened. This can increase employee satisfaction because subordinate jobs are more fulfilling when workers have greater responsibility and growth opportunities. From the organization's point of view, larger spans of control tend to reduce personnel and overhead costs and provide greater staffing flexibility. Everyone benefits if managers and staff earn each other's trust. High-trust environments foster better morale, demand less detailed supervision, and respond more effectively under crisis conditions.[9]

Of course, it is impossible to prescribe an "ideal" manager-to-staff ratio because the right span of control will depend on an organization's function and context. Nevertheless, a target ratio can serve to force government agencies to streamline operations. When Texas asked its agencies to trim their budgets by approximately $338 million over two years, most made cuts without streamlining their internal structures, reducing excessive management, or improving processes. To give them an added push in this direction, the Texas legislature enacted Texas Government Code Section 651.004, which required them to establish a goal of one manager or supervisor for every eleven employees.

In successful companies and in the military, the desire to be responsive to current developments is paramount and helps to shape the organizational structure. But in the civilian government, the pace of reorganization is slow and is disconnected from the external environment.

The IRS reforms in 2003 successfully reduced the number of hierarchical layers. This is an example of the kind of radical restructuring that is needed to bring the government in line with high-performing and even medium-performing organizations (see box 5-1).[10] And it shows that it is possible for government to streamline operations.

Perhaps the most important point to mention about streamlining efforts is that they are never "once-and-done." Rather, they are part of an ongoing process directed at improvement. Even the most carefully considered and customer-focused organizational designs must be open to change as an organization's challenges evolve over time. It is common practice for private sector organizations to restructure as often as necessary to align with new priorities and challenges. If anything, the criticism of the private sector is that companies reorganize too often and cause too much disruption for their employees and customers.

BOX 5-1. IRS Reorganized to Streamline Operations and Align with Customer Groups

The Internal Revenue Service (IRS) performed a personnel overhaul in 2003, in accord with the IRS Restructuring and Reform Act (RRA) of 1998. As part of this act, the IRS introduced measures to simplify its internal organization. It reorganized the agency into four new "customer-oriented" operating divisions to replace the fifty-year-old structure made up of districts, regions, and service centers. In addition, it reduced management layers by half. Approximately 400 mid- and top-level management positions were eliminated. Managers who had previously been split into separate GS-14 and GS-15 grades were placed into a single senior manager band, which eliminated hierarchical distinctions and gave the agency greater flexibility in making job assignments. Any manager in the senior manager band could be appointed to any other senior manager position. As a result of the reduction in management positions, the IRS was able to fund additional frontline positions and thereby improve service to taxpayers.

Source: James R. Thompson and Hal Rainey, "Modernizing Human Resource Management in the Federal Government" (Washington: IBM Endowment for the Business of Government, April 2003).

This kind of flexibility is far more difficult for the government to achieve because its structure is rigid and bound by the jurisdiction of congressional committees. In successful companies and in the military, the desire to be responsive to current developments is paramount and helps to shape the organizational structure. But in the civilian government, the pace of reorganization is slow and is disconnected from the external environment.

The Multisector Workforce

The federal government will also need to consider alternative organizational models for delivering services in order to deal with the impending staff shortages discussed in part I. Currently, the government uses a mixture of full-time federal employees, temporary employees, contractors, consultants, and nongovernmental organizations (NGOs) to deliver its products and services. Specific operations often hire extra personnel; for example, the decennial census hires more than 900,000 temporary employees and contractors to assist with counting the population.

This larger group of workers is often referred to as a "blended" workforce but in fact is better described as a multisector workforce operating under distinct rules and incentives.[11] The multisector workforce allows agencies to expand and contract and to draw on external sources to fill gaps in skills to some extent. Increasingly, this is being done through public-private collaboration and partnerships in which government agencies have to work more closely with each other as well as with private sector and nonprofit organizations to deliver public services.[12] Nevertheless, most government agencies have not changed their basic organizational structure, even when contractors and temporary personnel far outnumber the full-time employees.

The Core-Ring Model

One approach to managing a multisector workforce is the "core-ring" model.[13] This refers to an organizational structure in which the "core" of the workforce consists of a cadre of permanent career employees surrounded by a middle "ring" of full-time and part-time temporary government workers, who can move in and out of government.[14] The third, outer ring is comprised of the traditional contract workforce provided by the commercial and nongovernmental sectors.

There are several advantages to this model. First, those in the innermost ring are people performing inherently governmental duties. They develop expertise through job continuity and by specific, targeted training and investment over the course of a career. Second, the middle core provides a mechanism through which government (and government employees) can take advantage of the knowledge and expertise of the private and nonprofit sectors. As noted earlier, this is a key factor in recruiting college students into government. The middle core also offers a way for those whose careers are primarily in the private or nonprofit sectors to contribute their time and skills to the public good. This helps the government to attract people with hard-to-find skills who would otherwise be unable to participate. Another benefit is that a wider swathe of citizens will be able to understand and appreciate how the American system of government works. Finally, this model gives government agencies greater flexibility to expand and contract the workforce as needed, which can be especially important at times of national emergency. In a sense, the U.S. military already has a core-ring workforce that includes active duty military as well as reserves, national guard units, and contractors who train to be ready and highly interoperable at all times.

There is no real equivalent in the civilian sector. Today, even though the public, private, and nonprofit sectors all participate in providing government services, the government lacks many of the benefits of a core-ring model while retaining most of the drawbacks. The core ring is intended to help government increase talent in government and to distinguish between competencies that need to be purely governmental versus the skills that can best be acquired in a middle ring. (For example, most national intelligence skills would likely be deemed inherently governmental, whereas "claim processing" skills—for instance, to expedite education loans, tax filings, and social security claims—would not.)

There are many individuals—for example, retired veterans' claims experts and state and local tax experts—who would welcome the opportunity to contribute a few hours of their time every week to serve the country.

But in the current environment, there is a hodgepodge of relationships between the public and private sectors, with little strategic rationale. The government has some statutory authority in Title V to hire people into temporary positions for up to a year (with the possibility of an additional one-year extension), but there are no clear guidelines for when and how this authority is used. Moreover, the government lacks the flexibility to hire such employees on an hourly basis. But there are many individuals—for example, retired veterans' claims experts and state and local tax experts—who would welcome the opportunity to contribute a few hours of their time every week to serve the country. Such individuals could significantly improve customer service, particularly in rural areas. There is no reason why government should not allow part-time work in exchange for compensation or health benefits, or both, and provide longer periods of service for temporary full-time workers.

Of course, any model that increases flexibility also entails more attention to management and ethics. At present, the government lacks the business processes that would help it manage the core-ring system properly. But, as discussed in previous chapters, the government will be forced to revamp its management systems whether or not it adopts a core-ring model. And government supervisors will need to acquire network management skills supported by improved information sharing and documentation across sectors. Government also needs to figure out a way to coordinate mixed teams comprised of contractors and federal workers without violating procurement law. In short, many of the perceived disadvantages of a core ring are dilemmas that the government will have to grapple with even if it simply continues to use the current multisector workforce.

Proposed Organizational Structure

We propose that the boundaries between the core and the ring be made more permeable in both directions—that is, by allowing government workers to gain experience in the private and nonprofit sectors, and by allowing private/nonprofit sector employees to gain experience in the government. Under this new workforce model, the government would designate a number of positions for managers recruited from the private sector to serve a tour of duty of up to five years in government roles that carry all the authority and responsibility of these positions as if occupied by a career civil service employee. During this period, the temporary private sector "hires" would enjoy the same salary and benefits as their public sector counterparts, as well as the right to lifetime health care after five years of total public sector service. They would also have the same duties and obligations, including management and supervision of government employees assigned to them. We envision that this middle ring would start off small in relation to the total government population. For example, about 0.5 to 1.0 percent of the 1.9 million people (or about 9,000 to 18,000 people initially) around the United States would be in this category. This would be a select group of Americans who would contribute to public service in a unique way. The objective would be to achieve the kind of status and respect that is accorded Peace Corps and Teach for America volunteers.

Similarly, government employees could serve in the private or non-profit sectors for a period of time without having to compete to return to their government jobs. These periods of service would be viewed as career development opportunities, in that government employees would be exposed to different leadership and management environments, new technical knowledge, and a wider array of relationships through which to improve their ability to run government services. They could be part of a career development plan designed to further the growth of each employee in a chosen area of expertise. Exposure to the private sector and NGOs would enrich the experience base of government employees. In fact, so many government positions demand interaction with people in other sectors that a stint in the private or nongovernmental sectors could even be treated as a requirement for advancement. One retired federal procurement executive, Bob Welch, has suggested this very idea: "A year or two in industry should be mandatory before promotion to a certain level—probably GS-13."[15] Greg Rothwell, former head of acquisition for the Department of Homeland Security, would agree:

> If I knew then what I know now about the private sector, I would have insisted that all of my procurement personnel respond to a request-for-proposal before ever allowing them to write and issue one for the government. It ought to be a part of a normal government career path, certainly in procurement, to spend some time in the private sector. Why? Because adults are experiential learners, and because experiences in varied settings help to make people more adaptable, more flexible, and more confident in their own ability to cope with the unexpected.[16]

Years ago, the private sector had fewer incentives to participate in such programs. But today one of the major trends in business is "corporate social responsibility." Driven by intense pressure from shareholders and customers, companies are playing an increasingly vital role in problem solving. This trend has transformed the boundary between government and business in many areas, for example, in eradicating diseases, in addressing environmental hazards, and in delivering services. In addition, the large corporations are major contributors to the not-for-profit sector both through their own foundations and not-for-profit activities and by funding initiatives at independent NGOs like the Ford Foundation. Therefore the structure of governance has shifted over the past twenty years to encompass public, private, and nonprofit sectors in many disciplines. But the organizational structure of the federal government has not kept pace with these developments. By moving to a core-ring approach, the government can begin to build capacity to staff and manage multi-sector programs.

This type of system needs an ethical and legal framework in order to operate and to minimize the risks on both sides of the exchange. There are some easy steps that can be adopted. For example, government employees should receive an updated brief on ethics regulations before and after their private sector development assignment. Second, after working in the private sector on the same procurements as in the government, returning government employees should not be allowed to work on that contract for a year. Third, the host companies should recommit to the same ethical standards as participants do in the existing "loaned executive" program in government today. This would mean creating a firewall around returning private sector employees.

Upon completion of their tour of duty in government, private and nonprofit sector participants in this program should receive a nationally recognized "public service" award that would be a citation for their service, signed by their agency head. They could also be honored with a U.S. flag along with the award at a public event. The government employees would receive similar recognition for their commercial and NGO experience that would also be recognized by the secretary of their respective agency. Both groups would document their positions, dates, responsibilities, skills, and outcomes in a "human resources passport." Selection criteria for jobs and promotion in government would be modified to recognize the value of these opportunities and thereby create greater incentives for participation.

Introducing the private and nonprofit sectors more formally into the middle of government will inevitably produce some mistakes and the occasional ethics lapse, where someone will try to take advantage of their inside track information. But we believe that the overwhelming majority of those who are attracted to public service have a sense of honor and integrity. What is the value of penalizing, at great expense, 99 percent of the employees who are honest simply to weed out a few who are not? This is the approach currently used in dealing with veterans. Despite the fact that study after study has shown virtually no fraud in veterans disability claims, the Department of Veterans Affairs compels returning war veterans to prepare a twenty-three-page application with extensive documentation to verify even the most obvious disability, such as the loss of a leg. The department then subjects the veterans to a lengthy verification process that can take up to two years. In all, over 90 percent of veterans claims are approved after this protracted investigation.[17] By contrast, the private sector Blue Cross/Blue Shield processes 30 million medical claims per year, 98 percent of which are paid within sixty days.[18] It is able to do this because it accepts that in the interests of reimbursing doctors and hospitals quickly, it must tolerate a small amount of error and fraud.

> *The overwhelming majority of those who are attracted to public service have a sense of honor and integrity. What is the value of penalizing 99 percent of the employees who are honest, at great expense, simply to weed out a few who are not?*

Clearly there needs to be oversight, accountability, and ethical standards of the highest level. But allowing the public, private, and nonprofit sectors to work more closely together is recognizing the facts on the ground that the government now employs millions of private sector contractors. It makes little sense to maintain arbitrary separations and to deny honorable citizens the chance to serve on the remote chance that they might do something dishonorable. The public interest is poorly served by the current approach.

Challenges of Proposed Structure

At the same time, federal agencies will have to deal with a number of challenges created by the multisector workforce. One such challenge arises when government agencies and their contractors have a history of low trust, which makes it difficult to collaborate even though contractors are now an essential part of the government delivery system. Group dynamics can pose a challenge as well when federal employees find contractors doing the same work but operating under different expectations, standards, and compensation.[19] To add to these concerns, there are precious few models of how to manage in this context. Government agencies have few federal managers with the experience and the skills (particularly the acquisition, procurement, and program management skills) to oversee highly interdependent and complex contract-based relationships with nonfederal entities[20] By increasing the use of public-private networking, agencies would be better equipped to expand their areas of expertise through external employees as well as through the creation of relationships with other organizations and entities.

The third ring of the core-ring model is most effective when outcomes or the work tasks that contribute to the desired outcome can be clearly defined. The model has both succeeded and failed in augmenting the armed forces in Afghanistan and Iraq with contractors for a variety of operational and support functions. On the positive side, it has provided the government a means of rapidly expanding the number of linguists, information technology experts, and systems repair and maintenance workers, as well as less skilled people in food service, trucking, and construction who are needed for a temporary period of time. However, this increased reliance on contractors has also led to many problems, including the widespread profiteering by some of the largest contractors. But the "third ring" is indispensable to the functioning of the government: for example, the Pentagon now employs 190,000 contractors in Iraq alone.[21] Much better management and control of this "third ring" is the only way to ensure that the government reaps the benefits and avoids the pitfalls.

Enabling Cross-Sector Movement with a Passport System

The government could develop the flexibility to move between sectors by issuing portable "human resources (HR) passports" to eligible employees.[22] For existing workers, a formal exchange program would enable them to learn new skills quickly, gain greater breadth of experience, and better understand how their network partners operate. It would also help the government to attract young people: in our surveys, 80 percent of college students said they would be willing to work for the government if it allowed them to go back and forth between sectors.[23] For those serving in the not-for-profit or private sector, it would provide an opportunity for public service to the government.

The current system prevents this exchange because it was set up to prevent conflicts of interest. The overarching priority has been to make sure that government employees cannot directly influence an industry they interact with, for example, in purchasing services, regulating business practices, or reporting requirements. And the idea of allowing businesspeople to work in the government is at odds with the prevailing civil service culture. But government has lost sight of the fact that the vast majority of people are honest and law-abiding. Most federal workers would be the very first to make certain that their stint in the private sector did not create a conflict of interest. By the same token, if a private sector employee chooses to work in government for a period of time, he or she is probably motivated by a desire to serve the public mission or to obtain broader work experience—not for personal financial gain. The system has been set up backwards, penalizing honest employees in both sectors in a futile effort to prevent cheating.

Of course, many details would need to be worked out. The HR passport would need to be tailored to each agency, job, and employee skill. There would be limits on how many federal workers could be away at any given time. But at least the concept would bring a new philosophical approach to public service, fusing its interests with those of the private sector rather than conflicting with them, and demanding that public servants understand all the available avenues to their mission.

Above all, the HR passport would create an incentive for the best people to continue in public service without sacrificing their desire to explore new opportunities outside government. The passport would in fact be a set of fully portable documents including performance evaluations, credentials and certifications, and career planning records. In addition, passports would give employees who move in and out of the federal workforce a tool for maintaining security clearances, although the highest security levels would be exempted from the program. Similarly, private sector employees could use the passport to document the value of their experiences in the public sector. Companies should view this experience among their employees as they would any other development assignment.

In the military, officers must serve a joint tour in order to be promoted to flag rank. This means that all promotable officers actively seek to spend a few years in another service. The incentives clearly align with the organizational goal of promoting interoperability between the major services. And the result is a more broadly educated officer core as well as the transfer of promising practices between services. Similarly, government managers would benefit from a tour of duty in another agency—or in one of the nonprofit or for-profit organizations that form part of the network delivering the service. By not offering a pathway for federal employees to work outside their agency, the government effectively precludes opportunities for professional growth and advancement, new ideas, and greater organizational effectiveness.

The system has been set up backwards, penalizing honest employees in both sectors in a futile effort to prevent cheating.

Matrix Structures and Teams

Another approach to jump-starting engagement and productivity is based on a matrix structure, in which employees report to more than one supervisor: for example, a salesperson in Asia might report simultaneously to the head of sales and to the head of Asian operations. The advantage here is that employees are part of a functional team but can also join teams set up for specific projects. This arrangement allows the organization to be more flexible and responsive.[24] Matrix structures are most often used in organizations that need multidisciplinary teams on their projects. Professional services firms are a good example of matrix organizations because of their frequent need to construct new teams for each new project. These organizations tend to offer more variety of work for employees, which can stimulate innovation and high performance for people who thrive in fast-paced, rapidly changing settings. Employees who function well in a matrix also have a high tolerance for ambiguity and enjoy working in teams. The principal drawback of a matrix organization is that it is more difficult to manage. Employees may be participating in more than one team at a time and therefore may have conflicting schedules, priorities, and reporting relationships.

A number of government agencies have used matrix formats with some success. The Government Accountability Office (GAO) has used a matrix to assemble project-specific teams in order to examine complex and cross-cutting issues. Employees from various disciplines bring their specific expertise to the group, and there are no traditional organizational boundaries that would prevent the agency from assigning the right people to solve a problem.[25] The U.S. Department of Agriculture (USDA) also uses a matrix management structure in its Agriculture Research Service (ARS) to provide program guidance and line management in more than 100 office locations. That is to say, national headquarters provides the vision and research direction to ARS employees, while area directors and the line management they supervise are responsible for implementing the research programs, managing research units on a day-to-day basis, and ensuring the quality of research. Despite their different assignments, all parties (numbering as many as fifty on any one project) must work closely together to reap the benefits of matrix management.

A third example is the Air Traffic Organization (ATO) within the Federal Aviation Administration (FAA), which uses a matrix structure to counteract the effects of functional silos. The ATO's mission is to provide airspace services to FAA customers, implement advanced cost and performance tools and techniques, and focus on employee performance and accountability. To address issues in a rapidly changing aviation environment, the FAA needed to create a flexible work environment within the ATO. The matrix model has helped to reduce silos and promote a shared work experience among ATO employees. Decisionmaking and support are institutionalized across the FAA, which helps to break down organizational "stovepipes" and promote cross-pollination of expertise between service units.[26]

When matrix management works well, it has significant benefits. The military has used this approach for decades. Studies of the military cite benefits of the matrix approach, including reduced paperwork, faster response times, improved cooperation, perceived better empowerment, and project effectiveness.[27] However, the studies note that in order to enjoy these benefits, team members need to be fully qualified and trained before being matrixed, project leaders should be selected for their leadership qualities and openness, communication channels must be established for exchange of functional information, and new support roles must be designed for functional leaders.

The private sector is now well advanced in using matrix structures and training managers to use them. This has become increasingly necessary to deal with the issues of globalization and multiple time zones, cultures, and locations. However, a matrix approach requires significant management skills to structure and solve complex problems in teams. It can backfire if the lines of supervision are ambiguous. A recent failure was the massive financial loss at the investment bank Credit Suisse, where British authorities directly blamed the matrix structure's "multiple reporting lines leading to uncertainty as to supervisory responsibilities" and fined the bank $10 million.[28]

To date the government has had limited, but largely positive experience with matrices but few managers and supervisors who understand them well. The government requires an investment in training and experiments with this structure in order to add it to the government toolkit and to adapt it to the individual agency missions.

Promoting Innovation

The organizational needs of the federal government will continue to evolve to meet new requirements. It is essential that the government foster innovation as a means to meet these challenges. But rigid hierarchical structures are anathema to innovation. As numerous studies have shown, companies innovate more when they have a flatter, more people-centric organization.[29] To create such a culture, individual agencies must develop a tolerance for mistakes, that is, a willingness to recognize, report, and correct mistakes systematically. In addition, those who report mistakes must be protected to assure employees that it is safe to bring new ideas and innovations forward without fear of repercussion (see box 5-2).

Programs can also be introduced to reward innovation, along the lines of those established by the Coast Guard and the U.S. Navy. The Coast Guard's annual Innovation Expo Awards provide a venue for cutting-edge ideas that increase effectiveness and efficiency, improve processes, and aid in the development of best practices, the application of new technologies, or the containment of costs in meeting the organization's expanding missions and challenges.[30] The navy's quarterly Sea Enterprise

BOX 5-2. Learning from Mistakes to Promote Innovation

To build a more effective and accountable workforce, the Veterans Health Administration (VHA) has created a culture that promotes innovation within its medical centers across the country. Since the late 1990s, the staff of the VA National Center for Patient Safety has had to report mistakes or close calls in treating patients. This information was crucial for improving safety in VA hospitals, given that many medical errors occurred because of a flawed system rather than careless individuals.

The greatest challenge in making this improvement was to allay the concerns of VA employees reluctant to report a mistake for fear of some reprisal, either to themselves or to the person responsible. Although the VA needed to move toward an open, nonpunitive environment, the staff did not respond until top managers demonstrated they were serious by announcing that managers could be fired, fined, and even jailed for retaliating against workers who file mistake reports. Since then, more than 200,000 close calls and errors have been filed at the VA without anyone being punished. The reporting has also helped to draw out new ideas from caregivers, who now turn in a steady flow of improvement ideas. Overall, the newly transparent, supportive, and innovative culture has done a great deal to bolster the VA's reputation for high-quality medical care.

The *Annals of Internal Medicine* published a study showing that the VA had "substantially better quality of care" than other providers in many of nearly 350 indicators of quality, such as screening and treating depression, diabetes, and hypertension. Other hospitals have also noticed VA's improvements. Jennifer Daley, chief medical officer and senior vice president of clinical quality at Tenet Healthcare Corporation, is using the VA as a blueprint to improve performance at the nation's second-largest for-profit hospital operator.

Source: Christopher J. Gearon, "Military Might: Today's VA Hospitals Are Models of Top-Notch Care," *U.S. News and World Report,* July 18, 2005 (www.usnews.com/usnews/health/articles/050718/18va.htm).

Awards recognize and reward productivity and efficiency initiatives that transform navy "business." Winners receive a personalized trophy bearing the Chief of Naval Operations seal and a citation summarizing their accomplishments. Entrants may include teams comprising military, civilian, or contractor personnel of all ranks and grades. Joint initiatives of other services or agencies that improve navy business processes and effectiveness or that reduce costs are also welcome. In addition to offering a unique way to recognize innovative ideas, the program provides an invaluable database of lessons and solutions to some of the navy's most pressing business issues.[31]

Another way to stimulate innovation is to forge partnerships such as the one the U.S. Army has entered with Arizona State University to accelerate research, development, and manufacturing of flexible display technologies that will allow for real-time information exchange during military operations. The Flexible Display Center is the result of a multimillion-dollar, five-year cooperative agreement. Although the center receives core funding from the army, it focuses primarily on commercial applications. Innovation comes from the center's unique staff, which includes experts from the academic, industrial, and military sectors. The partnership not only gives the army an opportunity to broaden its technological capabilities while expanding its reach into the commercial sector but also brings innovation to a specific organizational task.[32]

Promoting innovation is part of making any organization work better. Front-line employees, who are closest to customers, gain insights about emerging customer needs as well as discover alternate ways of providing service. Middle-level managers spot patterns of performance that create opportunities to improve the efficiency of their units and then shared with others. Senior leaders can provide focus and attention on emerging problems, allocate resources to address them, adopt new strategies, and further shape relations with outside stakeholders when they foster innovation and embrace change.

The Chief Operating and Chief Human Capital Officers

Organizations that are more flexible and versatile need talented managers to ensure that operations run smoothly. Former comptroller general David Walker advocates creating a new position with the title of chief operating officer (COO) or chief administrative officer (CAO) as a way to bring more people into the government who are experienced in managing large organizations. He advocates that the individuals filling these posts be given "performance contracts and sufficient latitude and authority to get the job done."[33] We agree that agencies should have a career position focused on management, with a contract period of between five and ten years. The performance standards and objectives for the position would be set out in the contract. Candidates for these positions should have demonstrated skills in formulating strategy and managing change and a track record of results-oriented leadership. Ideally, the cadre of government COOs would be a mix of leaders drawn from both the private and public sectors.

Despite their title, many "chief human capital officers" do not participate in key agency decisions or have a central role in planning, even though the viability of every agency depends on having a workforce capable of executing the mission.

Following this same model, the newest members of the "C-suite" in government agencies are chief human capital officers, or CHCOs (pronounced Cheekos), who are intended to focus on strategic human capital. Despite their title, many do not participate in key agency decisions or have a central role in planning, even though the viability of every agency depends on having a workforce capable of executing the mission. In many agencies, this title has simply elevated the director of the same old second-class HR office, without making any real difference in how the agency functions. To address this problem, the GAO has called for better leadership in human capital to support agency goals.[34]

One such step would be to make CHCOs full partners in the senior leadership team of every agency where they could help establish key human capital management goals, develop associated strategies, and provide guidance on key issues. This is basically what CHCO Patrick Pizzella did at the Department of Labor when he placed human capital issues—such as hiring, retention, skills training, and workforce planning—squarely in front of the agency's top executives at their weekly senior staff meetings.[35]

Unfortunately, this level of attention to human capital management issues is not yet the norm in most agencies. CHCOs must play a greater and more meaningful role in all aspects of management in order to bring people issues to the forefront. Moreover, by integrating CHCOs more fully into the top leadership echelons of each department, the government will be able to recruit even higher-quality individuals to accept these positions.

Conclusions

The government is saddled with a hierarchical organizational structure that is not well suited to innovation and rapid activity. But the workforce itself has become a multisector operation, with civil servants outnumbered by contractors and working alongside the private, nonprofit, and local government sectors. Changes to date have been limited (such as creating the CHCO positions) and not terribly effective. Much more fundamental organizational reform is needed.

We urge the adoption of a core-ring approach that would force the government to choose areas that are purely governmental and to identify technical skill–based positions that could occupy a middle ring encompassing all sectors. This approach would improve governance by recognizing the role of private, public, and nonprofit employees, and by increasing confidence, understanding, and the quality of relationships among them. In addition, the wider use of common models such as matrix structures, where appropriate, may improve productivity in the government. We also urge the appointment of a term-limited COO with a performance contract to each agency to deliver progress on these organizational reforms. These changes will require much better management of the whole structure. If managed well, the kind of twenty-first-century organization we describe will have many widespread benefits for government and the people it serves.

6

Achieving Excellence in Human Resources

Anyone browsing through the business section of a bookshop will make a startling discovery: almost none of the books are about human resources (HR). CEOs may routinely say that people are the most important factor in their company's success, but apparently that is not what they are reading about on the plane. There are hundreds of titles on leadership, organization, teams, marketing, and management. There are aisles of books on accounting and finance. There are books on strategy, capabilities, and "enabling platforms." There are biographies of rock star CEOs and books about trendy companies like Google. There are thousands of "how to" manuals on starting a business and running a company. Even a quick check at Amazon.com confirms that HR receives less attention than any other business topic (see table 6-1).

Yet basic HR systems and procedures—ranging from planning, recruiting, and staffing to reward systems and diversity policies—have a direct effect on employee satisfaction and motivation.[1] Employees thrive when they work for organizations that provide competitive wages, excellent benefits, opportunities for advancement that are clearly spelled out, a system for dealing with poor performers, and rewards that are both intrinsic (in the nature of the work itself) and extrinsic (rewards for specific contributions).

TABLE 6-1. **Number of Books Listed by Amazon.com**

Topic	Number of titles
Management	788,453
Finance	601,277
Sales	567,908
Teams	497,171
Organization	480,441
Strategy	433,157
Accounting	365,448
Marketing	360,236
Leadership	265,981
Human resources	111,736

Source: Author search, www.amazon.com (June 20, 2008).

This chapter describes what the best organizations in the public and private sector do to recruit, retain, compensate, and reward their employees and examines some of the more innovative personnel practices that agencies in the government have attempted. Although specific practices vary, all of the high-performing organizations that we studied made a commitment to excellence in human resources. This typically involved elevating the role of HR in the organization, workforce planning, recruiting and hiring, compensation and rewards, retaining key employees, and creating HR systems for building job satisfaction (see also chapter 7 on training and chapter 8 on performance management).

Role of Human Resources in the Organization

Traditionally, the function of most human resources departments has been to provide support—for example, in the handling of payroll, employee relocation, records, and other transactions. The role is reactive, not proactive. By contrast, leading people companies give human resources a more central role in the executive suite, along with finance and law. These companies rely on HR to provide strategic insight, leadership, and creativity in deciding how the mission of the organization can be achieved. From this perspective, the role of the HR function is to maximize the contribution of employees to delivering the organization's goals.

At the two agencies we profiled, the Government Accountability Office (GAO) and the Defense Logistics Agency (DLA), HR has been integrated into the strategic center of the organization. At GAO, the comptroller general and the chief operating officer provide strategic direction for all the key HR functions (workforce planning, recruiting, hiring, compensation, retention, employee development, and so on). The line managers and the HR staff work together to execute the vision articulated by GAO's leadership.

The approach at the DLA has been to deploy technological innovations to leverage HR resources and to use the senior HR staff more strategically. Technology plays a central role. For example, DLA introduced a web-based exit survey for retiring employees. This survey revealed that many of those leaving were dissatisfied with their first-line supervisors. In response, the agency set up a two-year training program for new supervisors and revamped its requirements for supervisory positions to include qualities that employees considered important.[2] The DLA employed a similar survey to evaluate skills gaps and training needs and then designed further training programs to close those gaps.[3] Having automated much of DLA's hiring and HR transaction processing, Human Resources Director Jeff Neal reorganized his staff into a day-to-day operations center and a long-term strategic planning office. Neal stressed the need for a special HR office to deal exclusively with strategic issues. Otherwise, the role of strategic planner plays second fiddle to daily business: "If you have three things to do, one due tomorrow, one next week, and one in a year and a half, when are you going to do the one due in a year and a half?"

The GAO and DLA experiences demonstrate that organizations can reap benefits from placing a higher value on HR. But they cannot realize such benefits unless they recruit, hire, and train the HR workforce very differently. The old-fashioned support-function, paperwork-focused kind of HR department does not merit a seat at the head table.

Human resources has fallen short of its potential at most other organizations for several reasons. One is that HR staff seldom have a strong sense of what the organization is trying to accomplish. "Business acumen is the single biggest factor that HR professionals in the U.S. lack today," notes *Fast Company* magazine.[4] Another is that HR personnel spend much of their time documenting and measuring things that have little impact on the bottom line. Yet another reason that HR is taken less than seriously is that most staff are not even equipped to prove the cost benefit of investing in people (which is described in chapter 2 of this book).[5]

If HR is to become responsive, flexible, and strategic, the HR department needs to employ professionals who understand the mission goals of the organization and who have the skills to help it advance toward those goals. These skills typically include a foundation in budgeting and financial management, information technology, and organizational design. They may also include technical expertise (such as knowledge of a particular industry or subject) or regional expertise (such as an understanding of the demographics of a particular location). Above all, the HR staff must have detailed knowledge of compensation, benefits, matrix management, performance evaluation, psychology, rewards, penalties, and other subjects, with a strong sense of how to harness all these tools to achieve the organization's business goals.

> *If HR is to become responsive, flexible, and strategic, the HR department needs to employ professionals who understand the business goals of the organization and who have the skills to help it advance toward those goals.*

However, companies are unlikely to hire talent with this valuable set of skills for the HR function as long as HR is considered an organizational dead end. The catch-22 is that in order for HR to attract the best people and thus earn respect, confidence, and authority from senior management, senior management needs to empower the HR function. The experience of leading people-focused companies indicates that this is a task for the leadership of the organization. The challenge for government is that many HR departments are purely transactional, so agency leaders are tempted to simply outsource those functions and shrink the department's budget as senior HR managers retire. The government should be doing *exactly the opposite* for non-transactional work: hire outstanding HR professionals, invest in developing their skills, and bring HR into the center of strategic decisionmaking.

Workforce Planning

Most organizations plan ahead when it comes to staffing, and the most successful companies do the most workforce planning. These are the conclusions of a study conducted by D. Quinn Mills on a random sample drawn from more than 2,500 companies in the private sector.[6] Of the companies Mills examined, 85 percent do "some" human resource planning, and nearly half draw up formal management succession plans and prepare training and development plans for managers and supervisors. Most also include HR planning in their long-term business plans. Mills found that "the companies engaged in people planning do it because their top executives are convinced it gives them a competitive advantage in the marketplace. . . . Managers involved in human resource planning have difficulty understanding how other companies can do without it."[7]

Mills divided the companies that do HR planning into five cohorts. The highest-scoring companies, which he refers to as "stage 5," all do formal management succession planning. They typically plan three to six years ahead, and up to ten years ahead for managerial and professional staff. "The managers at the stage 5 companies," he found, "seem to be applying the same time frame to their human resource investments that they have commonly used for research and development projects and large-scale capital investments."[8] The stage 1 companies at the bottom of the scale hire or retrain only when they have vacancies. Ranked on Mills's scale, the federal government would be a stage 1 company—the very worst. Mills also compared the profitability of the top companies that included human resource goals in their business plans with that of companies that did not. Providing yet another data point to support the people factor thesis, he found that the companies that did the most human resource planning were more profitable than the companies (in the same business sectors) that did less planning.

HR Planning in the Federal Government

The expected wave of retirements from the government presents an unprecedented opportunity for agencies to rethink the profile of their workforces. In some places, this may be the first opportunity in their history to plan a targeted recruiting and development strategy that could produce a more strategic skill mix. But these departures will also place unprecedented pressure on existing personnel systems. To define the talent and capabilities needed over the next five to ten years and attract the right people to fill those needs, the government must have better planning systems, faster processes, and effective methods to compete for talent.

This is a tall order. HR departments across government have been downsized, outsourced, and not given much training or investment in recent years. Most government agencies are doing little real workforce planning today or have only recently undertaken such initiatives. Many agencies also lack the know-how and the technical infrastructure to support real investment in the HR process. As a consequence, few managers and staff have the information they need to map the skills available (and required) in their organizations and to plan for the future accordingly.

What Competencies Does the Government Need?

Starting with its strategic plan, each agency will need to analyze its existing staff capabilities and its expected needs. The result will be a substantive description of the skills gap between "as-is" and "to-be," including unmet requirements and unneeded capacity. An often-cited example of the rapid shift in needed capabilities is foreign language skills in the intelligence community. During the cold war, U.S. intelligence needed Russian speakers. Today, it needs more speakers of Arabic and Farsi.

Another purpose of workforce analysis and planning is to start a conversation about a topic that may be politically difficult to broach. Every large organization has subcultures, communities of interest, or siloed functional groups, each with its own parochial view of the needs of the organization. The process of developing a workforce plan can help agencies arrive at a consensus on agency-wide needs, which is essential in an increasingly resource-constrained environment. Because labor costs and attendant personnel development and support costs are, in most agencies, the largest single cost item in their budget, a workforce plan can provide vital data for budget submissions. Furthermore, agency managers can use the plan to communicate to employees what direction the organization is taking, what skills will be needed to do those jobs, and who will do them. Many high-performing organizations use Kaplan and Norton's acclaimed balanced scorecard to achieve this, focusing on the "learning perspective."[9]

There are many approaches to workforce planning, and some government agencies have already engaged in this process to some degree. A common trigger is impending retirements. When the National Aeronautics and Space Administration (NASA) realized that 75 percent of its workforce was over the age of forty and 4 percent under thirty, it launched a new staffing strategy. Each NASA center was asked to build its own workforce plan under agency-wide guidelines. These plans were based on five pillars: strategic alignment, strategic competencies, learning, performance culture, and leadership. The plans are now used to guide staffing decisions.[10]

The Social Security Administration (SSA) adopted workforce planning when budget cuts forced a 22 percent downsizing over five years. In response, the SSA developed a Future Workforce Transition Plan to give managers better data on workforce composition and needs. Its analysis was instrumental in persuading Congress to grant the SSA authority to institute an "early-out" program and to rehire 130 retirees to train new employees. Among the results attributed to this plan were high rates of employee satisfaction (94 percent said they felt valuable to the agency), a new-hire retention rate of 90 percent, and redesigned training for new employees and managers that incorporated a mix of classes, on-the-job training, and rotational assignments (starting with GS-9s).[11]

The Office of Personnel Management (OPM) and numerous government agencies have already begun to study their workforces and plan for the future. But it is clear that in most cases these efforts are paltry compared with the systematic, robust skills-mapping and succession planning that many leading organizations practice. Moreover, these efforts are led by staff members, whereas the best people-focused companies make sure that line management is fully engaged in workforce planning. Perhaps most important, leading people companies spend money on planning for their future workforce, both directly (in planning budgets) and indirectly (by ensuring that line managers participate in the process). By contrast, the federal government has actually been cutting human resource budgets—just when far more resources are needed.

In addition, the government needs to invest in technology that helps managers analyze their workforces more easily. Currently, individual agencies are developing their own technologies, with much duplication of effort. For example, the Department of Justice (DOJ) has developed an automated planning model that generates employee head counts, expected separations, five-year staffing targets, and hiring/workforce gaps. The DOJ can then run "what-if" scenarios to project future needs and set up a workforce metrics dashboard that top executives, budget officials, and human resources managers can use to drive improvement initiatives.[12] The Defense Logistics Agency also has a state-of-the-art HR technology system. But rather than operate in isolation, such tools need to be made available throughout the government and shared among agencies that recruit people with similar backgrounds.

Defining the Role of the Federal Worker in the Future

The task of planning in government is complicated by the changing nature of governance itself. During the 1980s, the private sector went through a decade of restructuring and reengineering that radically changed the way the business world operates. Today, societies are reexamining how to achieve public goals—experimenting with a mixture of public-private partnerships, NGO-led initiatives, regulatory incentives, and other innovative combinations. The interplay of these forces is shaping how the government gets work done, but defining this boundary between public and private has generated a highly charged debate. During the George W. Bush presidency, the President's Management Agenda (PMA) encouraged more outsourcing of "non-core" activities in federal agencies. But the line between "core" and "non-core" is unclear. The war in Iraq has employed a larger number of contractors than ever before, with private security forces engaged in seemingly core activities such as protecting U.S. diplomats, interrogating prisoners, and repairing secret weapons systems.[13] Meanwhile, some of the president's most successful and well-funded global initiatives, such as the fight against HIV/AIDS and tuberculosis in Africa, have involved joint efforts by government, nonprofits, and the private sector.

Planning, in the government context, is not simply a matter of mapping out skills and the details of succession. It must also establish which jobs absolutely need to be led, managed, or conducted by government employees.

This boundary issue has important implications for the role of the federal employee. Planning, in the government context, is not simply a matter of mapping out skills and the details of succession. It must also establish which jobs absolutely need to be led, managed, or conducted by government employees. What are the criteria for such jobs and how should the government ensure that it has a pipeline of qualified personnel to do them? If this kind of planning is not begun now, mission-critical work will increasingly be performed by contractors, NGOs, and others, simply because the government lacks the manpower, skills, or technical expertise to do it.

Recruiting and Hiring

Workforce planning gives people-focused organizations a head start in attracting top job applicants and selecting the ones who will best fit their organization. Over the next decade, there will be intense competition to hire talent—and the federal government will lose out unless it overhauls its recruiting and hiring processes. The current system almost seems designed to thwart talented applicants, with its poorly worded job announce-

> *O*ver the next decade, there will be intense competition to hire talent—and the federal government will lose out unless it overhauls its recruiting and hiring processes.

ments, hiring processes that take an average of months instead of weeks, barriers to transitioning interns into full-time employees, disincentives to midcareer recruitment, inflexible work arrangements for new hires, and other impediments.

In addition, most government agencies divorce the recruiting process from daily operations, leaving it largely to the HR department. This practice is quite the opposite of the attitude at top private sector companies. Consulting firms such as McKinsey and Booz Allen assign their top consulting staff—the smartest, most engaging, and energetic ones—to lead the recruiting effort. This is seen as a plum role, which receives kudos and attention from the most senior partners at the firm. These top consultants will spend anywhere from six to eighteen months flying around the world interviewing job applicants, answering their questions, and trying to persuade them to join the company. And they do this instead of regular work because these organizations believe that recruiting is more important. Similarly, they view their summer intern programs as recruiting investments—with senior members of the company taking the time to learn about the personal interests and aspirations of prospective employees.

The same is true in academia, where the most distinguished professors are asked to lead search committees. Faculty are given generous amounts of time off from teaching and administrative responsibilities if they agree to serve on panels that interview, negotiate with, and generally woo potential new faculty members. At knowledge companies across many sectors, the responsibility for recruiting rests firmly with the line managers, who are judged by their results. Such an approach is almost unthinkable in the federal government.

Moreover, leading people organizations try to hire candidates who not only meet the technical requirements of a job but will also contribute to the spirit and culture of the organization. To that end, writes David Maister in *Practice What You Preach,* hiring itself must take on a new spirit, as reflected in the comments of people he surveyed: "Involve the whole team in hiring"; "In recruiting ask questions like 'What kind of people do you like to work for? What kinds of people do you like working for you?'"; and "Hire people with enthusiasm, excitement, sparks, energy, spirit, a sharing style, smarts, personality, compatibility and vision."[14] This excitement in recruiting seems all but absent from much of the government.

The federal government is well aware of its challenges in this area. The Office of Personnel Management, the GAO, and inspector general offices in a number of agencies have documented the situation in some detail. Some impressive and innovative work has already been done to identify problems in the hiring process and to develop solutions. The cases profiled in this section, particularly the work done by the Partnership for Public Service (PPS), highlight some of this work.

Partnership for Public Service: "Extreme Hiring Makeover"

The PPS Extreme Hiring Makeover project, launched in September 2004, was a cooperative venture of several private sector recruiting and hiring experts: Monster Government Solutions, ePredix, CPS Human Resource Services, AIRS, Brainbench, the Human Capital Institute, and Korn/Ferry International. The goal of the makeover was to transform the recruiting and hiring processes of three federal organizations facing serious hiring challenges: the entire Department of Education (box 6-1), the National Nuclear Security Administration (Department of Energy; box 6-2), and the Centers for Medicare & Medicaid Services (Department of Health and Human Services; box 6-3).[15]

B O X 6 - 1 . Department of Education

The Extreme Hiring Makeover team found that hiring a single employee at the Department of Education took 114 steps. By the last one, many prospective employees were no longer available or interested. To make matters worse, the process did not deliver the high-quality candidates that department managers needed.

Many of the steps consisted of getting multiple approvals for each new hire. To reduce the time wasted in seeking these approvals, the makeover team asked senior managers to prepare and follow approved annual staffing plans. This mapping not only reduced the back-and-forth steps but also uncovered communication gaps between hiring managers and HR specialists. Information relayed from managers to HR specialists usually focused on the position's occupational series and grade, not the "essential education, skills, and experience required for success." Once the hiring manager and the HR specialist began conversations about a specific job's needs as a first step in hiring, the entire process worked better.

As a result of these and other reforms recommended by the makeover team, the department reduced the number of steps required to hire an employee by more than 50 percent and expects to see a marked improvement in the match between applicants and the skills needed.

The extreme hiring makeover suggests that, with some guidance and outside help, it is feasible to improve the federal government's ability to recruit and hire. However, it also shows the extent to which improvement is needed in order to replicate the PPS effort throughout the federal government. Most agencies desperately want to improve their systems—but apart from the ones that benefited from the "extreme makeover," they do not know how to do it. The PPS effort shows that government needs to focus on four measures to get hiring and recruiting right:

1. *Identify the skills and competencies that each agency needs.* Then ask line managers to work closely together with the human resources managers to search for suitable job applicants. Supervisors need to define the specific skills and experience they are looking for in candidates—not just the position's occupational series and grade.

2. *Communicate with recruits in clear, jargon-free language that people outside of the government can understand.* Potential candidates need

BOX 6-2. National Nuclear Security Administration

Because the National Nuclear Security Administration (NNSA) is responsible for the security of the government's nuclear programs, it needs to be able to identify and hire professionals with uncommon scientific and technical skills and experience. In recent years, the NNSA's search for highly skilled people has become a struggle. And with more than a third of its personnel eligible for retirement, the agency has been facing a serious threat of lost knowledge. Not only is there a dearth of technical skills needed by NNSA, but its facilities are in remote locations unappealing to most people. Consequently, the agency had to start with a small pool of potential candidates, many of whom had never heard of the NNSA because of its low profile, or of the opportunities it offers.

To help build a pipeline of potential candidates to meet NNSA's long-term needs, the Extreme Hiring Makeover team focused on developing internship and competitive university recruiting programs. To meet the organization's more immediate recruiting needs, the makeover team first worked with NNSA managers to simplify and clarify the highly technical, multipage job announcements for specific NNSA jobs so that applicants could better understand which jobs they were interested in and qualified for. The new announcements outlined the critical mission of NNSA, the major features and selling points of the job, and the most important skills and experience required of candidates. The team then helped get the announcements out to the right people, especially to experienced candidates who had posted their résumés on various job boards. NNSA also ran advertisements in *Government Executive* magazine under the tagline "Where Engineering, Science, and National Security Intersect in a Challenging Career."

The early results from the team's efforts have been very promising, with one senior scientific position yielding an eightfold increase in applicants. The team felt the proactive targeting was particularly successful.[1]

---

1. Partnership for Public Service, "The Science of Marketing: The National Nuclear Security Administration" (Washington, April 7, 2006).

to understand the types of tasks they will be asked to perform and the skills and competencies they will be expected to have.

3. *Seek out qualified candidates actively.* Most highly qualified professionals have a choice of good job opportunities, and they can afford to be picky. They are probably not even aware of the opportunities available

BOX 6-3. Centers for Medicare and Medicaid Services

When the Extreme Hiring Makeover team began working with the Centers for Medicare and Medicaid Services (CMS) in 2004, the organization was still reeling from the largest expansion of Medicare since its inception. Under the Medicare Prescription Drug Improvement and Modernization Act of 2003, the CMS was to grow by 10 percent (500 employees) in two years. This challenge was compounded by the many retirements expected during that period. Hiring managers were already unhappy with the time it took to hire new employees and the quality of the applicants; they did not believe the system in place at the time could support such an increased demand for new hires.

To help the CMS meet these critical short-term demands, the makeover team recommended several of the same reforms that were successful at the Department of Education and NNSA: streamlining the current process, job announcements in plain English, and active recruiting of qualified candidates whose résumés appeared on various career databases. However, the team's main concern was to help the agency define the process for "effective selection and assessment" needed when the volume of applicants increased significantly.[1]

To identify the best candidates, the team and CMS developed questionnaires that could screen out approximately 15 percent of the applicants. Those who were successful with the questionnaire took an online skills test. The scores from the questionnaire and test were then combined to rank the applicants. After the hiring manager reviewed the applicants, those chosen for an interview were asked to complete an additional assessment that measured "behavioral competencies and cognitive abilities."[2]

As a result of this makeover, applicants increased in number and quality, and the process for evaluating them and getting them hired speeded up. The CMS now had the foundation for a system robust enough to meet its enormous hiring demands.

1. Partnership for Public Service, "Extreme Hiring Makeover: Prescription for Hiring Success" (Washington, March 2, 2006).
2. Ibid.

in the federal government. It needs to advertise on popular websites, review résumés posted on databases, and generally employ twenty-first-century tools.

4. *Shorten the hiring process.* Most qualified applicants are not willing (or financially able) to wait the months it often takes the federal

government to make hiring decisions. This is especially true of college graduates—85 percent say they need to have a job within two months.

Recruiting Midcareer Staff from Outside Government

Government agencies usually recruit and hire for senior positions from inside their own ranks. This practice is accepted within the civil service where government employees take it for granted that everyone around them has been working in the government for their entire careers. But outside the government, most companies aim to keep a balance between the continuity that comes from internal hires and the fresh approaches that external hires bring to an organization. Even companies that promote primarily from within have systems to bring in outside talent for specific needs.

This propensity for insiders can have dangerous consequences for the U.S. government. According to the 9/11 Commission, "The FBI's tradition of hiring analysts from within instead of recruiting individuals with relevant education background and experience was one of the reasons we failed to thwart the 9/11 plot."[16]

However, the government will be forced to change—thanks to the combination of retirements and a shortage of inside candidates. But it will require new recruiting techniques to identify, attract, and then integrate external recruits successfully. The government needs to incorporate its midcareer cohort into workforce planning and make certain sensible changes that would enable experienced senior people to join the government. These range from providing a wider menu of HR benefits to bypassing rules that restrict vacation time, flexible working hours, or staffing assignments to midcareer entries. The government should also reach out to programs—such as the midcareer program at the Harvard Kennedy School and executive training programs at leading universities— to establish pipelines to highly educated candidates who are already in a period of career transition.

Currently, the main vehicle for hiring employees from outside government is the temporary or "term" appointment, which allows the employing agency to hire appointees for up to four years. The stated reason can be special project work, an extraordinary workload, scheduled abolishment of a position, reorganization, uncertainty of future funding, or contracting out of the function.[17] In some cases, government leaders have special flexibilities with their term appointees. The GAO, for example, has the authority to hire up to fifteen people at a time on term appointments and to specify the salary, duties, and geographic location for each individual. Up to now, however, there has been a certain "second-class" stigma attached to many term appointments. It is assumed that term appointees are hired only because they could not obtain permanent employment.

We advocate a complete reversal of this mindset: the government ought to reach out to talented Americans in many disciplines and encourage them to spend a period of time serving their country in the government. The government is coping with many problems that could benefit from this expertise. The Veterans Benefit Administration, for example, has a backlog of more than 400,000 pending disability claims. It uses a cumbersome, twenty-three-page, paper-intensive process that takes an average of six months just to adjudicate the claims of returning wounded veterans. It would make a lot of sense—and help a great many veterans— if the government were to hire some of the best health care claims specialists from the private sector for a short while, not as contractors, but as employees with full benefits and responsibility in positions where they can teach, train, and manage other employees. Surveys indicate that a number of Americans would volunteer for such positions. But the federal government has very limited mechanisms to allow this.

Where they exist, such programs have been successful and popular. In Canada, the Recruitment of Policy Leaders (RPL) program is designed to bring exceptional graduates into the public service. The selection process involves detailed applications, careful screening, and the personal involvement of senior managers in one-on-one interviews. The program seeks individuals to perform in areas highly sought after. In general, the Canadian government recruiting materials are easy to use and make it very clear that they are looking to attract talent at many levels. At the top of the Canadian civil service recruiting website, it states clearly:

> Whether you're a student looking to gain work experience, a recent graduate beginning your career, a seasoned professional looking for a change, or someone seeking a fulfilling position that contributes to the wellbeing of all Canadians, the public service of Canada should be number one on your list of potential employers. We may have just what you're looking for!

The United States would stand to benefit from emulating its northern neighbor in this area.[18]

The nonprofit sector has long adopted this practice. For example, the Loaned Executive Program at the United Way gives the private sector an opportunity to make a different kind of charitable contribution. During the United Way's peak campaign season for thirteen weeks during August, September, and October, its individual chapters call upon corporate partners to lend their best and brightest employees. These employees are called "loaned executives." They assist local companies in running United Way campaigns and become spokespeople within the community. Firms may also sponsor a loaned executive by donating the funds necessary for United Way to hire a high-quality temporary employee.[19]

In the U.S. government, the GAO has introduced a two-way Executive Exchange program that shows the benefit of this approach. As David Walker explains,

> The program is intended to help with hiring more from the outside. Half of my direct reports came from outside GAO. We are looking for people in finance, IT [information technology], transformation, and financial auditing. We hope to draw from investment banks, consulting firms, and IT firms. The idea is that people would take sabbaticals from their firms. We pay only a GAO-rate salary; the firms may make up the difference, or if they see the appointment as strategic for their firm, they may pay the entire salary.[20]

Under regulations known as Schedules A, B, and C, the federal government also has the authority to fill special jobs or to fill any job in unusual or special circumstances: "These excepted service authorities enable agencies to hire when it is not feasible or not practical to use traditional competitive hiring procedures, and can streamline hiring."[21] Schedule C, the best known of the three, covers the hiring of political appointees. Although Schedules A, B, and C provide valuable flexibilities for hiring under special circumstances, they tend to be underutilized. Supervisors should be trained and empowered to use these hiring authorities much more aggressively to help fill positions with innovative recruits.

Another mechanism for importing knowledge and skills into government is the "hybrid" employee, whereby an individual is shared and compensated by, for example, a government agency and a nonprofit organization. This kind of approach can make sense in fields where people need to work across organizational boundaries, as do scientists working in research teams or aid workers in humanitarian disasters, as well as at semiautonomous government institutions.[22]

Whatever method is used, bringing experienced professionals from the outside into government is likely to present some new assimilation challenges. It is one thing to take young college graduates with little work experience and teach them how things are done in government. All that one can expect of these entry-level recruits is that they are bright, energetic, and ready to learn what the current staff has to teach them. It is something else entirely to hire and assimilate someone with substantial work experience. Organizations expect far more from an experienced hire, yet the assimilation challenges are still likely to be difficult, perhaps even more so, precisely because the new hire has already developed a particular way of doing things that may conflict with the manner in which the new organization operates. One way to counter this effect is to create midcareer internship and fellowship programs that allow more professionals to experience work in the government environment with a minimal commitment on both sides.

Expanding the Use of Internships

In the private sector, internships are an effective way to attract entry-level professionals who fit the organizational culture. Internships can help test the "fit" between the candidates and a given agency, thus establishing a key qualification for the work. Indeed, internships have been especially successful in recruiting entry-level employees. Private sector programs for college students convert approximately 36 percent of their interns into permanent employees. Although the federal government has several programs employing well over 50,000 interns annually, the rate of conversion to permanent employees is less than half that of its private sector competitors. Some federal programs are not even structured to offer full-time employment opportunities following the internship.[23]

Research shows that college graduates who interned with their employer before accepting a full-time position have a higher retention rate than all other hires.[24] When large numbers of new hires may be needed, it makes sense to develop and finance a steady pipeline of qualified candidates.

The federal government should also create a separate midcareer internship or fellowship program. Midcareer fellows would be hired for a specific period and paid a fixed salary. Throughout the program, the hands-on experience would be fortified by the usual benefits of such a program (lunchtime lectures, network building, and mentoring). At the end of the program, the most promising fellows would be offered full-time positions.

At least two government departments have initiated effective internship programs to recruit and develop a cadre of future managers and leaders. The Emerging Leaders program at the Department of Health and Human Services (HHS) selects 50–60 people out of 2,000–3,000 master of public health (MPH) and master of business administration (MBA) applicants each year. The program offers a robust two-year training experience and at the end offers trainees a job. It has proved to be an effective recruiting tool, despite the initial skepticism of HHS executives and managers. According to its former HR director, Bob Hosenfeld, the department retained approximately 90 percent of its first class of interns.[25]

The Department of Labor's (DOL's) MBA recruiting program has also enjoyed a strong response from potential candidates: the department received almost 700 applications for its first fifteen MBA openings. The DOL marketed its program to current MBA graduates and to MBA alumni groups (to target those who are in career-changing mode). New MBA recruits start out on six-month rotational assignments. Some quickly move to permanent positions, some continue rotations, and some leave the agency. Overall, according to Chief Human Capital Officer Patrick Pizzella, the program has been very successful at increasing the number of MBAs in DOL and has, over time, won over the skeptics in the department.[26]

Compensation and Rewards

The correlation between job satisfaction and organizational performance is well documented. What is also clear is that job satisfaction depends in part on satisfaction with one's own compensation and rewards. But the relationship between the two is complex. According to HR experts Michael Beer and Richard Walton, the degree of satisfaction with one's compensation depends on four factors:

1. The employee's own expectations.

2. Employee perceptions of their compensation in relation to what other people are paid.

3. The values an individual brings to this comparison: others may seem to be worth more or less (in relation to oneself) than their compensation reflects.

4. The overall mixture of rewards, including monetary compensation and nonmonetary rewards such as recognition, promotions, status, and respect.[27]

According to these four criteria, federal employees have ample reason to be dissatisfied. They currently receive a hodgepodge of compensation and benefits based on historical decisions regarding fair pay for certain skills. The system covers a mixture of exempt and nonexempt positions, wage-grade and salaried staff, and political and career senior executives. This system, notes the OPM, "was established at the end of the 1940s, a time when over 70 percent of Federal white-collar jobs consisted of clerical work. Government work today is highly skilled and specialized 'knowledge work.'"[28]

This legacy has given rise to numerous inconsistencies. As a result, many federal employees feel that they are not being compensated fairly in comparison with others on the government staff. In addition, many work alongside federal contractors who earn significantly higher salaries for what they see as similar work.[29] Whatever dissatisfaction emerges from such inequities, whether perceived or real, it will precipitate morale and performance problems.

There are pay inequities within government and between the government and other sectors. Within government, for example, pay inequities are discouraging members of the career senior executive service from seeking jobs as inspectors general (IGs). In an interview with the *Washington Post,* the retiring inspector general of the Environmental Protection Agency, Nikki L. Tinsley, said, "Serving the president as an IG has been an honor . . . and working to improve federal operations provides great job satisfaction." However, the article noted that in her office, "the top SES aide earns $23,000 more than she does . . . . In addition to the pay comparability issue, IGs drawn from the ranks of the SES have not been eligible for bonuses since 1984. The double whammy can be costly: as much as $80,500 a year, she estimated."[30]

Pay inequities have also triggered intragovernmental competition. OPM senior policy adviser Doris Hausser recalls that the banking regulatory agencies were successful in drawing talent away from other agencies because they were able to offer more competitive salaries. Another example: TSA drew staff away from other law enforcement agencies because the skills needed for the TSA jobs were available elsewhere in the government. The increased turnover in at least one agency placed mission-critical functions at risk.

Pay parity with the private sector is also an issue for the Pentagon, where the uniformed military competes for experienced combat veterans with private contractors like Blackwater who can pay much higher salaries. "The irony," says HR executive Roger Blanchard of the U.S. Air Force,

> is that we reduce active duty strength levels and then engage in an operation that exceeds our capacity. So we hire contractors and pay them at much higher rates (because we have to) to do the same work. This creates internal competition and forces us to find ways to compensate active duty forces [with retention bonuses, for example]. This shows we do not have, and do not operate from, a total force management perspective, which includes contractors in the total force equation.[31]

Public Sector Wages versus Private Sector Wages

Harvard professor George Borjas examined the issue of wage structures in the public and private sectors between 1960 and 2000. One of his insights is that the wage structures in the two sectors have evolved very differently over the past decades, with the wage dispersion rising at a much faster rate in private sector jobs than in public sector jobs.[32] This has had the consequence of discouraging highly skilled private workers from joining the public sector and incentivizing highly skilled public sector workers to leave. He concludes:

As the wage structure in the public sector became relatively more compressed, the public sector found it harder to attract and retain high-skill workers. In short, the substantial widening of wage inequality in the private sector and the relatively more stable wage distribution in the public sector created magnetic effects that altered the sorting of workers across sectors, with high-skill workers becoming more likely to end up in the private sector.[33]

This finding is confirmed in the recent work of another Harvard labor economist, Jack Donahue, who shows that wages in the private economy have sharply exceeded those in the public sector in highly skilled jobs and have lagged far behind in low-skilled occupations. This can be seen in his analysis of congressional salaries relative to the private and public sectors. Congressional salaries form a kind of unofficial wage ceiling in government—all senior executives, cabinet and subcabinet officials, indeed, everyone but a handful of top officials (the president, vice president, justices of the Supreme Court) are pegged to earn less than members of Congress. Donahue points out that the average member of Congress is earning three times the income of the average family of four. This 3:1 ratio has persisted for three decades. (Whether consciously or not, Congress has kept its salary tethered to the average income of its constituents.) But top private sector salaries have diverged sharply from congressional pay during this period. Thirty years ago, the salary for a member of Congress was roughly equal to the average income for the top 5 percent of U.S. families. Today, that compensation is *less than half* the average income of the top 5 percent.[34] This reflects the extraordinary growth in income in the upper echelons of private companies.

Donahue argues that the disparities at both ends of the labor market contribute to the government's performance failures: "It limits the government's access to the human assets required for custom tasks and it hobbles government's flexibility to alter commodity tasks. Public missions that demand highly qualified workers are frequently performed less adroitly than they ought to be . . . or performed less accountably than they ought to be. Simpler public missions that require unspecialized labor are performed less flexibly and more expensively than they ought to be"[35]

There is no "quick fix" to solve a wage gap problem that originates in the private sector. But most analysts who have looked at the government compensation system have recommended giving departments and agencies more flexibility in designing, testing, and offering competitive compensation levels and structures.

Market-Based Pay. Competition for key skills varies over time by occupation and by locality. In recognition of this fact, the Federal Employee Pay Comparability Act of 1990 (FEPCA) took a first step toward introducing a form of market sensitivity into federal compensation practices. FEPCA allows the government to adjust pay in response to local differences between public and private sector compensation based on pay grade, but not on occupation.

> *By failing to adjust wages for market shortages or excesses for specific skills, the federal government will find itself unable to compete for the best candidates to fill a specific job and overpaying for more prevalent skills.*

This approach is dated. As the federal workforce becomes increasingly specialized and highly skilled, it is less useful to scale compensation against the prevailing wage for the private sector equivalent of a GS-12 (which has no real private sector equivalent) and more useful to be able to draw distinctions between an employee with budget skills and an employee specializing in IT systems administration. By failing to adjust wages for market shortages or excesses for specific skills, the federal government will find itself unable to compete for the best candidates to fill a specific job and overpaying for more prevalent skills.

The federal compensation system should also be able to adjust salaries in accordance with an agency's special circumstances. If it is having trouble locating employees for a mission-critical category despite offering competitive wages for that occupation, it should be able to offer additional incentives and compensation. Indeed, in its study of human capital flexibilities in the federal government's twenty-four largest departments and agencies, the GAO recommended three incentives to help the government hire mission-critical employees: recruitment bonuses, relocation bonuses, and superior or special qualification appointments.[36]

Performance-Based Pay. One of the most appealing concepts in business is the idea of paying employees according to how well they perform, or "pay-for-performance" (PFP). This idea is attractive because, at least in theory, it can help to motivate the best workers, attract and retain high performers, incentivize certain behaviors, and penalize those who do poorly. In theory, performance-based pay would give the federal government an important mechanism with which to use limited resources efficiently to attract and retain top performers. Top performers have come to expect performance-based compensation in the private sector; its absence in federal jobs confirms the perception that the federal government does not prioritize the development, advancement, and retention of top performers. However, as Beer and Walton point out in their study of rewards and the role of compensation, "there is a wide gap between the desire to devise a pay-for-performance system and the ability to make such a system work."[37]

Many federal managers and staff will find it difficult to change from automatic step increases to pay based on performance ratings (see chapter 8). The latter system will not work unless employees have confidence in the fairness of the evaluation process and the capability of their supervisors to conduct it. To create this confidence, the government will need to provide extensive training and establish a formal credentialing program to certify that it is able to evaluate performance.

Individual pay-for-performance makes sense when individuals have real control over the outcome, but this is usually not the case in government. Most public servants are in occupations where the outcomes are influenced by many factors outside their control. This makes it difficult, if not impossible, to set meaningful individual performance targets that can be linked to compensation. Despite the theoretical appeal of paying more for better performance, we believe it is too difficult for the government to implement such a system in practical terms, at least at the current time.

Group pay-for-performance is much more attractive. At the organizational level there are many benefits to using forms of performance pay. For example, "gainsharing"—whereby the financial proceeds of performance improvements are distributed among members of an organization—has been used successfully in many parts of the world. In the United Kingdom, several government agencies have been permitted to reinvest savings achieved over a three-year period.[38] Typically, employees and management work together to introduce a new process that improves efficiency. In a similar vein, the U.S. government could permit agencies to retain some of their budget savings earned for the taxpayer as a result of a cost-saving, waste-reduction, or productivity effort.

This kind of system requires trust and cooperation between labor and management. As Beer and Walton point out, "Organization-wide incentive plans that are part of a philosophy of participation require strong labor-management cooperation in design and administration. For example, the Scanlon Plan, the oldest and most widely used gainsharing arrangement, requires a direct employee vote with 75% approval before implementation. Without joint participation, commitment to any organization-wide incentive plan system will be low, and its symbolic and motivational value will be diminished."[39]

Other performance-based awards can produce immediate benefits. Incentive tools suggested by the GAO include cash awards to motivate and recognize exceptional performance by employees. Cash awards can mirror performance bonuses paid in the private sector after an annual performance review period, or they can be awarded more opportunistically, as events warrant. Cash awards can also be issued to individuals or to a group. Group incentives help supervisors encourage teamwork and innovation in support of specific organizational goals. Given the current benefits structure in the government, one-time cash bonuses are not reflected in the calculation of retirement benefits.[40]

Bonuses and Adjustments. The private sector generally pays whatever it takes to hire someone it really wants. Common incentives include bonuses, stock options, relocation pay, and compensation to even out differences in the cost of living between one job location and another. Many companies help spouses find jobs in a new location or even employ them.

In government, these everyday tools are largely out of reach. Yet agencies like the National Nuclear Security Administration, with facilities in remote locations, could make their jobs more appealing if they offered relocation and signing bonuses. But the government remains by and large restricted in this regard. To remedy the situation, the GAO suggests paying retention bonuses to employees who are uniquely skilled or employed in difficult-to-fill positions, as is already done to some extent in the military. It offers certain highly trained special operations personnel reenlistment bonuses of up to $150,000 in exchange for a multiyear commitment.

This bonus represents significant savings to the military when compared with the cost of recruiting and training replacement troops, or hiring private contractors at even higher salaries.

Such retention pay should also be used in regional settings where the job market is highly competitive. For example, if the government wishes to retain IT specialists in a region with a buoyant tech-based economy, or in a location where a major technology corporation has just built a new plant, it would make sense for the government to have the ability to pay a one-time retention bonus to its most valuable employees. (This could be made repayable to the government should the employee leave within twelve months.) This kind of simple tool, widely available in the private sector, may help the government retain needed staff and avoid recruiting, hiring, and training costs.

Senior Executives. Borjas's study showed that the wage gap between the private sector and the public sector has increased significantly for women, and slightly for men, over the past forty years. He also found that the top wages in the public sector have compressed in comparison with the private sector.[41] This disparity has not only prompted a few top government managers to leave government service for the private sector but has also limited the pool of highly trained senior managers who are willing or have the financial ability to take up a career or political job in the government. These are precisely the kind of experienced, skilled leaders that the government badly needs.

In the political arena, it has become a truism that only millionaires run for the U.S. Senate, with the House of Representatives not far behind. By restricting the pay of political managers, such as assistant and deputy assistant secretaries, the United States is rapidly creating a system in which only the wealthy can afford to serve in government. It is shooting itself in the foot by allowing the most experienced and talented senior executives to "retire" so they can work as consultants, often on a less demanding schedule. Instead, the government should be providing an attractive option that would enable older, experienced government workers to contribute their expertise on a paid, part-time basis. If the government offered more flexibility in the structuring of work, it might be able to retain more of these individuals.

Buyouts

While buyouts and early retirements may seem unusual ingredients for a retention strategy, a GAO report on their use in non-defense federal agencies suggests otherwise.[42] Before 2002, they were used primarily to facilitate the downsizing of federal agencies but since then have helped reduce payroll costs in some occupations. This frees up limited budget dollars for new initiatives, new staff with hard-to-find competencies, and rewards to help retain existing staff whose skills are at a premium. In short, buyouts can be used to reshape the workforce to help retain workers.

Retaining the Best Employees

Any high-performing organization should have a targeted retention strategy. It needs to be both proactive (must reach out to key employees) and reactive (should focus on reducing turnover). Most organizations are eager to reduce turnover, because it costs time and money to recruit and screen applicants and then train newcomers. Further costs arise when positions remain vacant for long periods in the form of overtime pay for current employees or absenteeism due to burnout because of the extra work. The government generally does a poor job of addressing these issues. The Department of Veterans Affairs, for example, has a high turnover of new claims specialists, with attrition rates at the Veterans Benefits Administration reaching 49 percent at some regional offices.[43] The training of new employees takes a minimum of eighteen months, but the department is not retaining those it trains. Similarly, the Patent and Trademark Office is experiencing a high turnover of skilled patent attorneys. The State Department, which continues to attract new recruits without difficulty, is facing a serious problem in retaining midcareer foreign service officers. These individuals often face dual-career pressures and other family commitments that make them easy prey for the aggressive recruiting tactics of companies that hope to poach their language and cultural skills.

The key to retaining good workers is to provide an environment that is rewarding and flexible—both financially and personally. A National Academy of Public Administration (NAPA) study found that once reasonable pay comparability is achieved "nonmonetary issues become more important. . . . [M]ost of the factors that cause people to stay or leave an organization are under the control of their immediate supervisor. People want training, career development opportunities, open communication, and flexible work arrangements. They want to be involved in decisions and in setting goals."[44] These are the same issues that we have cited throughout this book.

NAPA's observations are also consistent with a Gallup study of managerial behavior and organizational effectiveness, which found that responses to the following five questions were linked to employee retention:

—Do I know what is expected of me at work?

—Do I have the materials and equipment I need to do my work right?

—Do I have the opportunity to do what I do best every day?

—Does my supervisor, or someone else at work, seem to care about me as a person?

—At work, do my opinions count?[45]

In the past, the only way to reward top performers over time with pay increases and prestige was to promote them into management ranks. But this is a slow process. In fact, the government has very few carrots at its disposal to create an enticing environment. Some agencies—notably the Treasury Department, the National Geospatial-Intelligence Agency, the Central Intelligence Agency, and the National Security Agency—have created dual career tracks for technical experts, with separate career paths for their senior executive (managerial) and senior technical (nonmanagerial) positions.[46] This is attractive to some people, but not most. Young people would prefer to be able to move among the private, nonprofit, and government sectors to obtain training and experience at all three, as shown in our study of college students.

Support and Mentoring from Supervisors

No one has a greater impact on retention than an employee's immediate supervisor. Supervisors communicate the expectations of a job, define specific duties, and provide day-to-day commentary and coaching. They are responsible for functional matters, such as approving requests for materials and equipment. As the person who most closely observes a staff member's work, a supervisor is in the best position to understand where an individual's skills lie and to solicit and act on input from staff members. Beyond the day-to-day responsibilities, supervisors can take on the role of coaches and even mentors. Most organizational studies show that good coaching and mentoring improve staff retention and morale.

Formal mentoring programs can help key employees develop a larger network of supportive contacts in the organization, but these programs are often difficult to institutionalize. The military, however, has managed to embed the concept of mentoring into its culture. The sense of obligation that military officers feel toward their subordinates all the way up the chain of command is an essential part of the rapid development in leadership supervisory skills that junior officers undergo in their first tour of duty. In the course of a twenty-five-year career to flag rank, an officer will receive years of coaching and mentoring. The process of frequent changes in duty assignments, ample training, and the mentorship and coaching from superior officers and noncommissioned officers ensures that the opportunity to ask hard questions, as well as to be held accountable for results and the highest ethical standards, is a constant positive influence in the military work environment. How many people remember a good boss who pulled them aside and made a penetrating observation about a challenge or opportunity that resulted in a step-change in their management capabilities? In the military, this is not a simply random occurrence, but an integral part of the design of formal and informal systems, training, and operational and performance evaluations throughout a military career.

How many people remember a good boss who pulled them aside and made a penetrating observation about a challenge or opportunity that resulted in a step-change in their management capabilities?

It is unrealistic to expect the civilian government to provide the same degree of coaching, mentoring, and detailed supervision as the military does. But the military does provide a model to which the civilian government should aspire. Government workers need to work together effectively, and to support each other, in order to accomplish their mission. Students say that what they most want in a job is "an organization that cares about me." This all points to the need to develop a more structured and formalized approach to supervision, coaching, and mentoring in government. It also means that the government should encourage, rather than frown upon, the informal gatherings, off-site development workshops, and other mechanisms through which its teams can develop better informal communication.

HR Systems for Job Satisfaction

Satisfied employees not only perform better, but they also make better team members, co-workers, mentors, and colleagues.[47] They are more cooperative, enthusiastic, energetic, innovative, and loyal to their employer. For all these reasons, it is in the best interests of an organization to pay attention to all the factors that determine job satisfaction and to devote resources to them. In addition to compensation, these are the factors that we grouped under "intrapreneurship" in earlier chapters. They include flexibility of work structure, staffing, and hours; personal benefits such as healthy living, child care, and elder care; and rewards and recognition for individual and team contributions.

Work and Staffing Schedules

The federal government is one of the least progressive organizations in the United States when it comes to providing flexible work schedules. Outside the government, the standard five-day pattern is giving way to full-time, part-time, overtime, and flexible schedules and shifts. Yet the federal government by and large still requires a traditional 8–5, Monday–Friday schedule. This means that taxpayers who want to contact a government office outside of regular business hours are out of luck and that government workers with inflexible hours will continue to contribute to Washington's serious traffic congestion and environmental impact. Many countries around the world and many state governments in the United States permit greater flexibility than the federal government. Canada allows its employees to work flexible hours, and alternative work arrangements, such as telework, are commonplace. Utah has adopted a four-day workweek, and many other states and local governments are experimenting with flexible work schedules.[48]

But in the federal government, flexibility is quite limited. The main permitted "alternative" is the compressed work schedule (CWS), which allows employees to work eighty hours over nine workdays, thus providing a Friday off every other week. In other compressed schedule programs, employees work ten hours a day, four days a week. Managers agree that these programs tend to reduce absenteeism because employees have scheduled time off during regular business hours to complete necessary personal tasks.[49] However, this flexibility is quite limited compared with that of the leading people organizations.

Leading companies have accepted the reality of the world's new technologies: computers and cell phones make it possible for a vast number of employees to work from home and to be in contact with their customers/clients from locations other than their cubicle. They can even reside in other countries, as demonstrated by call centers and help desks located in India. It should be just as possible for the U.S. government to allow its employees some flexibility to work from their homes.

Telecommuting

Telecommuting—which replaces physically commuting to work with working from a remote location through a telecommunication link—would appear to be an excellent idea for the government. Employees would save commuting time, not to mention the money spent on transportation, buying lunch, and related personal expenses. It is also good for the environment. But to date, less than 14 percent of the federal workforce is telecommuting.[50]

Although popular with federal employees, telecommuting worries managers and supervisors, who think it reduces productivity and creates logistical obstacles to teamwork and good management. In our view, this is simply because managers have not received training in managing the modern connected workforce. As the GAO points out, those who have been exposed to telecommuting programs are more receptive.

Indeed, the experience of federal agencies that have fully embraced telecommuting has been very positive. In 2002 the DLA began to permit eligible employees to perform their official work duties at alternative sites such as their homes or telecenters one to five days a week, or intermittently.[51] As of March 2005, 6,717 civilian employees (31 percent of the agency's civilian population) were identified as telework-eligible, and 1,072 were actively telecommuting. Although telecommuting is only one piece of the people package at DLA, productivity has soared since it was implemented. The DLA's former director, Vice Admiral Keith Lippert, has been a vocal advocate of the program as a way of increasing productivity and worker satisfaction while meeting recruitment and retention objectives.[52]

To judge by its participants, another telecommuting program that can claim success is under way at the Treasury Inspector General for Tax Administration. Initiated in 2001, the program now has 35 percent of the agency's 950 employees working away from the office at least two days a week, and more than 90 percent of the agency's workforce participates in the program.[53]

Teleworking has also been introduced at the U.S. Department of Agriculture (USDA). Teleworking employees there save an average of one hour a day by not commuting to work. If the average round-trip commute came to 50 miles a day, say, teleworking at the USDA could reduce vehicular travel by 103,100 miles a week, or 5,361,200 a year for the entire agency (based on 2003 estimates). The practice has the potential to reduce absenteeism, attract new applicants, retain current employees, reduce office space requirements, and benefit the environment. It has already allowed the USDA to hire employees outside of the Washington, D.C., metro area to perform duties remotely.[54]

Job Sharing

Job sharing is another flexibility practice seldom used in the federal government. The OPM has laid out guidelines to help government agencies determine whether job-sharing arrangements are feasible. But the idea has fallen far short of its potential. Leading people companies use job sharing to meet various work-

Paying attention to the basic well-being of people in the workplace is an integral part of improved organizational performance.

force circumstances. Most notably, it enables women with small children to remain employed by sharing a job with another flex-time employee, lets individuals desiring semi-retirement to work part-time (this may involve training the new person at the same time), and prevents redundancies when jobs are no longer needed full-time. In all three cases, the federal government could use job sharing to its advantage. But supervisors need training in how to make it work and how to manage the career path of a person who is sharing a job. One agency that has begun to explore this practice is the Department of Justice. It has created an electronic job-sharing bulletin board where employees can express interest in or views on sharing a position. The website is part of the DOJ's Worklife Program.[55] Other experiments with job sharing are under way at the U.S. Fish and Wildlife Service, the Federal Aviation Administration, and the USDA. However, much more needs to be done in this direction.

Wellness

Another tool for increasing the effectiveness and efficiency of the federal workforce is to invest in its health. Although federal employees have access to health insurance benefits, these should be supplemented by a variety of healthy living benefits. Such benefits are designed to strengthen the physical, mental, and emotional well-being of employees through both preventive and corrective care. For example, programs could be established to provide a range of free confidential counseling and referral services for employees whose personal problems may be affecting their health and job performance. Such programs could also address a variety of other issues: smoking cessation, promotion of exercise, weight and fitness management, vaccination, and stress-reduction programs, or subsidies with proven benefits. Some programs of this nature have already proved successful at the IRS and among civilian and uniformed personnel in the air force.[56] Universities such as Harvard provide a wide range of wellness benefits for their employees, including free flu shots and subsidized counseling, acupuncture, massage therapy, weight-loss clinics, nutrition consulting, meditation, emergency child care, elder care, transportation subsidies, and optometry assistance.[57] Companies like IBM pay employees to participate in wellness programs, including those directed at fitness, weight loss, and smoking cessation.

Employee health and assistance programs are particularly important when employees are facing major transformations in their work environment. The scope and scale of the changes proposed in this volume could temporarily heighten stress and anxiety across government. Since illness and absenteeism are known to increase during such changes, the effects of a long transition to a new personnel system, if ignored, could in turn precipitate serious emotional health issues.

Leading private employers have long invested in the health of their workforces. A majority of large U.S. companies now provide on-site health clinics. It is obviously more convenient for an employee to see a doctor for minor problems right away, on the premises. Even most schools larger than 250 children employ a school nurse. Yet Washington is filled with buildings that employ 4,000–5,000 workers but do not even provide an on-duty nurse to handle routine ankle sprains, hay fever, rashes, insect bites, sore throats, and other minor ailments. Employees end up taking a whole afternoon off work to deal with these problems. Providing basic health care creates a workplace in which well-being is an integral part of performance. It is another way that an employer can demonstrate that it values its workforce.

Child Care

Working parents cannot function effectively without knowing that their children are under good care. Employees need assistance with child care over a long period: from pre-school ages that require full-time care to teen years that need supervision after school and during vacations. Working parents also have to juggle the demands of children when they are ill or when the regular child care provider is not available. A parent with two children born three years apart will therefore have these responsibilities from birth to the age of eighteen for each, for a total of twenty-one years—or the majority of the parent's career.

The leading people organizations understand that child care is not simply a matter of providing an on-site day care center for babies and toddlers (though this is helpful). It is about creating an atmosphere in which the company acknowledges that working parents must have the flexibility to take care of their children when necessary.

Much has been written about the demands placed on working parents (especially mothers), and we cannot begin to address the full range of issues here. What can be stressed is the widely demonstrated positive impact of child care assistance on job satisfaction and loyalty. Parental responsibilities need to be fully recognized. A parent should not have to fabricate a dentist appointment in order to attend parent-teacher conferences during the regular workday.

Harvard University, which consistently ranks at the top of *Working Mother* magazine's parent-friendly employer list, uses several techniques to support working parents. Most important, it allows up to $5,000 a year to be deducted tax-free from an employee's salary to pay for child care expenses. It also maintains a corporate account with an emergency babysitting service (Parents in a Pinch) that enables any employee to obtain an emergency babysitter on a priority basis. Harvard subsidizes eighty hours a year of this service and provides a wide range of additional services, including day care centers for preschoolers, summer and vacation camps for school-age children, and special services for parents who need to travel. Admittedly, Harvard is a wealthy institution that can afford the best. But the basic principle remains the same: in order to get the best productivity from its workforce, the federal government should aim to provide the best possible level of child care assistance. Assistance should also be available to employees who are the primary caregivers for aging relatives or spouses who are seriously ill.

According to agency and union officials surveyed by the GAO, providing federal workers with on-site or near-site child care decreases absenteeism and allows employees to better focus on their job responsibilities.[58] These centers need not be government operated, nor must they rely solely on government funding. Several corporate child care providers already provide services to the government. For those agencies that do provide child care, demand often outstrips supply.

Some employees question whether it is fair to support working parents, the implication being that the non-parents get stuck with the extra workload. We believe that precisely the opposite is true. Without such assistance, parents will be forced to choose between their children and their work, which means the co-workers are likely to be picking up the slack.

Despite these and other benefits, an employee may fail to understand the value of a total compensation package (including base salary, retirement benefits, transportation subsidies, child care subsidies, and time-off bonuses). The GAO and the military services within the DOD provide their employees with an annual summary of their annual total compensation.[59] This kind of report helps employees and job applicants make realistic comparisons between the total compensation packages offered by the government versus those of other employers.

Managing Diversity

At the front of its website, the Canadian government states: "The public service is committed to being representative of the population it serves." This sums up the philosophy that should underpin the federal workforce. This means a workforce whose make-up in terms of age, gender, race, faith, disability, and sexual orientation compares with that of the country and the civilian labor force from which it is drawn. The federal government's workforce grew more diverse in fiscal 2007, but many groups, including women and Hispanics, are still underrepresented when compared with the civilian labor force, according to a new report from the Office of Personnel Management.[60] Meanwhile the country as a whole is growing more diverse—"minority" groups will make up nearly half the population by 2050.[61] Several quasi-judicial bodies help to enforce this goal, including the Equal Employment Opportunity Commission (EEOC), the Merit Systems Protection Board, and the administrative judges who frequently preside over cases involving alleged discrimination.

Despite the fact that most people in the federal government accept the theoretical requirement for diversity, it is not clear that the majority of the workforce truly understands the benefits that diversity can bring or knows how to unleash them. The federal government used to be seen as a leader in recruiting and promoting a diverse workforce. But that is no longer the case. Here again, private people-focused companies have taken the lead.

Most high-performing companies know that greater diversity in the workforce is necessary to sustain a competitive advantage in the marketplace. This is especially true for companies involved in retailing, marketing, sales, distribution, and service industries. Their bottom line is that diversity is *necessary,* not just "nice to have."

Successful private sector companies also understand that it is more difficult to manage a diverse workforce than a homogenous one.[62] As a result, they have invested in new tools to hire and retain good personnel, to harness the creative energies of employees, and to form a common bond among diverse members of the labor force.[63] In many cases, this has involved retraining managers and teams to communicate, negotiate, and handle disputes in different ways than they did previously.

The military is also light-years ahead of the federal civilian workforce in this regard. The fundamental methods of recruiting, training, working, and promoting are such that diverse teams are literally forced to work together or perish. Of course, the military still faces some challenges, such as the failure of the "don't ask, don't tell" policy. But except in professional sporting teams, few organizations exhibit the comradeship among diverse backgrounds, races, and religions that the U.S. military forces do.

The federal government frequently emphasizes the importance of diversity in its ranks, urging its workers to attend all kinds of diversity celebrations, and endeavors to hire "diverse" candidates. Despite its enthusiasm for achieving this goal, the government lacks the ability to build diversity through outreach, recruitment, and hiring and has yet to develop fully the capability to maintain diversity through training, career development, rewards, recognition, and a positive management environment.

The government has devoted little effort to studying the impact of diversity on organizations, including its influence on decisionmaking, team building, and success of the enterprise. Recognizing that the private sector had made great strides in this area, the U.S. Equal Employment Opportunity Commission appointed a task force in 1997 to study the employment opportunity policies, programs, and practices of private sector employers. The task force examined recruitment and hiring, promotion and career advancement, terms and conditions, termination and downsizing, and the resolution of disputes.[64]

The task force identified numerous practices that could be adopted by the government. In recruiting, for example, it recommended greater use of internships, targeted recruitment strategies, education and training programs, mentoring, and career enhancement initiatives. In the area of "terms and conditions," it supported tools used in the private sector such as disability and religious accommodation programs, pay equity, insurance, employee benefits, and work-life and family-friendly policies and practices. In its section on "termination and downsizing," it urged retraining and placement programs for employees displaced by downsizing programs, nondiscriminatory early retirement programs, and insurance. "Alternative dispute resolution" focused on early resolution of employment discrimination complaints and voluntary and effective alternative dispute resolution programs.

Above all, the task force found that these best private sector firms had an overarching management commitment to equal employment opportunity (EEO) policies, programs, and practices. In examining commitment, it looked at what management was saying *and* doing—in other words, accountability. The task force also looked at tools such as performance appraisals, compensation incentives, and other evaluation measures to reflect a

> *The leading private sector companies were not simply trying to comply with the law; they were using diversity as a source of strategic advantage.*

manager's ability to set high standards and demonstrate progress. According to these and other indicators, the leading private sector companies were not simply trying to comply with the law; they were using diversity as a source of strategic advantage. The commission coined the acronym SPLENDID to describe the actions that conscientious employers can take to address EEO and diversity issues: it stands for study, plan, lead, encourage, notice, discussion, inclusion, and dedication.

The public service has accepted the ideal of diversity, but it has not yet invested resources, time, or hard work into leveraging a diverse workforce to achieve higher productivity for the U.S. taxpayer. This is where the next stage of the effort must concentrate.

Summary of Recommendations

The government should borrow the best techniques from the public and private sectors aimed at recruiting, retaining, and rewarding employees. When adapted for government, these practices will lead to excellence in human resources. The four most important priorities for the government HR system to adopt are:

1. *Require strategic workforce analysis and planning.* Every agency needs an organization-level profile of its workforce to support its strategic direction.

2. *Streamline recruiting.* The government will have to make the process of screening and qualifying candidates faster, more efficient, and transparent. It will also have to reach out to a broader pool of candidates.

3. *Enhance flexibility.* The government needs to convert from a stodgy bureaucracy into a leading-edge twenty-first-century organization that people want to join. This will require major reforms such as increased compensation for certain types of jobs plus numerous small changes such as telecommuting, flex-time, child care, and wellness benefits.

4. *Deal promptly with performance problems.* Agencies and unions must actively coach, counsel, and train employees with performance problems. There must be realistic time-bound objectives for improvement; if this fails to bring about the necessary improvements, employees should be offered help to find more appropriate roles.

7
Training

raining and education are the most powerful levers for reform in government today. This applies to employees at all levels, particularly managers and supervisors. In the military and in top private sector companies, it is nearly impossible for an individual to be promoted into the managerial ranks without receiving training in how to lead, manage, and evaluate subordinates. But in the federal government, such training is rare. Even when government leaders set aside money for this purpose, training budgets are the first to be cut.

Fortunately, the government has attracted some extremely dedicated and talented managers throughout its history. Indeed, many of them make the task of managing a complex government organization look deceptively easy. The government has also made a great deal of information accessible online, and it has made some strides in other areas. But the pace of change, especially in technology, is much faster than the government's efforts. Looking ahead, it is hard to imagine how the federal workforce will ensure high quality on a consistent basis without providing adequate training and resources.

This is especially true because the private sector has transformed the quality and timeliness of customer service that the public has come to expect. Today's citizens are accustomed to printing out boarding passes online and tracking Federal Express package deliveries to the minute. They expect that a veteran checking the status of his claim should be able to do it with the same level of precision. Younger taxpayers have grown up using simple and secure online systems to pay for goods and services and to file their taxes. They find it incredible that the Census Bureau still has no capacity to accept forms over the Internet. The public also wants to be confident that the equipment used by the government to evaluate air or water quality is state of the art, accurate, and being used correctly. They want a government in which federal regulators can evaluate the financial transactions on Wall Street. Such a level of service can only be delivered if training of the federal workforce moves to the top of the political agenda.

Therefore the model for reform requires training at every level. Training should encourage employees to take personal responsibility for career growth while they also engage in their day-to-day activities. Effective training should increase the capacity of personnel to face new challenges, including the ability to transition to a new personnel management system, and should strengthen their ability to operate in that system. At the same time, it should provide managers with the skills they need to guide their organizations through change successfully. In short, training is vital to organizational performance and for success of the reform effort.

The Training Deficit

Unfortunately, the federal government's record of investing in training merits a D minus. Until recently, agencies and departments did not even have to track or report their spending on training and development. As of December 2007, however, spending on training must be reported to the Office of Personnel Management (OPM) to remain in compliance with Title V (section 410.701). OPM has consolidated and published reports on training spending. We expect the new figures now being compiled will continue to be far lower than the amounts spent on training by their military and private sector counterparts. With so little money available for training at any level, good training programs are in short supply, especially for federal workers residing outside Washington.

Because the federal government has not tracked spending on work-force training until very recently, data on the subject remain scarce. Furthermore, because training continues to be undervalued, any funds budgeted for it are at risk for cuts. As a result, managers have long been inclined to conceal training money, making it even more difficult to track and control how it is spent.

In its survey of investment in training in 2005, the American Society for Training and Development (ASTD) estimated the amounts spent, broken down by industry, using its "government" category as a proxy for the U.S. federal government (acknowledging that it may include some state and local data). The ASTD calculated that investment levels in training in the private sector averaged 47 percent higher per employee than in the public sector, and that private sector employees averaged 25 percent more learning hours a year. Even more striking is the difference that emerged when the government was compared with companies that the ASTD categorizes as "demonstrating a clear link between learning and performance": these companies invested an average of 137 percent more on training than the government, and their employees received 37 percent more learning hours a year.[1]

Of course, the cost of training, especially technical training, varies greatly, given the nature of the job and the equipment required to provide the training. Managerial and supervisory training can be conducted relatively inexpensively through online or classroom sessions, or both. But highly technical training, such as learning how to use new environmental testing equipment in the field, is very expensive. This difference can be better appreciated by comparing the cost of training military personnel with that of their private sector counterparts. The Pentagon invests about $2,500 a year per person in training military personnel, or 160 percent more than the ASTD's average private sector benchmark, and 281 percent more than its government benchmark.[2] Given the unique tasks required of the government, private sector investment levels should not be seen as a ceiling but merely a benchmark for the government. Depending on the tasks required of federal employees, the military model may be more relevant in highly specialized fields and in overcoming skills deficits.

The government's long-tolerated training failure can be traced to three factors. First, training has typically been viewed as a cost or even a perk—

not as a critical strategic investment in getting the mission accomplished. Second, in the absence of a serious commitment, the little training that is offered is seldom fully integrated into the workings of the organization and therefore becomes a tempting target during a budget squeeze. Third, and perhaps most important, few in government fully understand the outcomes that training can produce.

Investment levels in training in the private sector averaged 47 percent higher per employee than in the public sector, and private sector employees averaged 25 percent more learning hours a year.

By contrast, the U.S. military has been providing a very high level of training for decades. Training is provided across a wide range of subjects, including leadership, management, personal development, and technical competence in military operations. Training budgets are generally large and well protected. Like mentoring, training is deeply embedded in its culture. It is also viewed as a necessary requirement for advancement—not as a gift.

However, not even the Department of Defense (DOD) places the same emphasis on investing in its civilian workers. As Roger Blanchard, a senior HR executive in the U.S. Air Force, points out, "With civilians, DoD expects to hire them already knowing how to do the job we are hiring for. On the military side, we expect them to come in knowing nothing, and we concentrate considerable time and effort on development toward meeting our requirements."[3] Today, DOD civilian personnel are at a crossroads where hiring, training, and development must be improved to preserve and enhance the career defense civilian service.

This observation raises a key question. Must the government build (that is, develop from scratch) the skills needed in the civilian federal workforce, or can it buy those skills in the talent marketplace? The question for employers is not only how to build or buy the talent they need, but how to make the best use of the talent that they already have. Adding contractors to a networked organization is no panacea for these challenges. While the multisector workforce provides government with more flexibility, it adds complexity because the workforce needs to manage its own employees and must manage and train commercial partners about the requirements and standards for working with the government. We believe that the federal government needs to do both: it must be at least as robust as the military—capable of hiring and training personnel from scratch, and flexible enough to add new competencies to its existing workforce and to purchase and to manage expertise from outside the government when necessary.

The labor market is already forcing the government to invest in the skills of its workforce. In the coming century, the country will face increased competition for its fair share of talent. Young people now entering the workforce no longer want or expect to stay with the same organization for an

Training has typically been viewed as a cost or even a perk—not as a critical strategic investment in getting the mission accomplished.

entire career. They change jobs, on average, every two to four years.[4] As a result, employers have every right to expect new hires to become productive quickly, but employees have high expectations as well. They want every job to provide opportunities for them to learn and develop their professional skills so that they can succeed in their current jobs and prepare themselves for the next. Therefore we focus on the design of a training program that will develop better supervisors and managers from among the career civil service: those already serving in government and those who will be recruited in the future.

Core Competencies Needed for Better Leadership and Management

Good training aims at reinforcing or creating a set of behaviors that help employees achieve the organization's mission. One of the best ways to determine which specific skills and competencies lead to better results is to study those demonstrated by successful managers and supervisors. For example, the IBM Corporation introduced a process in 1996 to "define what IBM leaders must be, know, and do in the areas of leadership and people management to execute [IBM's] strategy and win in the marketplace."[5] As a first step, IBM gave managers a validated survey and feedback instrument. Subsequently, it held focus groups for newly appointed executives and high-performing first-line and upline managers. The company identified the top 300 performers from among an executive team of about 4,000. Then it brought in a team of experts to provide analysis and advice.[6] The firm identified several common attributes that set these individuals apart in terms of the business results they achieved and how they were viewed by their superiors, colleagues, and subordinates. Ten top competencies emerged around three core values. One of the top competencies was "collaborative influence."[7]

IBM then built an entire performance evaluation process and reward system to foster these traits and to reward those who demonstrated them consistently in action. A robust training program was also established to further nurture these traits. Training materials were developed for the skill level and position of employees at every level of the organization. Following this example, the government should identify the traits of its most successful leaders and managers, recognize their key competencies, and develop a system to evaluate and confer special status on those who achieve the same level of competence.

Create a Public Manager Credential Program

We believe every manager who supervises or manages other workers beyond a certain level needs to be certified in basic supervisory and management skills. Currently, there is no standard of competence for management or supervisory positions in government. Credentialing would lead to a widely recognized and well-regarded validation of a recipient's level of proficiency that would lead employees, managers, and supervisors to expect a certain level of competence. Such credentialing will help to build trust among managers and employees. In interviews, Kennedy School students who were previously federal employees at the GS-14 level noted that they would not trust managers and supervisors to complete performance evaluations fairly unless they had participated in a freestanding, well-thought-out credentialing program that taught them how to perform this task.

The competency standards required for credentialing should be derived from demonstrated behaviors of effective leaders, managers, and supervisors in the government, the military, and the private sector (see box 7-1). The standards selected must be measurable, and when they are met, the credential can be awarded (regardless of current position and responsibilities). They can be based on a variety of existing certification

B O X 7 - 1 . Certified Public Manager as a Credentialing Model

Existing programs—like the Certified Public Manager (CPM) program—are highly valued credentialing tools for government employees. This program is specifically designed for employees in federal, state, and local governments. Its purpose is to develop leaders who are prepared for the changing expectations and goals, reform promotion and implementation, and the business orientation of today's government.

The CPM program is offered through the Graduate School of the U.S. Department of Agriculture (USDA), in partnership with the George Washington University (GWU). It requires 234 hours of study in areas of public management, such as general administration and organization, analytical and conceptual skills, technical and quantitative skills, and human skills. CPM participants must also complete an agency or community and professional development project for 40 hours, comprehensive exams for 11 hours, and elective course work for 40 hours.

Once the program is successfully completed, participants become members of the American Academy of Certified Public Managers, and people who review their credentials will have a clear understanding of what skills they can be expected to have.

criteria such as the Certified Public Manager (CPM).[8] These standards should be established to guide the quality and efficiency of management in government. Nongovernmental organizations such as the National Certified Public Manager Consortium can provide and monitor accreditation standards, facilitate development, encourage innovation, and develop linkages with programs and organizations with similar concerns.[9] The requirements for certification should include the completion of class work for theory, practical experience on the job, and a review by a panel of experts of actual job performance.

Once the desired competencies are established, training can be targeted at specific skills. These will be tactical in nature for the most part and will address questions such as: Does the employee know how to use the various information technology (IT) tools needed to accomplish mission objectives as well as the overall performance and management objectives of the organization? Does the employee have the necessary communication skills? Does the employee need to refresh previously mastered skills such as evaluating individual performance, writing performance evaluations, counseling employees, developing remedial plans, coaching to improve performance and motivating employees to develop new skills and try new opportunities to enhance their proficiency? This exercise is likely to be easier than identifying required competencies, although a broader range of skills may be needed across occupations and roles. Four types of training are discussed in more detail later in this chapter.

Before training and education begin, it is important to determine the employee's current level of skill and competency. Training and education that are either too basic or too difficult are a waste of money. They demotivate students and fail to result in improved performance. Therefore skill and competency assessment tools should be employed to target training to student needs and organizational priorities. These tools can take many forms, such as 360-degree reviews, self-assessments, and reviews by expert raters and coaches (see box 7-2).

We suggest that a wide array of community colleges, colleges, and universities compete to deliver this standardized training curriculum. This would give government employees easy access to training at or near their place of work, thereby lowering the cost of attendance and improving its relevance to the management team's agency and community. This decentralized approach to the delivery of a centrally controlled and updated curriculum will ensure nationwide consistency and value. The large number of participants is also likely to create price competition and innovation among training service providers.

Measure Performance

The desired outcome of management and supervisory training is, of course, a better-run government. There are several ways to measure the outcomes of such a sweeping program. One is to employ existing employee surveys instituted by OPM and the Partnership for Public Service. Successful training should lead to different behavior and an improved work environment. Innovative third-party providers that measure and report performance are emerging as trusted partners in the tracking of national performance such as the State of the USA organization.[10] These and other sources can be used to measure the effectiveness

B O X 7 - 2 . IRS Manager Competency Training

One element of the IRS overhaul that began with the IRS Restructuring and Reform Act of 1998 was a plan to transform the agency's leadership. The plan called for four key steps:

1. Build a set of guiding principles to govern the activities of the new organization.

2. Identify the requirements of leadership and the new competencies necessary to manage the transition and future operations.

3. Develop an organizational model to carry out the new dual role of customer service and compliance more effectively.

4. Redefine all leadership jobs in the new model to make them consistent with the new competencies.

As this plan was implemented, the IRS developed five core management responsibilities and corresponding competencies for its executives and managers. The competencies were derived from the IRS's mission, guiding principles, and transformation requirements. They also incorporated many elements from the OPM executive core qualifications.

The new core management responsibilities and competencies were used to rewrite job descriptions for all leadership positions. Senior leaders and executives were then required to reapply and compete for the redefined jobs. The competencies became the basis for executive selection, development, and performance management. The result was a roadmap both for managers' professional development and for improved organizational performance.

To develop competencies, the IRS now relies on a variety of tools, including classroom and electronic education, developmental assignments, coaching, leadership simulations, and on-the-job practice. Each manager also receives assistance in crafting an individually customized leadership learning plan as his or her career advances. By consciously focusing on its obligation to develop leadership skills at all levels, the IRS ensures that individuals are prepared for the increasing responsibilities and demands of their positions, both before and after they are promoted.

Interestingly, as it began implementing this new program, the IRS found that all participants reported individual progress such as increased effectiveness. However, the results with respect to management improvements were more mixed. To achieve better results across the board, the IRS critiqued and

(continued)

B O X   7 - 2   *(continued)*

reevaluated its development plan. The original list of twenty-one competencies identified for development were whittled down to the five determined to have the greatest impact on management performance. With resources focused on these five competencies, the IRS saw consistent improvement.

The results of this effort have been encouraging. Since 1999 the IRS has seen its employee satisfaction rates jump from 50 percent to 60 percent, while customer satisfaction has risen even more dramatically: from 37 percent to 61 percent. The IRS's former director of leadership and organizational effectiveness, Jim Trinka, credited much of this success to the new leadership model and programming efforts: "The improvements in customer and employee satisfaction track directly with the number of managers we've trained." Indeed, the IRS has gone from having roughly 500 of its employees trained under the new leadership model in 1999 to nearly 5,000 in 2005—which is close to half of all its management positions.

of the training effort and make adjustments to the standards, curriculum, and training program.

Initiate Four Types of Training

To make sure that the government's managers know how to structure work and supervise employees, we recommend serious investment in four types of training—leadership/management, supervisory, technical, and general transformation training. These courses will improve not only individual team performance but also the ability of managers to work across stovepipes in the federal government.

Leadership and Managerial Training

Leaders have to enlist the hearts and minds of their employees to accomplish the objectives of the organization with passion and enthusiasm. Their efforts encompass values, culture, and innovation as well as the disciplined execution of resource allocation, business processes, technology, and work tasks. This combination of strategic thinking and problem solving, along with the ability to inspire and motivate employees, is something that can be taught. One of the best ways for an organization to improve the quality of life and performance of its workforce is to leverage the effect of strong leaders and managers. Leaders influence large numbers of people through the organizational chain of command. For this reason, leadership training is the highest priority among the four types of training.

Leadership and managerial training consists of substantive improvement in the knowledge, skills, and competencies that every senior executive in the government should possess in order to lead and manage well. This includes training in how to structure work assignments; set goals and objectives; measure, monitor, and evaluate performance; motivate employees; and handle poor performers. It applies equally to career and political appointees.

This training helps individuals guide and direct the activities of others with greater understanding and insight. Awareness of the strengths, weaknesses, opportunities, and threats to an organization, as well as of the capacity of employees and contractors to deal with them in a coordinated fashion, is an essential ingredient of successful management.

Supervisory Training

Supervisory training focuses on developing, managing, and evaluating overall employee performance and linking those evaluations to compensation and career progression. Federal workers who do not possess this certification in supervisory skills should not be permitted to evaluate their subordinates. They can advance as technical experts, but without this core managerial responsibility.

Those who run large organizations know they are dependent on a cadre of managers and supervisors who work "north, south, east, and west" of their position in the organizational hierarchy as well as outside of the organization. We define supervisors as those managers who are primarily focused on the day-today aspects of product and service delivery, rather than strategic issues. These supervisors are responsible for the operational requirements of disciplined and repeatable performance. They are the people who translate organizational goals into concrete tasks with measurable outcomes.

Supervisors deal with well-defined work tasks delivered through the coordinated application of human talent. They tend to be the daily source of communication, direction, encouragement, and accountability that employees associate with the "boss." The importance of their impact on the working environment cannot be overestimated. As much as individual employees help nurture the relationship with their supervisor, a capricious, unethical, or, more commonly, an incompetent boss has the power to sour the work environment and divert creative energy away from work tasks and to foment conflict, discouragement, and a sense of failure.

Training supervisors to conduct performance appraisals is the essential first step in remedying the government's decades-long inattention to the development of strong people-management skills. To some extent, this lag can be explained by the General Schedule (GS) system, which limits the involvement of supervisors in decisions affecting employees' annual raises and thus gives them less reason to provide meaningful performance feedback. The role of supervisors in the military has been interpreted quite differently, even though they are not responsible for setting pay either. First-line supervisors there feel a direct responsibility for training their subordinates in all the skills that will make it possible for them to be promoted to the next level. The civilian government needs to undergo a cultural change that would encourage first-line supervisors to provide meaningful performance feedback to subordinates and help them to succeed. Furthermore, supervisors need training in the basic tools for accomplishing this.

The civilian government needs to undergo a cultural change that would encourage first-line supervisors to provide meaningful performance feedback to subordinates and help them to succeed.

Some organizations acknowledge that not everyone can master these skills, which are usually learned and developed over time, and they give out work and developmental assignments accordingly. The GAO, for example, decided not to make all managers "performance managers," carefully selecting those who were most likely to be successful in this important role.[11] Because of the time involved in mastering supervisory and mentoring skills, government leaders must now begin to establish the necessary recruiting and development programs that will, within ten years, produce the desired cadre of government supervisors to oversee the next generation of civil servants.

Technical Training

There is a tremendous need for technical training throughout government given the array of complex systems for which the public sector is responsible. These include satellite tracking stations, supercomputing systems, and biological weapons labs. If the government is to perform at the highest levels, it needs to invest in the best, state-of-the art technical training for the people who do the work.

High-performing organizations invest in technical training as a matter of basic practice. For example, the U.S. military has a sophisticated training structure for military weapons systems. These are generally complex engineering systems that integrate sensors, command and control elements, and hydraulic vehicles into an integrated capability. The elements are themselves complex, the interactions among elements in the system even more so. The military breaks down the system into manageable parts and then develops detailed training at each level in the system to operate and maintain it. Responsibility is allocated in a pyramidal structure with basic training provided for new members and extended training for senior members of the team. The training encompasses both "book" learning from textbooks and manuals and operational training. The result is that the military creates master technicians supported by a layer of experts in specific functions. Training is provided over the course of an entire career.

Similarly, technical specialists in the nonprofit and corporate world require training to master basic skills as well as additional training to keep up to date with new developments in their field. Whether an art restoration expert at a museum, a dental technician, or an accountant, no one should be expected to perform a job well without periodic education over the course of a career.

Common sense dictates that personnel be trained in the appropriate skills when asked to learn a language, master a new computer system, operate a complex machine, interpret a complex policy for the sake of determining program eligibility, or manage a billion dollar project. Yet the government relies largely on sporadic on-the-job training, personal initiative, and trial and error to fill the gap. This simply is not sufficient to sustain the massive technical infrastructure of the U.S. government.

General Transformation Training

In order to fully participate in the people-focused organization we are proposing, all federal employees will need a set of basic skills for coping with major organizational change and mapping out and achieving their career objectives in their new environment. This training is critical to the success of the transformation. Without a widespread understanding and acceptance of the necessary reforms and knowledge of how to accomplish them, federal employees will be much less willing to embrace the new system.

Leverage Training to Recruit Better Hires

Developing a list of competencies for government managers and providing systematic training along with feedback are also useful means of identifying desirable traits in potential new hires in the recruiting process. Once hired, new personnel should receive focused training to speed their integration into the agency's culture and accelerate their effectiveness. Internship programs for both entry-level and experienced hires will attract strong candidates and be useful in assessing the "fit" of each candidate. Although the investment in training these candidates is usually high over the internship period, this cost is easily outweighed by the costs of high turnover or the negative impact on organizational performance when an unsuitable hire stays on.

The Emerging Leaders Program at the Department of Health and Human Services (HHS) is one example of an experiential learning and training program that allows new recruits fresh from college to rotate through jobs in several parts of the agency. This allows them to develop a better understanding of the scope of job opportunities at HHS and of agency work. Recruits quickly build their network of agency contacts and, most important, can use their new knowledge to select a permanent job that matches their skills and interests.[12] The Department of Labor (DOL) offers a similar rotation program to new employees directly out of business school. The DOL rotations last six months, with some employees quickly moving to permanent positions and others continuing on rotation to acquire broader exposure to department opportunities.[13]

Allow Cross-Training

Cross-training, sometimes referred to as lateral training, allows workers to learn the jobs of their co-workers and serves as another useful learning tool. It enables motivated and capable employees to develop skills beyond their current area of competence, which enhances their value to the organization and their overall professional marketability. Employees who need to explore the requirements and suitability of a new job or learn skills outside of a particular agency find that, remarkably, such training is rare.

Sometimes the government bureaucracy defies common sense. For example, federal regulations prohibit offering training for a job unless the employee is already in it. As David Chu, DOD undersecretary of defense for personnel and readiness, has noted, this regulation is antithetical to good human resources management. Experi-

> *Sometimes the government bureaucracy defies common sense. For example, federal regulations prohibit offering training for a job unless the employee is already in it.*

ence at the Internal Revenue Service (IRS) and in the military has clearly demonstrated that the professional development of employees—independent of its relevance to an employee's current job—brings real value to both the employer and the employee. These are practices that civil service laws and regulations should encourage, not restrict. Unless these regulatory barriers are removed, the U.S. federal government will continue to lag behind other developed countries in its investment in training and education and will fail to reap the benefits of these investments.

Moreover, cross-training has great potential to improve collaboration in government if made part of the formal training and development expectations for all managers and supervisors. One example of such a systemic approach to training and career development that worked for the military came out of the Goldwater-Nichols Act (P.L. 99-433) of 1986.

Goldwater-Nichols prompted a major reorganization of the Department of Defense in an attempt to fix problems caused by interservice rivalries that became more evident during the Vietnam War and subsequent conflicts. It demonstrates that training can reshape a culture, in this case, by breaking down well-established organizational stovepipes. Among several major reform elements, it forced the military to place its best people in joint billets and encouraged cooperation and interoperability across the services through extensive joint duty assignments and joint military education requirements for promotion to senior ranks. While it is not perfect and service parochialism still exists, the emphasis on joint training brought about by Goldwater-Nichols has had a great impact on interoperability of the services' procedures and technologies and the use of combined arms on the battlefield.

The positive outcomes achieved by the military since implementing Goldwater-Nichols prompted the former vice chairman of the Joint Chiefs of Staff, General Peter Pace of the Marine Corps, to suggest similar legislation for all of the federal government to improve the way the country responds to terrorism.[14] Subsequently, John Negroponte, former director of the Office of the Director of National Intelligence (ODNI), mandated that intelligence community employees serve in joint duty assignments to qualify for promotion into the government's senior ranks.

This directive is one of several steps ODNI has taken to better integrate operations among the sixteen federal agencies that make up the intelligence community and to break down the barriers between them. Ronald P. Sanders, one of the leading personnel experts in the intelligence community, has argued that integration of human resources will be essential to the transformation of the intelligence community: "Almost by definition, a leader's abilities are improved when he or she has an enterprise-wide perspective."[15] These legislative and administrative actions suggest a heightened awareness by some government leaders that forcing employees out of their comfort zone to cross organizational boundaries plays an important role in developing the collaboration skills and scope of understanding most needed in today's workforce.

Higher-Quality Training for Better Results

Over the past decade, a growing segment of the private sector has benefited from innovations in workplace training and education. But most of the public sector has been slow to adapt. Workplace training and education are not synonymous, but they are complementary. Training focuses on present or past skill gaps or specific task requirements. Education prepares employees to anticipate and deal with unknown or future challenges. Preparing individual employees for unknown situations is just as important as skill-specific training because it builds an overall capacity for flexibility and responsiveness. To date, the military has expanded workplace training and education, but civilian agencies have lagged far behind (see box 7-3).

The delivery of training and educational programs has been transformed by technological advances, making it far easier to reach government employees dispersed throughout the United States and the world. The widespread use of web-based delivery, for instance, has helped organizations not only reach more employees more quickly but also control the costs of deploying these learning programs. Several programs already in place can serve as useful models for the government in all its locations.

In 2001 the U.S. Army launched e-Army University. This program is designed to offer eligible enlisted soldiers the opportunity to work toward a college degree or certificate during their off-duty hours—it is globally accessible 24/7. Soldiers and officers select from more than 148 certificate or degree programs from a base-degree-granting institution while taking courses from twenty-nine regionally accredited colleges and universities.

Another good model is the Defense Acquisition University (DAU), designed for the DOD's acquisition, technology, and logistics (AT&L) workforce. The DAU is a multicampus university that provides continuous training and career management through certification and assignment-specific courses. Equally impressive, it promotes career-long learning, offers consulting and training, and facilitates knowledge sharing through online resources.

The DAU follows what it calls the AT&L Performance Learning Model, which provides a network-centric learning environment to overcome the barriers of time, location, and distance. It has developed a partnership with several universities, including Boston University Metropolitan College, Southern Methodist University, and Howard University. The DAU has won various awards over the years, including Best Overall Corporate University, Best Virtual Corporate University, and Best Use of Technology, plus Most Innovative Corporate University (second place) from the Corporate University Best in Class (CUBIC) awards in 2002.[16]

The curriculum for all training and education programs must be updated periodically. Therefore it is essential to regularly review the effectiveness and content of training programs and to update curricula to meet new requirements in order to achieve a dynamic and relevant training

BOX 7-3. Naval Personnel Development Command

The U.S. Navy has created an extensive training program in response to four challenges: the increasing need for technology-savvy sailors, mounting pressures for efficiency and cost control, the changing nature of warfare, and new requirements for high-performance teams. To meet these challenges, the navy developed a strategy and implementation plan to revolutionize training. The plan had three overarching objectives:

1. Develop a lifelong learning continuum that exploits technology, optimizes sailors' time, minimizes students' time away from their parent commands, makes the best use of limited resources, and produces motivated and well-trained sailors.

2. Determine the most effective learning strategy and delivery methods to ensure that sailors possess the knowledge, skills, and abilities to do their jobs.

3. Provide recommendations for developing the most effective and efficient training organization with features that enhance innovation and facilitate rapid implementation of revolutionary ideas.

The plan resulted in a series of training programs administered by the Naval Personnel Development Command, including the Navy Leadership Development Program (NLDP), which serves senior leaders of the service; the Leadership Management Education and Training (LMET), which helps junior and midcareer officers develop basic leadership and supervisory skills; and the Naval Leadership Training Unit (NLTU, formerly NAVLEAD), which is designed to teach more experienced sailors (E-5 and E-6 sailors) leadership and management skills. Since 9/11, the navy has refocused key aspects of the programs to better address the threat of terrorism and keep participants abreast of current events.

One particularly interesting feature is that instructors continue working with students after the course is completed. This extends the learning process and provides students with a useful resource should they encounter relevant challenges while on the job.

Also, the military approach to naval officer subspecialties is designed to allow officers to focus on a skill or area of expertise outside their normal warfare specialty. This opportunity entitles them to enroll in degree-granting programs, attend specific navy training, and compete for assignments in which the job experience will enhance their skill in and knowledge of the subspecialty.

program over time. Web-based training programs are particularly easy to update and revise, given the central control point for distribution and the economics of web delivery.

Political Appointees and Congressional Staff

We have argued that government career managers and supervisors should receive effective training, aimed at achieving better results for taxpayers. The people who lead and oversee the federal personnel management system and the operations of the executive branch agencies—the political appointees and members of Congress and their staff—should also receive training. The appointees and congressional staff typically have a range of skills, and many have training in law, business, or other disciplines. But they seldom have HR experience or training in the people management aspects of the agencies they look after. They, too, need to improve their base of knowledge so that they can be more active and effective in their de facto role as the board of directors for the executive branch.

Training and education for political appointees, members of Congress, and their staffs should include a program with the following three elements:

1. An orientation with in-depth review of existing policy, process, and organizational structure affecting government agencies in a training session like the one that the Council for Excellence in Government already sponsors for new political appointees. Other examples of this kind of training are the Harvard Institute of Politics training sessions conducted for new mayors and new members of Congress.

2. Continuing education courses and seminars on the theory and practice of human capital management in both the public and private sectors. For example, this could be developed in conjunction with the Partnership for Public Service and the National Academy of Public Service.

3. A library of best practices. At the Department of Commerce, we reassigned more than thirty senior executives in order to help the department achieve important management goals such as a clean financial opinion. This was one of the first instances of this technique being deployed successfully in the federal government. A best-practice library would gather such examples and make it possible for new political appointees

and congressional staff to make changes without reinventing the wheel. The library could be maintained by a government agency such as OMB, or a nongovernmental agency such as the Partnership for Public Service or National Academy of Public Administration.

This training and education will provide appointees and congressional members and staff with the tools they need to strengthen legislation and operational performance of the government's agencies and departments.

U.S. Public Service Scholarship Program and Public Service Academy

Scholarship opportunities should be available to a broad segment of students interested in public service enrolled at leading colleges and universities across the country in much the same way that the Reserve Officer Training Corps (ROTC) is designed. These Public Service Scholarship recipients would follow a standard curriculum to augment their normal course of study at leading academic institutions. The goal of the scholarship program is not only to provide another source of qualified and motivated candidates who meet certain common standards for public service, but also candidates from more diverse backgrounds with a broader range of educational experience.

The Public Service Scholarship Program would create a program to prepare undergraduates for public service in our nation. The country would gain a source of well-qualified candidates prepared to make a difference from their first day of duty. The combination of students at a formative time of their lives together with good leadership and a rich set of learning opportunities should combine to build a strong *esprit de corps*. The students themselves would gain increased access to higher education without incurring the debt that frequently prevents them from serving in the public sector after college.

Another interesting new proposal is the Public Service Academy.[17] The academy is envisioned as an undergraduate institution devoted to developing civilian leaders for the public sector. The academy would offer four years of tuition-free education in exchange for five years of civilian service following graduation just like the nation's military academies. Competition for seats in the incoming freshman class each year would be conducted using a congressional nomination process by state, like that already in use for the military academies. Candidates for the program would be evaluated on their academic record, fitness for public service, and desire to serve.[18]

The curriculum would focus on service and leadership. Its core curriculum would focus on service-learning and international education. It would include extensive requirements for international education, including mandatory study abroad and foreign-language fluency for all students. The curriculum would encompass law enforcement, emergency management, and civic education. The combination of academic theory and practical service would produce students with the character, academic training, and leadership experience they need to serve the public.[19]

The level of investment in a new academy is significant and the time to create the program long. But we have seen how powerful institutions such as Annapolis, West Point, and the Air Force Academy can be in molding and preparing some of our best and brightest to serve our country. Judgment about the net value of cost—in terms of budget, leadership attention, and political capital, should be made in the context of an overall program for reform. This would not be the first thing we would do to invest in our civil service. Until then, the concept merits further study.

Conclusions

Training is the single most important step the country can take to reform personnel and to strengthen the civil service. The benefits of training are well established in the private sector, the military, and management literature. We propose a national standard for management and supervisory skills for the nation's public managers and supervisors. Here "training" is defined broadly, to include teaching the skills of leadership, management, supervision, and transformation, and the technical skills that government mangers need in order to produce better results and to create a better work environment. We also propose a modest training program for political appointees, congressional members, and their staff to recognize their shared ownership in creating better results in government. We support the creation of a Public Service Scholarship Program. Investing significant resources in training government workers will produce a high return for taxpayers—in the form of better performance and greater efficiency in government.

8

Managing Performance

Perhaps no other topic has attracted as much study and effort as "performance management," the drive to improve how well organizations and the people in them can function. This is a broad area, encompassing improvements at many levels, including individuals, teams, departments, and the overall organization. Leading experts in the field define business performance management as all the processes, information, and systems used by managers to set strategy, develop plans, monitor execution, forecast performance, and report results in order to achieve sustainable success, no matter how success may be defined.[1] In government as well, an organization's mission and strategic objectives are the starting point for lower-level plans and measures, which then provide the basis for creating plans and objectives that support overarching organizational goals. Effective performance management (that is, appraising, counseling, and rewarding or sanctioning behavior) happens largely within the context of an effective management system.

In this chapter we focus primarily on individual employees and supervisors, and on the processes through which they control performance. In particular, we address issues that are relevant to making government work better for the public, such as setting performance targets, measuring progress, and motivating public servants to achieve higher productivity.

We discuss four building blocks from a people factor perspective that can help implement performance management systems in the public service: (1) developing performance plans that make sense to employees and align with organizational goals, (2) conducting performance appraisals that are fair and insightful, (3) providing feedback to employees that is specific and concrete and that serves as the basis for future improvement, and (4) linking performance to reward, including, when necessary, dealing with poor performers.

Some of the most intractable problems in government today are caused by the absence of effective performance management. Correcting this situation is possible but will require a commitment of resources and will. The private sector, the military, and governments around the world have devoted years to this challenge. The for-profit world has a very different set of tools to control performance, and as noted in previous chapters, it has a different time frame and much simpler standards for measuring success. Therefore simply importing concepts such as "pay-for-performance" is not easy in a government setting. Many policy outcomes are hard to quantify and often beyond civil servants' direct control. Further, there are ceilings on the amount of rewards that can be offered to high performers. Finally, various obstacles undermine efforts to discipline and fire low achievers.

Unlike many problems that have been ignored by government, performance management has attracted a number of reform efforts. Both the Clinton and the Bush administrations tried to introduce systems for setting performance targets and measuring progress toward desired outcomes. Innovative initiatives in the United States and the United Kingdom have achieved some significant improvements in government service through a performance management approach. However, these efforts have not been embraced universally, and unions have largely opposed the efforts. In our view, this opposition is not because they or their members oppose accountability, but because they do not trust their managers to fairly and accurately appraise their performance. This sentiment has a basis in fact because, as we have shown, managers and supervisors generally have not received adequate training and have not met any consistent standard of performance themselves. The discussion that follows is premised on the call for extensive training and effective certification.

Prior Reform Efforts

Over the past fifteen years, there have been two major attempts to implement performance management reforms at the organizational level in the U.S. government, each with limited success. Both initiatives focused on establishing new requirements for analysis, oversight, and reporting.

The first was the Government Performance and Results Act of 1993 (GPRA), which required strategic planning and performance measurement in the federal government. For many agencies, this was their first experience with strategic planning. The goal of the program was to improve public confidence that agencies were spending money to achieve specific and measurable results. Agencies were required to plan their work, publicly state their goals, and then report on their progress a year later. GPRA was enacted with lofty and worthy goals. These included providing greater visibility into the link between budget and program results and improving service quality and customer satisfaction. It was supposed to improve congressional decisionmaking on programs by making it possible to assess the relative effectiveness and efficiency of federal programs and spending. The combined effect was to improve internal management of the federal government.[2]

The second reform, the Performance Assessment Rating Tool (PART), was developed with the help of the Office of Management and Budget (OMB). PART was designed to identify a program's strengths and weaknesses in order to inform funding and management decisions aimed at making the program more effective. The PART review was expected to look at all factors that affect program performance, including program purpose and design, performance measurement, evaluations, program management, and results. Because PART included a consistent series of analytical questions, programs were able to show improvements over time and could be compared with other similar programs across government.[3]

These two initiatives produced important information about government programs and performance at the agency level. They also forced budget personnel to justify budgetary requests in terms of improved efficiency, outputs, and outcomes. The GPRA revealed the lack of adequate performance planning at the agency level, while PART drew increased attention to the results expected from government programs, sparking a difficult but ultimately productive dialogue between agencies, OMB, and Congress.

Despite calling greater attention to performance, both GPRA and PART had major failings. First, neither program adequately linked budgetary decisions to performance management. This raises a question: when a program fails to achieve its objectives, is this a signal to shut it down? Or should government spend additional resources, time, and attention to get it right? Without linking performance management to the budget, the investment analysis required under GPRA and PART becomes largely a paperwork exercise. Moreover, it is an exercise that is fraught with political difficulties when a lawmaker's pet project is identified as a poor performer or as an endeavor lacking a sound business rationale. Second, GPRA and PART failed to address performance management at the individual level. They focused largely on the performance of agencies and on process analysis while missing the critical people factor: namely, investing in and improving the performance of people who contribute to the mission. Third, most government agencies did not possess the skills or staff to design strategic plans, set performance targets, monitor them, and redesign programs. So they outsourced much of this work to outside management consultants, thereby limiting the effectiveness of the GPRA and PART initiatives.

Issues in Individual Performance Assessment

Few agencies have effective systems for assessing individual performance. Managers are not trained to practice performance management and do not have the incentives to make the hard judgments or hold the difficult discussions necessary to turn performance around. Consequently, many agencies treat the appraisal system as irrelevant and thus open the door to rampant grade inflation. Not infrequently, close to 100 percent of employees consistently receive the highest rating (for example, "outstanding").

Both the GPRA and PART initiatives have encountered a number of challenges arising from unique aspects of performance management in government. First, government performance itself has complex parameters because it rests on a relationship between a worker's immediate actions and the delayed outcome of a particular mission. For example, those working in the juvenile justice system will not fully know whether their work has reduced recidivism for a generation. Government workers who are involved in trade promotion, poverty reduction, scientific research, and education, among many other activities, may find it difficult to pinpoint the effects of their efforts compared with the impact of global and economic developments.

Second, the right measures are difficult to find because many of the key outcomes desired by government programs are not easy to measure directly. Government organizations have traditionally measured only the output of their procedures (such as the number of cases or claims processed and number of containers inspected) as opposed to their outcome (such as security and safety).

Third, under the current statutory system, employee performance is measured against standards established for the particular government position without taking into consideration the context in which the employee is operating (such as a team or a specific assignment).[4] This leads performance assessment to focus solely on individuals without regard to the overall effectiveness of their team or the desired organizational outcome. Clearly aligning individual effort with organizational goals is the way to improve performance. This requires that the goals be set for the team or the unit that is tasked with the objective, and that individual performance targets are designed in a way that complements the others on the team.

Fourth, the system not only focuses on the wrong level of performance (individual versus unit), but it does not train managers to learn and practice performance management. The government fails to teach managers how to make hard judgments or to have difficult discussions with employees about their performance. Nor does it teach individuals how to best contribute to a team. This is perhaps one of the most striking differences with the private sector, where companies devote considerable time and effort to "team-building skills" in the way of offsite retreats, sporting competitions, games, workshops, and so forth. In government, such exercises are typically regarded as frivolous, even though they have demonstrated value in enhancing team performance.

Fifth, few employees trust their supervisors to fairly and accurately appraise their performance. This is not surprising, since most supervisors are poorly trained and have not been required to meet any consistent standards of performance themselves.

Lessons from Outside the Federal Government

Despite the limited success of the government's own efforts to date, there is a broad consensus that it will perform significantly better if it can set clear objectives for employees and measure performance. Many government organizations have adopted initiatives to improve performance management at the macro level—some with good results. These include the national measurement initiatives introduced in the United Kingdom, as well as "stat" programs such as Citistat in Baltimore, Maryland, Compstat in the New York City Police Department, Somerstat in Somerville, Massachusetts, and dozens of similar programs in municipalities around the world. These programs gather information on a variety of key performance indicators, including response times for services such as filling in potholes, answering emergency phone calls, and collecting litter. Next, the information goes into computerized databases, and maps are constructed to zero in on areas of underperformance. Managers from each city department then meet with the mayor's office every two weeks to answer questions about their results.

The stat programs have delivered very strong improvements in performance. In its first year of operation, the Baltimore program saved the city $13.2 million, $6 million of it in overtime pay alone. In New York City, the Compstat program is credited with helping to reduce crime and improve the training and morale of police officers. With the help of its program, the city of Somerville, Massachusetts, has shed its reputation as "Slumerville" and become that state's best-run city, according to the *Boston Globe*.[5]

This approach is well entrenched in the private sector. Senior corporate managers view their investment in performance management as an integral part of a winning strategy. The firms pick and choose from among a range of special tools and techniques. They focus their attention on business process and systems that empower employees to act in ways that are consistent with the interests of the organization. This disciplined approach is a characteristic of winners of the prestigious Malcolm

Baldridge National Quality Award, given to companies that demonstrate an ongoing commitment to better performance and higher-quality service through rigorous performance management.[6]

Performance Management at IBM

IBM, for example, is widely recognized as a leader in people-management policies. The firm employs a number of performance management techniques to ensure that the performance of its 325,000 employees aligns with corporate policies and business goals. IBM follows highly disciplined and data-driven strategic and operational planning procedures in shaping its business targets and corporate investments. Assiduous attention to detail goes into business case analysis in order to meet the standard of an "investment-grade decision."

Underpinning this planning process is a highly supportive people strategy built around the concept of a personal business contract (PBC) and an Individual Development Plan (IDP). The personal business contract shows how each employee plans to achieve all or a portion of the nested goals that roll up into achievement of overall corporate goals. Every IBM employee is required to draw up a PBC and is then assessed across a range of performance categories in relation to PBC achievements: from "unsatisfactory" through "solid contributor" to "top performer." These grades tie into IBM's conditional compensation system, which includes bonuses, special recognition, and awards, as well as stock that represents a significant portion of total income.

The IDP, which is drawn up separately, is designed to help employees plan their long-term career and meet short-term training requirements. It might include a long-term goal (such as earning an MBA at a leading university) as well as an immediate training need (such as enrolling in a week-long training program to help achieve a sales quota for the year). The value of this document is clear: the IDP links the growth of abilities for the individual employee to the objectives of the company. Employees are tracked using a detailed system of competencies, supported by training and experience, and tested by committees of subject matter experts before receiving certification at the next level in areas such as information architecture, strategy and change, and human capital management. The executive team reviews every employee to determine his or her next step.

Every year, the CEO engages in a five-minute drill for all IBM executives to plan possible career moves that meet the needs of the company and the desires of the individual. Succession planning is built into these annual performance reviews. The entire process is facilitated by a set of web-based tools that track compliance with due dates and provide related training to refresh information on policies, practices, and procedures. The tools remind every manager and supervisor to schedule personal sessions with employees in order to discuss their progress and provide guidance. The system facilitates substantive interaction with employees about their performance and its relevant to company objectives. The technology system makes it easier to handle the volume of documentation related to performance management.

The IBM example shows that the systems used to guide, monitor, and measure performance can be an integral part of the way managers operate at all levels of the organization. IBM has devoted decades to designing this system and continues to invest heavily in refining it. IBM is not alone: most leading companies do the same. Effective performance management—which consists of appraising, counseling, and rewarding or sanctioning behavior—takes place largely *within the context* of an effective management system. There is an enormous body of literature on this subject providing guidance on how to customize performance targets for different types of personalities and tasks. Most leading companies have also adopted a balanced scorecard, which helps align the strategic goals of the company with the individual priorities of the individual.

Of course, performance management is not always successful, even in the corporate sector. In a Watson Wyatt survey of 265 large U.S. companies, 92 percent said that their performance management programs are designed to link pay to performance, but only 52 percent indicated that their managers actually tie pay to performance. Furthermore, the vast majority of performance management programs (82 percent) are designed to include career development, but only 37 percent of employees say their managers are effective in this regard, and only 31 percent of employees say their companies offer career development.[7]

But in the federal government, most employees do not have a customized individual development plan at all. Where they do exist, few supervisors have been able to spend the time and effort required to take these plans seriously.

Four Ways to Improve Performance Management in Government

Four key elements of sound performance management drawing on the people factor philosophy can improve how government works:

1. Developing realistic performance plans that align with organizational goals so that people know how their work fits in with the goals and priorities of the organization.

2. Conducting performance appraisals that are fair and insightful so people are confident of where they stand.

3. Providing feedback to an employee that is specific, concrete, and actionable so that people know how to improve their performance and their value to the organization.

4. Reinforcing successful performance with rewards and discouraging poor performance, while providing training and other opportunities to improve performance in the future.

This investment in performance management is a continuous cycle. It needs to be renewed as standards change with new technology, business processes, competitive pressure, and customer demands. Moreover, organizations are dynamic: they are constantly evolving—bringing in new people, ideas, and strategies. Performance management needs to be frequently updated to respond to the changing environment.

Realistic Performance Planning

Performance plans at the organizational, work group, and individual levels make performance expectations explicit and show how the activities of individuals and groups help achieve organizational goals (box 8-1). This is sometimes referred to as the "line of sight" between organizational and individual performance. As pointed out in a 2003 report by the Government Accountability Office (GAO), a defining feature of effective performance management systems in high-performing organizations is

BOX 8-1. The Internal Revenue Service Targets Individual and Work Group Performance

As part of its transformation efforts in 2000, the IRS developed balanced measures to evaluate the performance of each organizational unit in achieving its new strategic goals. In 2001 the system was expanded to include all front-line employees. The new measures focused on critical job elements (CJEs) reflecting the organization's new mission and values for every position in the IRS. Unique features of each work group and individual position were used to tailor the new elements to the performance of specific employee occupational groups. Today, the agency uses these CJEs together with its retention standard and other data to evaluate employees annually. This is one way the IRS is cascading its organizational objectives down to the employees in a measurable, comprehensible manner.

Source: Partnership for Public Service, "IRS: Performance Management Drives Change in Agency Culture" (Washington: Performance Management Solutions Center, 2003).

that they align daily activities with broader results.[8] The most important element of such systems is the set of measures used to evaluate performance. What gets measured gets done, and measures define what data must be collected to monitor performance.

It is often difficult to find the right measures. The challenge is to link the actions of the individual to the outcome, even in situations where the final result may not be evident for a long period of time, such as a poverty-reduction program or scientific research. It is equally challenging to keep the number of measures limited to those that will make the greatest contribution to the organization's overall strategic goals (see box 8-2). Too many measures can divert attention from the most important indicators. In any case, the costs of collecting excessive or wrong data are prohibitive. A good rule of thumb is that it must be cost-effective to collect the necessary data for the measure.

In this respect, the private sector has an advantage, because it is easier to find the right performance measures there. Howard Risher, a performance-based systems expert, points out that private sector managers

BOX 8-2. Occupational Safety and Health Administration Finds the Right Measure of Workplace Safety

Under its original mandate, the Occupational Safety and Health Administration (OSHA) is committed to improving safety in all workplaces. But until recently, only about 2 percent of workplaces received an inspection visit from OSHA each year. So OSHA revised its business model from an inspections/compliance approach to a more highly leveraged partnership/education approach. This had the effect of improving workplace safety nationwide, not just in selected companies.

Initially, OSHA measured safety by the number of fines and citations issued, which, given its limited number of inspections, was a poor indicator of nationwide workplace safety. Its revised measure consists of the number of workers' compensation claims, which is a far better indicator of OSHA's desired outcome and also allows it to assess the real impact of the shift in its business model.

operate in an environment where measuring business performance is a central concern. They are rewarded, in some fashion, for performance results, which in turn gives them a much higher level of interest in the performance of their people and confidence in their performance judgments. Risher also notes that private companies usually have job-specific performance measures (often in the form of goals), which may lead to greater clarity and agreement on expectations. When managers and employees agree on what is to be accomplished (the performance criteria) and on the basis for assessing performance, they are less likely to disagree on the final rating.[9]

By contrast, the government's performance standards tend to apply to a broad group of positions that carry the same title but that on close analysis may differ enough to merit different criteria. Only in the past few years have public employers begun to develop more realistic performance criteria.[10] Furthermore, it is difficult to distinguish individual performance within a group and to strike the right balance between individual, work group, and organizational performance. Performance measures that overweigh the performance of individuals or of distinct work units may "downplay the combined performance of the entire organization and lead units [and individuals] to ignore the value of cooperation."[11] But increasingly the government needs to cooperate across organizational and work unit boundaries in order to be efficient and productive. Performance measures and rewards need to take this into account. The private sector tries to create incentives for such cooperation. For example, at Boston Consulting Group and at IBM, partner and executive remuneration is based on the performance not only of the individual, but also on the office, business practice area, and the country and region where they are based, as well as worldwide annual profits. Thus each partner and executive has an incentive to help everyone else.

These rewards do not have to be pecuniary. Another way to boost cooperation is to take it into account in performance evaluations that influence career opportunities. Over the past decade, the military has invested heavily in trying to get the services to function together smoothly. Many military operations (such as amphibious assaults, protecting embassies, and launching, tracking, and recovering satellites) cannot be carried out without joint operations. To achieve proficiency, the military conducts joint operations in different theaters around the world every year. These exercises test the effectiveness of the combined organization in achieving objectives. They can thereby indirectly measure how well the participants are able to collaborate and cooperate. The exercises are graded by independent observers, who feed these results to the commanding officers, who in turn incorporate the results into the performance evaluations of each individual. Despite much progress in advancing "jointness" among the services, however, there are still significant shortcomings that the military is trying to improve. By contrast, the federal civilian workforce lacks the ability or incentive to foster, measure, and reward collaboration across most areas of government.

Fair and Insightful Performance Appraisal

The system most organizations use to collect, document, and feed performance data back to individuals and groups is often termed "performance appraisal or performance assessment." Our focus here is not on the documentation per se, but on building the capacity of managers to provide meaningful performance feedback to individuals and groups.

A credible performance appraisal system has three essential ingredients: (1) a set of procedures for establishing performance ratings considered to be fair by those receiving ratings, (2) a complement of "raters" with the necessary skills to make these judgments and to provide feedback that supports the ratings, and (3) access to credible data to measure inputs, outputs, and outcomes related to the job.

Applying ratings consistently based on objective information is viewed as a mark of fairness by employees and makes it easier for appraising managers to compare performance across agency boundaries. In a study of performance management practices in medium and large companies conducted by the University of Southern California Center for Effective Organizations, human resources (HR) managers identified "calibration meetings"—a type of second-level review—as valuable tools for standardizing appraisals, thus helping to ensure that the system is operating fairly across the entire organization.[12]

In recent years, many cities have adopted "stat" programs to set meaningful targets that produce desired outcomes (see box 8-3) and to hold regular meetings that shine a spotlight on the people responsible for meeting these targets. This critical step converts each manager into a problem solver dedicated to finding ways to achieve the outcomes that are vital to the organization. Management can then focus on ways to remove barriers to improved performance and recognize and share success. Employee performance measured against data obtained through this system is credible.

The goal of performance appraisals is to create this credible environment on a miniature scale for every employee. That means translating lofty strategic objectives into specific bites that the worker can achieve. Done correctly, performance appraisal reviews force every employee (supervisors and subordinates) to think about the mission of the organization and how his or her own performance relates to it. Performance appraisals should also encourage employees to discuss how best to achieve things. Like the stat programs that draw attention to each program and the results it is achieving, performance appraisals for individuals can help them to become problem solvers. It is also an opportunity to bring to light issues that might otherwise be overlooked in the course of daily business. For example, do employees have the appropriate training

B O X 8 - 3 . Performance Management Saves Baltimore More than $70 Million

Several U.S. cities have implemented a comprehensive performance management "stat" tool after the success of the "Citistat" program in Baltimore, Maryland. Baltimore implemented Citistat in 2000 as part of the mayor's strategy to better manage city resources. The program sets specific targets for city services, measures the performance of all municipal agencies against these targets, and provides a weekly forum for Baltimore's operational managers and decision-makers to discuss the obstacles to meeting these targets. The program has enabled the city to reduce costs, increase revenues, and improve the quality of municipal services. In doing so, the program has promoted a culture of inter-governmental cooperation and coordination. Another benefit is that it provides an ongoing opportunity to evaluate progress in achieving the city's goals. Since the program's inception in 2000, Baltimore has saved more than $70 million through reduced overtime costs, the elimination and reduction of program redundancy, generation of new revenues, and increased efficiency.

Following Baltimore's success, cities such as San Francisco, New York, Chicago, Somerville, Mass., and Phoenix have implemented the system. Many individual agencies within cities, such as the New York City Police Department, have made significant improvements through the use of this tool.

Sources: City and County of San Francisco, Board of Supervisors, "CitiStat Technology Systems" (www.sfgov.org/site/bdsupvrs_page.asp?id=21916); Harvard University, Kennedy School, Ash Institute for Democratic Governance and Innovation, "Citistat" (www.ashinstitute.harvard.edu/Ash/citistat.htm).

and education, tools and infrastructure, authority and guidance to achieve their objectives? Are these the right indicators of progress toward the organization's goals?

If this dialogue is to be fruitful, managers and supervisors must be carefully trained to perform transparent, meaningful, and fair evaluations based on objective, fact-based information. They must understand the context in which the work was conducted, including factors such as resource limitations or unexpected roadblocks. Evaluations must also be reviewed to ensure consistency and fairness. This is especially important in the first few years after implementation, when managers are learning how to make the performance distinctions that are the basis for ratings and pay. The GAO, for instance, has multiple levels of review: "Before performance ratings are finalized, they receive second-level reviews . . . [that check] if raters have consistently and reasonably applied the performance standards. Subsequently, the Human Capital Office and the Office of Opportunity and Inclusiveness review the performance ratings and pay decisions across all of GAO to determine whether there are any irregularities or potential adverse impacts to be addressed."[13]

The GAO has also implemented a standardized scoring system to ensure consistency. The standardized rating score (SRS) "indicates the employee's position relative to the average rating of that employee's team. Employees in different teams with the same SRS have the same relative performance, thus achieving better comparability in ratings across teams. Employees' SRS and the midpoint for their pay range are key factors in calculating their performance-based compensation for that year."

The desire for consistency was a primary factor in the Department of Labor's (DOL's) decision to revamp its separate agency rating systems.[14] All thirty-two DOL agencies now use the same rating system with a set of universal criteria against which all employees are rated, although each agency also includes some rating factors that are specific to the agency's mission.

Specific and Concrete Feedback

Once fair procedures for performance ratings are in place, supervisors must take the next steps to have substantive conversations with their employees about the employee's actual performance. In our focus groups, most government employees complained that they had never really had a substantive conversation with someone about their own work. Lack of personal attention is a problem. Employees do not get the coaching and insight into their own performance that enables them to turn a failure or substandard performance into an opportunity to learn and improve. More likely, they get a vague pat on the back without the hard analysis that would enable them to improve.

Once employees have a clear sense of how they performed, they need to know specifically what steps they can take to improve their performance. The burden is clearly on the supervisor to identify and explain what was not correct in their employee's performance and then describe what would have been right in order for the employee to remedy the situation.

Reinforcing Successful Performance

Once a solid performance appraisal system is in place and employees actually are having insightful and constructive discussion about their performance, it is essential to motivate them to continue to do their best. Rational, resourceful employees will do more good if they see clear incentives for doing the right thing and disincentives for acting in ways that do not promote the mission and well-being of their agency. Reinforcement includes both pecuniary compensation and nonpecuniary recognition. We begin with a discussion of pay-for-performance.

Pay-for-Performance. In the discourse on civil service reform, no single issue has been as controversial as pay-for-performance. Implementing pay-for-performance poses some unique challenges in government. On one hand, the theory is appealing: it promises greater accountability and greater rewards for individual contributions to the achievement of an organization's goals. Watson Wyatt's comprehensive study of the subject finds that companies that link pay to performance do better in the market. On the assumption that it would have positive organizational outcomes, Comptroller General David Walker made pay-for-performance a critical component of his reform efforts at the GAO.

Theoretically, rewarding individual performance does provide a direct incentive to perform better. But there are substantial obstacles to making this simple and sensible formula work in government. We have already recounted the challenges of measuring performance and of assigning a direct causal link between individual performance and outcomes. Is there any less challenge in reaching agreement on desired outcomes? How can people be held accountable for things they do not control? Individual pay-for-performance makes sense when individuals have real control over the outcome, but this is usually not the case in government. Most public servants are in occupations in which the outcomes are influenced by many factors outside their control. For example, would the absence of a terrorist event during a specific reporting period be a positive indicator of performance for an executive at the Department of Homeland Security? How can one measure the contribution of a scientist working on technology advancements that will be ten years in development? How should one measure customer satisfaction among prison inmates? Many agencies complain that it is difficult to identify individual contributions to a group effort or to develop meaningful measures. This makes it difficult, if not impossible, to set meaningful individual performance targets granular enough to be linked to individual compensation.

There is a difference between providing individual rewards (such as cash or non-cash bonuses and perks) for special achievements and linking a person's career progression and salary to specific performance targets. As we described in chapter 6, it makes sense for managers to have the ability to reward employees with bonuses when the situation warrants it. There are many circumstances in which team-wide or department-wide bonuses can help to incentivize and celebrate success. For example, a city might choose to reward its snowplowing team for an especially effective effort after a blizzard, or the police might receive extra compensation for achieving a crime control target. But these are group rewards, in which there is no effort to drill down into how well each person performed.

By contrast, introducing a pay-for-performance system throughout government would require a massive upgrade in the capabilities of the system. The government as it is currently configured lacks virtually all the capability needed to underpin such a system. In theory, it seems clear that top performers should be rewarded for superior results (and that the worst performers should not receive pay increases). But this leaves a vast group of employees whose performance falls somewhere in the middle. It may be next to impossible to distinguish between the top 20 percent of performers and the next quintile, especially when the workforce is highly driven by the mission. And how would one draw the line between those in the top 20 percent compared with the top 30 percent without discouraging many extremely valuable employees?

Fair treatment will depend on one's definition of "pay-for-performance" itself. Harvard's Robert Behn argues that the term is actually inherently ambiguous because its meaning has at least twenty variants. The government's rather open exchange of information about employment evaluation only complicates things. Furthermore, managers who want to provide honest data-based feedback are handicapped by the general stigma of judging people as below average (or even as average, for that matter). Pay-for-performance also threatens many of the safeguards developed over the years to protect government workers and government operations from political infighting. While those safeguards were intended to meet real needs, they must now be redesigned to achieve their important mission and foster a new level of efficiency in government operations. More important, rewarding individual performance runs counter to the team-oriented culture of government: by design, it takes many players to deliver a single government service.

There are too many practical flaws in the current environment—including inadequate information technology and HR tracking systems, training, and measures—to warrant an experiment with the morale of the career civil service. Instead, the focus must be on building a performance system and an outcome-oriented culture based on team efficiency and effectiveness. At some point in the future, when these underlying capabilities have been squarely addressed, it may be possible to introduce pay-for-performance in certain specific and well-defined situations. That point is far off in the future.

Therefore we recommend that pay-for-performance not be implemented until an agency has a cadre of well-trained managers and supervisors who know how to evaluate performance and its employees are confident that these people can do it fairly and well. This will take many years. Once this first step is accomplished and performance measurement systems have improved, incentives can be introduced to reward people for teamwork. Teams could be evaluated and held accountable for working together to achieve mission goals. Agencies could be held accountable for leadership and the results they achieve on overall mission objectives as well as their demonstrated ability to invest in people. GPRA and PART tools are well suited to this process when they are firmly linked to the budget process and coupled with the budget reforms we propose in chapter 10 to capture the fully loaded cost of personnel and line-item tracking in the budget. Individuals then can be rewarded for controllable aspects of performance such as interpersonal relations, courtesy, and reliability in customer service.

The argument for delaying pay-for-performance should not be confused with the fundamental need to hold employees accountable for their integrity and honesty as public servants at all times. Nor should it be used as a means for management to defer badly needed investment in the training and development of personnel. The compact with the civil service has been broken on this count for a long time and must first be restored if programs to tie performance more directly to individual reward are to be credible and not an exercise in applying tenuous private sector experience to a totally different public sector environment.

The argument for delaying pay-for-performance should not be confused with the fundamental need to hold employees accountable for their integrity and honesty as public servants at all times. Nor should it be used as a means for management to defer badly needed investment in the training and development of personnel.

Addressing Performance Shortfalls. On the opposite end of the performance spectrum, government managers must deal effectively with poor performers whose presence on a team can have adverse effects on morale and overall customer service. Managers everywhere resist dealing directly with performance problems. Many say this is their toughest challenge. Is it any wonder that so many managers avoid or sidestep problems in the workforce rather than take action to fix them? If there is a need for an attitude change among federal managers on any subject, it is on the value and usefulness of giving timely and meaningful performance feedback and following this up with specific actions by both the manager and employee designed to help the employee improve. Unfortunately, most employees with performance problems are unable to solve them alone. They need help from managers, colleagues, and union representatives to change their behavior. Withholding help from employees who need it can have insidious effects, building frustration in the troubled employees and resentment among their colleagues. This results in poor morale. And while there is no one right way to address performance problems, protracted adversarial procedures are rarely needed and nearly always destructive. This poses both a short-term HR problem and a longer-term issue about how to properly view employee performance when it suggests that an employee is failing.

As a result, some scholars question the usefulness of annual performance appraisals altogether. Bob Behn, for one, argues that annual performance reviews undermine an agency's ability to fire truly bad employees. Current systems, says Behn, give managers only two real choices: "launch an all-out attack—using the full powers (and convoluted rules)

of the personnel system to get [the employee] fired, or shrug off the problem," rate the employee as "meets expectations," and get back to work.[15]

According to Behn, managers base their decision on how much effort
and energy and sometimes political capital they are willing to expend to
get rid of problem employees. A manager attempting to fire a poor performer may well be forced to battle with the union. Not infrequently, the
employee will file a formal complaint or even a lawsuit. Behn's observation raises important questions about the effectiveness of traditional performance appraisal techniques that need careful attention throughout the
reform program.

In the 1999 National Performance Review Employee Survey, only 28
percent of respondents reported that corrective actions were taken with
poor performers. Furthermore, nearly one in three managers cited the
lack of upper management support as the reason they had not terminated
a poor performer.[16]

One reform in particular would go a long way toward addressing the
poor-performer issue: streamlining appeals and the adjudication of grievances. We are encouraged by the current trend in the federal government
away from highly formalized, adversarial, time-consuming, and expensive adjudication processes for resolving grievances and the movement
toward various forms of alternative dispute resolution (ADR). In our
experience, the best approach to a workplace dispute is to intervene early
with a fair, independent, and confidential resolution process that can qui-
etly find solutions to problems and rectify inequities before they disrupt
mission-critical work.

One of the more successful ADR methods relies on dedicated ombudsmen or "ombuds" to address grievances and minimize formal appeals. As
the GAO explains, "Federal ombuds offices deal with a wide range of
workplace issues, from helping employees get answers to questions about
agency policies and cutting through 'red tape' to more serious situations,
such as allegations about employment discrimination, other prohibited
personnel practices, and workplace safety issues. Ombuds work to
resolve disputes between individuals as well as within work groups."[17] In
a review of the work of the ombuds at the National Institutes of Health,
the International Broadcasting Bureau, and the U.S. Secret Service, the
GAO found that these organizations were able to resolve between 60
and 70 percent of their cases.[18] Ombuds can also be very useful to senior

leadership by alerting them to emerging issues that are affecting groups of employees and could lead to larger problems.

Another strategy to ensure that both managers and individuals with performance problems get the attention they need would be to provide targeted training and coaching for the manager. This might then translate into better supervision and training for the employee. In particularly difficult cases, a fresh start may be warranted, or a period of time added to a special projects unit to allow low-performing employees to work with capable new managers, learn new skills, and take on new assignments, with careful documentation of their performance.

In the military, a soldier with chronic performance problems may be reassigned to an administrative unit or placed in a situation that allows the soldier to improve. This reassignment will also relieve the commanding officer (manager of the poor performer) of the burden of close monitoring and special remedial training. Some form of this program could be developed in civilian agencies in order to ensure that individuals with performance problems get the attention they need and opportunities to improve without putting essential day-to-day operations at risk. Unions could play an important role in addressing performance problems and helping employees get a fresh start. To this end, unions could help identify and develop the content and approach of a remedial program and thereby increase the likelihood of achieving the desired effect: a successful and productive employee.

An atmosphere of resolve to genuinely improve performance (rather than a thinly disguised desire to fire the employee) will go a long way toward producing the best outcomes for managers, employees, and their organization. Ultimately, the right decision for all parties may even be for the employee to pursue a career outside the agency or outside government altogether. The government manager should not shrink from decisive action on poor performers, but managers should approach the situation with care and respect for the employee, as well as appreciation for the mission and resource limitations of their agency.

Performance Management and Performance Budgeting

Establishing a robust performance management system is a prerequisite for introducing performance budgeting. (Performance budgeting means taking it to the next step by linking the budget to how well an agency or a program is actually performing.) There is evidence that the PART program has already had some positive effect. A recent study by John Gilmour and David Lewis found that PART scores had a statistically significant impact on budget decisions within OMB, particularly on budget decisions regarding small and medium-size programs.[19] However, they also found that the section of the PART scores that most influenced budget allocations was not the "results"—but the "program purpose." They point out that this finding "tends to contradict the goal of performance budgeting to redirect resources to programs that produce results." The lack of impact of the "results" component may be due to problems in defining good outcome measures, or it may be a combination of historical, political, and practical factors that ultimately influence budget decisions in Congress.

To remedy this situation, the government must tackle the disconnect between performance management and the budget appropriations process. (This wider issue of budget reform will be the subject of another book.) But even without massive budget reform, the government should at least take steps to allow agencies to retain some of the savings they create through higher productivity and cost savings—and to reallocate these funds to other priorities that serve the mission. A strong link between resources that matter and organizational performance will provide some of the missing incentive to make the performance management system work.

The benefit of such an approach can be seen in any national park. Each national park receives its own line item in the budget, and all the parks are chronically underfunded with a long wish list of needed repairs and educational and conservation projects. But if a park superintendent is especially efficient and saves a little money in the operating budget, he or she is not permitted to use that money to pay for a repair or another project—no matter how worthwhile. Instead, Congress would be likely to conclude that the park could get by with less funding, and it would cut the park budget for the following year. Thus the superintendent is actually penalized (rather than rewarded) for efficiency. Unless this problem is addressed, it is difficult to put teeth into even the most thoughtful performance management program.

Many government entities at the local, municipal, and state level have found ways to introduce some form of "gainsharing" in which employee work units share in savings. In Indianapolis, this approach led to sustained performance improvements by the public works department, without increased costs, for a decade. Yet the federal government has lagged far behind in this critical area.

Conclusions

The government needs to build a performance management system that reinforces each agency's strategy, operational needs, and core values. This requires that it set performance standards, measure them, and use compensation, benefits, and recognition programs to reward success. For the organization, this is an opportunity to reinforce the things that matter to the mission. For the individual, this is an opportunity to be treated fairly, as an intelligent, participating human being who wants to make a difference in the world. The investment in designing and rolling out a robust performance management system should not be viewed as a cost, but as a source of long-term strength to the country and the important work it carries out. This will not happen without commitment from the president to forge an agreement among the many stakeholders.

PART **III**

Enacting
Public Service Reform

eforms of government-wide systems—whether they are financial, information technology, policy, budgetary, or human capital systems—require determined leadership. They are difficult to achieve in the United States because its system of government discourages radical change. It empowers many stakeholders in the system to slow or block change; yet no stakeholder has a preponderance of power to make change happen. Instead, many stakeholders with a wide array of interests must be consulted. That said, we believe that personnel reform can be achieved through vision, skill, and leadership.

In part I, we made the case for action, explaining why the personnel management system needs to be overhauled and what benefits it can achieve. In part II, we described the endgame by identifying needed reforms. As any government practitioner knows, however, it takes more than a vision and a case for change to produce results. Large-scale efforts also require focused leadership in order to mobilize support among stakeholders, pass necessary legislation, obtain the necessary financial resources, and build the management infrastructure. This aspect of the reforms we envisage is the subject of part III.

We have written this section of the book as a set of recommended actions for the new president. Others—members of Congress or the cabinet—could lead the changeover by breaking the effort into smaller, more focused reform initiatives. Working alone, however, they are unlikely to muster the support needed to lead a total transformation of the system.

Presidential support for a people factor initiative will motivate both the political appointees and career civil servants. As with any comprehensive shift, the president will have to understand the situation and work effectively with Congress. This means he will have to identify the stakeholders, understand the issue, and assemble a top team of people to lead the transformation. But in this instance, the president must do a few additional and very important things because the challenge of overhauling the federal personnel management system is different from most other large-scale policy reform efforts.

First, people factor transformation would affect everyone. It would alter one of the three largest categories of government spending. It would entail sweeping change across the far-flung federal system. Bureaucracies are resistant to major structural changes by design, and have many tools at their disposal with which to oppose them. In this case, decades of congressional and executive rule-making and labor negotiations have left a legacy that many users of the system, even the specialists, are reluctant to change. And public servants are skeptical about new proposals because hyped changes often turn out to be superficial and fail to address the problems they face.

Second, control over people is distributed throughout the system. Although the executive branch reports to the president, the president essentially delegates this responsibility to department heads who, in turn, delegate their authority into their organizations. As a result, the responsibility for managing people is diffused, and no one except the president is really in charge of—or responsible for—the overall health of the human resources system.

Third, the stakeholder groups that support personnel reform are fragmented. Those who have advocated people reforms range from members of the two Volker commissions and the Partnership for Public Service to unions and specific reformers in each administration, such as Al Gore and Clay Johnson. Despite their good efforts, it is difficult for this diverse group to form the strong coalition that is a prerequisite for success. As in many movements for reform, the supporters must be willing to adjust their positions on the edges in order to come together at the core and thus gather the power to move things forward.

Part III provides a roadmap for a leadership team determined to bring a people focus to the federal government. It is organized into three chapters. Chapter 9 explains the legitimate concerns of different stakeholders, and how to engage them in the reform effort. Chapter 10 lays out the specific financial and statutory requirements. Chapter 11 suggests ways to galvanize public opinion in order to implement this bold vision.

9

A Job for the President
Engaging Stakeholders
to Reform Public Service

t is almost a truism to say that public service is important. But fundamentally restructuring the government to prize and reward public sector employees requires leadership from the top and a coming together of the many interested parties.

This is especially challenging when the constituencies that are affected are fragmented and the subject matter is not too captivating. Everyone agrees that it is important, but it is just not a "hot" topic.

To bring urgency to the problem of climate change, former vice president Al Gore produced the film *An Inconvenient Truth*. His challenge was to find a way to bring the American public out of its complacency and into a state of awareness about the environment. He needed to inspire people sufficiently to summon the enormous will required to make immediate fundamental change, invest in alternative energy, and see the world differently.

The president faces a similar hurdle in inspiring the country to tackle the people factor in government. Most Americans want the U.S. government to work better and would agree that this topic is important. But they are complacent about the federal workforce. To drive change on this subject, the president will first need to educate the public about the crisis in the federal workforce and how it affects our ability to fix the economy and achieve key goals.

An additional problem is that the people who understand the federal workforce and are already committed to reform have different opinions about what that reform should look like. There is a very wide range of perspectives among the various constituencies. The president faces a formidable challenge in bringing these groups together and engaging them in a way that produces consensus.

> *A*mericans want the U.S. government to work better and would agree that this topic is important. But they are complacent about the federal workforce.

Gain Command of the Issues

The president will need to learn the key features of the civil service system and its variations, the legal and procedural constraints, and the lessons of previous attempts to change these systems—both successful and unsuccessful. The president will also need to cultivate constructive relationships among the key stakeholders in human capital reform, including Congress, the unions, the media, the executive branch, and academia. By developing these relationships, the president will not only gain an understanding of the concerns and needs of stakeholder groups but also create an environment in which consensus is possible. This is a complex process that requires consultation, expert advice, personal "face time" between the president and different constituencies, and the development of a core team within the administration to lead and manage the change.

Create the "Container"

The reforms in public service that we are advocating are on as large a scale as the Great Society and the New Deal —so vast that they can only move forward if the president marshals all stakeholders to support the reform. The president will need a dedicated team to guide the transformation effort and to liaise with the different stakeholders. From the beginning of the process through its implementation, this team must be on the job, driving reform, identifying areas of potential compromise, and mustering the political will inside the White House, in the cabinet agencies, and on Capital Hill to remove roadblocks to reform.

The goal of leadership for this team is to motivate and engage a network of people in a problem-solving process that is flexible enough to enter into disagreement but strong enough to reach compromise and resolution. In effect, the team creates a "container" in which the participants can reach compromise. The president has to set skillfully the boundaries of the debate around the core problem and opportunities of personnel reform and then work within these boundaries to forge a consensus.

Part of Lyndon Johnson's genius in the Senate was his ability to create such a container—one strong enough to contain the animated debates among the diverse constituencies involved in the early battles over the civil rights reform bill of the 1950s. He realized that action had to be taken and that the Senate needed to begin the difficult dialogue on the first civil rights bill in eighty years.[1] He had to do it while maintaining and building trust and eventually reaching agreement on a course of action through compromise. Johnson was tough and forceful. But the parties did not walk away; in the end, they made a deal. Historian Doris Kerns Goodwin writes: "The forces were closely matched and fragmented among themselves. The manner in which the issue was conducted was vital in adding support and moderating opposition. And it was Johnson's leadership that determined the manner and terms of conduct, which alone made it possible . . . to pass a bill."[2]

President Johnson used a similar approach to urge the country into enacting the Economic Opportunity Act:

> [He] worked incessantly to make poverty an issue of public concern. He met with groups ranging from the Daughters of the American Revolution to the Socialist Party, from the Business Council to the AFL-CIO. He made dozens of speeches. He made personal visits to poverty-stricken regions. What had largely been the concern of a small number of liberal intellectuals and government bureaucrats became within six months the national disgrace that shattered the complacency of a people who always considered their country a land of equal opportunity for all. From this base, Johnson went to the Congress to declare an "unconditional war on poverty."

As Kearns Goodwin points out, "By shaping the political consensus beforehand through an elaborate courtship of leaders of the relevant groups, he paved the way for legislative success.[3] Of course, this is easier said than done. Just ask Hillary Clinton—who despite enormous personal commitment and leadership on the health care issue was unable to create a container for all the competing interests when she tried to enact sweeping health care reforms during the 1990s. These and other reform successes and failures can guide the president as he embarks on the significant leadership challenge of personnel reform.

In our vision, the president would lead the effort to create the "container," together with, for example, the deputy director of the Office of Management and Budget (OMB), the director of the Domestic Policy Council, a key cabinet secretary (for example, the labor secretary), a union president, respected former members of Congress (preferably with experience on the Government Affairs Committee), the head of the Office of Personnel Management (OPM), the director of the Partnership for Public Service (PPS) and other nongovernmental organizations (NGOs) dedicated to improving public service, and White House staff, including the heads of congressional liaison and communications.

The team will need to create a charter to define its mission and responsibilities. As the work proceeds, the leadership team will use the power of presidential attention and interest to keep stakeholders, the media, and the American public aware of and engaged in its work. The most important work of the leadership team is to develop a detailed strategy for enacting people reform. The team will need to construct specific legislative, regulatory, and programmatic reforms and initiatives and shepherd them through Congress. In developing this package, the team will draw on the combined resources of the relevant White House offices and agencies, the work of a presidential commission convened to study and make recommendations for reform, and the expertise of the various stakeholder groups, including the unions and Congress.

To be successful, the rationale for change must be seen as both bipartisan and independent. It must, above all, be compelling. To build this case, the president will need to seek the advice and participation of all those who have a stake in personnel reform and, where appropriate, to appoint people to commissions, teams, and advisory groups. Representatives of these constituencies will then need to work together to build national awareness of and consensus on the need for investment in public service. The business case is the set of arguments that explains why the *value to the nation* of making this change exceeds the *cost* needed to get it done. It forms the core rationale for the transformation that will be used to build public support. And it provides the narrative line of a large-scale effort to persuade and educate the public.

> *The business case explains why the* value to the nation *of personnel reform exceeds the* cost *of getting it done.*

Seek Advice and Participation

The various stakeholders have differing opinions on how to reform the federal workforce. The president should seek the advice and participation of all of them. This is important not only to solicit ideas but also to build trust and relationships with various groups, some of which have been badly frayed in recent years. Drawing from this group of stakeholders, the president needs to assemble a team that can analyze the existing federal human capital management system and needs to develop recommendations for wide-ranging strategic and tactical reform. This task could be completed by a presidential commission, an internal task force, or some other working group. A presidential commission would be an obvious choice for the job because such entities hold a significant place in the American political system. As scholar David Flitner Jr. explains, task forces of this nature "have provided the basis for legislative and administrative reform as well as affecting the very social climate itself via their sometimes forceful role as public educators. They may promote redefinition of critical social and political issues, increase awareness, lend legitimacy to previously marginal points of view, and actually inspire the national conscience."[4] The president might consider negotiating a charter in the style of Defense Base Closure and Realignment Commission (BRAC) recommendations that would be considered only on an "up or down" basis.[5]

The resulting recommendations would lay the foundation for the transformation effort. They would provide the initial definition of the priorities of the transformation, the necessary legislative and regulation reforms, and the resources and funding required, as described in chapter 10.

One of the key characteristics of the Johnson strategy was that it sought advice from a bipartisan group of experienced opinion leaders. Having created a core team inside government to guide the personnel reform effort, the president also needs to engage this second critical group: outside experts with deep, relevant expertise on the subject of personnel reform. These are individuals who have the capability, reputation, and interest to shape and validate the president's plan for action. They may also have specialized knowledge of the complex federal system that is essential to inform the judgment of the leadership team. And they are the individuals to whom the media will turn in order to understand, evaluate, and judge the effort.

This cadre could be drawn from a list of leaders such as former OPM directors, secretaries and deputy secretaries of federal agencies, academics, members of think tanks, leaders from the private sector who are already engaged in the political process (such as members of the Republican and Democratic National Committees), former political leaders, senior civil servants, state and local leaders, and union leaders. The coalition should also engage organizations dedicated to good government, such as the National Academy of Public Administration (NAPA), the Council for Excellence in Government, and representatives of the career civil service, including the Senior Executives Association, the Federal Managers Association, and others. This group of leaders can help look for common ground by identifying opportunities for agreement and compromise.

Identify Stakeholders

Steve Goldsmith learned during his tenure as mayor of Indianapolis that a vital step in leading political change is to identify the critical stakeholders and their interests early and accurately.[6] However, one of the major impediments to personnel reform is that the stakeholders who have the most authority have little interest in the issue, and those with the interest have little authority. Congress, the White House, and the OMB have the power to make reform happen, but little expertise in human capital management. By contrast, the unions and nongovernmental organizations (including NAPA, the PPS, the General Accounting Office, and to some extent OPM) have the knowledge and expertise, but limited direct authority to improve the system. This misalignment of power and under-standing—exacerbated by insufficient cooperation between unions and government leaders—has impeded the design and implementation of per-sonnel reform to date. In the next sections, we identify the major stakeholders who need to be involved in a successful personnel reform effort.

> *One of the major impediments to personnel reform is that the stakeholders who have the most authority have little interest in the issue, and those with the interest have little authority.*

Political Appointees

Implementing personnel reform will be the job of both the limited-term appointees in executive positions and senior civil servants. As former political appointees ourselves, we believe that the vast majority of individuals who are appointed have a sincere desire to contribute to public service. Unfortunately, many political appointees have little appetite for undertaking major organizational change because "it is difficult, results are not guaranteed, and it is contrary to what political appointees are 'hired' to do by a president, which is to create public policy that differentiates one president from another."[7]

Appointees are rarely chosen for their skills in managing large entities or major organizational changes. Many appear to focus on crisis management and quick successes. As discussed in part II, the tenure of most appointed leaders in the U.S. government is far shorter than that of their employees. Moreover, political appointees favor activities that will produce results within their tenure and that enhance the political capital of the agency head (and the president). People factor reform is a long-term, messy, and complicated effort that does not fit this profile.

Political appointees probably do not think about the personnel system very much when they first enter government. Many have technical experience in the field of their appointment and have political goals to achieve, in addition to the specific mission objectives of their agency. Many are drawn from the ranks of law firms, congressional staff, think tanks, and political campaigns and have little experience in managing large bureaucracies.

In general, political appointees want to make a difference. But what they need is speed and flexibility: the ability to pull the levers to move the bureaucracy to accomplish their goals. This means they must have the power to hire and fire senior staff quickly, to redeploy senior executives to meet different needs, to adjust performance goals, to staff up new initiatives, and to reward the people in the organization who help them. For many political appointees, the federal personnel rules are an impediment to getting things done.

There is an inherent conflict between the desire of political appointees to move boldly and quickly and the basic structure of the bureaucracy, which is programmed to move cautiously and conservatively. Bureaucrats tend to be more concerned about the consequences of change than about making change happen fast. They tend to worry about operational constraints, compliance with law and regulations, avoidance of unintended consequences, and other issues of practical implementation.

Therefore the only way the president can guarantee that the political appointees will take people factor issues seriously is to make people management a performance requirement for this group. In other words, the president must specifically ask senior political appointees to spend their time, effort, and political capital in this area. The president can also reward those who pay attention to this issue with awards, recognitions, and promotions.

By making people reform a personal priority, the president can directly motivate political appointees to focus on this issue. But even political appointees who are fully committed to the goal of personnel reform may lack the length of tenure or the expertise in this field to be able to lead change on their own. Their success therefore depends to a significant degree on the cadre of senior executive service (SES) managers and other civil servants.

Senior Civil Servants

The SES is one of the most critical constituencies in strengthening public service. First, the SES is itself badly in need of reform. When Congress enacted the 1978 Civil Service Reform Act, its intent was to create a versatile group of senior civilian managers who could be deployed across government to tackle important challenges. It was modeled on senior executives in industry, who expect to work in assignments throughout the company, wherever they are most needed, and on flag officers in the military, who are expected to redeploy to different missions in response to the immediate needs of the country and the military service. These rotations were supposed to be an integral part of the design of the SES, allowing individuals to gain experience and versatility. However, the SES has evolved into a set of entrenched senior civil servants who typically remain at one agency for their entire careers.

Therefore senior executives are now the people who run the government on a day-to-day basis. More than 90 percent of them are located in the Washington, D.C., area, typically working in the headquarters of a department, agency, or bureau. Personnel reform cannot succeed without their active participation and leadership—but they do not have strong incentives to fix the system. Senior civil servants fill the leadership gap whenever political leadership is absent (for example, they take on the job of "acting" assistant secretary, administrator, and so on, in the period between administrations and appointments), but this has, over time, created a culture oriented more toward stabilizing their organizations and maintaining the status quo rather than changing them, as was evident in our study.

Senior civil servants whom we interviewed expressed considerable resistance to personnel reforms for several reasons. One executive who has worked on such reforms for a number of years commented:

> Many SES members don't want these reforms. When the SEA [Senior Executive Association] and FMA [Federal Managers Association] testified on proposed personnel reforms, they did so from roughly the same perspective as the unions. Lots of their members didn't want the extra work implied by more rigorous and demanding performance management requirements, nor did they believe that a business case had been made for reform. It's at this level that the rubber meets the road.[8]

Another reason for their opposition to reform is that SES members have spent a lifetime acquiring detailed expertise on the current system and learning how to manipulate it to get things done. Any effort to dismantle the system is therefore a threat to their effectiveness. In some respects, it would also diminish their authority if their hard-won knowledge would no longer differentiate them from their subordinates.

During the IRS transformation, the president of the SEA "voiced strong opposition to the use of critical pay authority," which would allow the government to pay higher salaries for certain hard-to-get managerial and technical skills.[9] During a month-long seminar for SES candidates held at the Harvard Kennedy School, these future leaders voiced concern that the planned reforms would most likely produce more paperwork and little real change. Many predicted that reforms would add time-consuming—but meaningless—people management tasks that would draw their attention away from what is really important: their agency missions. These comments suggest a cultural bias against change among senior career civil servants, who may be personally invested in the work that would have to be changed, redirected, or scrapped altogether to make way for the new initiative.

How, then, can senior civil servants be expected to lead the transformation of government organizations when their historical role has been to maintain the status quo? We believe the answer is that operational managers from the SES level down to line supervisors must see the link between human capital reform and accomplishing the mission more clearly. Once these managers are involved in developing the strategic human capital plans, and once they are held accountable for addressing people issues, they will be able to see whether personnel management contributes to or detracts from achieving strategic objectives.

The midlevel professionals that the government needs to retain are in a bind: they are at once potential allies while also likely opponents of personnel reform. The result is inertia in the system, which cannot be shaken until this group is engaged and motivated.

Most managers in government today—including executives, supervisors, heads of HR operations, chief human capital officers, and others—are well aware that the personnel system is broken. However, they are also apprehensive about the possibility of reform. They experience first-hand the difficulties in hiring, firing, and dealing with poor performers. They recognize that they will bear the brunt of the cost of reforming the system, even as they are forced to work within it to bring about near-term change. This cost provides a powerful disincentive to implement reform. Unless this issue is addressed, personnel reform could double the workload of these managers without providing them with additional pay, resources, or career enrichment. As we discussed in chapter 6, the pay gap between senior government careerists and their private sector counterparts has widened over the past two decades. Shrinking this gap will be an important tool in gaining support from senior managers. In addition, resources need to be made readily available so that managers can strengthen their teams and provide training and performance incentives. The midlevel professionals that the government needs to retain are therefore in a bind: they are at once potential allies while also likely opponents of personnel reform. The result is inertia in the system, which cannot be shaken until this group is engaged and motivated.

The Workforce

As noted in part I, the federal workforce is a large, disparate group of nearly 1.9 million individuals performing an extremely wide range of functions in many locations around the country. For the most part, the career civil servants now running the government have become successful in achieving the government's missions despite their highly constrained environment. The majority can use the system to create the outcomes they want, within limits. Others find they cannot use the system effectively and fail. For the first group, their knowledge of the arcane rules and regulations of the existing system ensure their value to the organization. They have a minimal incentive to create a more open environment in which their unique ability to operate will be of less use. Many government employees also feel a sense of entitlement to their specific positions independent of the overall needs of the organization. Proposals that change this fundamental relationship or alter the "rules of the game" (particularly late in a career) are viewed with suspicion.

Unlike the senior executives, this workforce is highly diverse and geographically dispersed. (Only 15 percent of these employees are located in the Washington area.) Not surprisingly, this group contains a spectrum of viewpoints, which vary according to type of job, region, and the individual agency and work unit. However, most share certain concerns about any proposed reforms. These include a desire for closer pay parity with their private sector counterparts, opportunities for personal growth and education, job security, and job satisfaction. They want more recognition from the public (and the media) of the important contribution they make. They also share a concern about the competence of their immediate supervisors to operate fairly and effectively in a system that ties employee performance to pay.

Unlike their counterparts in the private sector, federal workers have, until now, been sheltered from the major upheavals that have transformed industry during recent decades. (As we have noted, this has led to a growing pay differential between the public and private sector, and to a lack of investment in public sector employees.) Another result is that federal employees are likely to be anxious about the prospect of fundamental personnel reform. They will raise questions about whether it is worth exchanging pay, benefits, and promotion opportunities for the unknown and unproven attributes of a new system. They are also skeptical of any proposed reform because they have seen many reform efforts over the years that ultimately were unsuccessful and made little difference in their lives.[10]

Not only do current federal employees need to be engaged in the reform effort, but there is a second category that must be involved: the people whom the government is trying to recruit. With the expected retirements in the existing force in the next five years, the government will soon have to hire hundreds of thousands of new employees.

To engage the existing employees and to allay their fears about structural reform, the president and senior political leaders will need to enlist the "opinion leaders" within the current workforce. This is the cadre of people present in any organization who help their colleagues deal with periods of transition. Their insights into workplace events and issues have gained the deep respect of their coworkers. These opinion leaders are often long-time employees with technical expertise or organizational savvy. While they may not hold formal leadership positions, their influence on employee attitudes can be considerable, and employees will rely on them to help interpret the often-ambiguous events surrounding a major organizational change.

The second constituency—those the government hopes to recruit into the federal workforce—is also a diverse and wide-flung group, composed primarily of students and young people. As we discussed in part I, our survey of college students shows that these recruits value how they are treated and have high expectations. They want an organization that cares about them, rewards their contributions, and allows them to rise to the top on the basis of merit.

To engage this audience, the president needs to make a direct appeal to young people to join the civil service. There are organizations that can help; for example, the PPS is bringing attention to government work—and making it seem meaningful and prestigious—through its awards and recognitions. But there is no substitute for a direct appeal by the president. John F. Kennedy inspired the generation of Americans who are now retiring from government. The new president needs to reach out to the new generation. There are also dozens of mundane ways to engage this audience—from streamlining the hiring process to making job descriptions more enticing, performing more recruiting online, and using web technology.

Federal Employee Unions

Although less than one-quarter of the federal workers are dues-paying union members, the unions represent about half the workforce, to some extent.[11] The Department of Defense (DOD) alone has 1,500 bargaining units, 43 unions, and approximately 400,000 unionized employees. The Department of Homeland Security (DHS) has 50 bargaining units, 15 unions, and approximately 44,000 unionized personnel. These and other unions that represent federal employees do not believe the case for reform has been made yet. In their view, most government agencies already possess many personnel flexibilities that go unused. Meanwhile, unions argue that the government should be focusing on pay comparability with the private sector and the cost of benefits, especially the rising co-payments for health care.

No major personnel reform effort can succeed without the acceptance of the unions. This is evident from the recent history of the three major personnel efforts during the Bush administration: the Homeland Security Department reform, the DOD personnel reform, and the Working for America Act. All three initiatives faltered from the lack of union involvement.

At the DHS, four unions sued to stop personnel reforms in January 2005, charging that the rule changes developed by the agency and OPM violated specific provisions of the Homeland Security Act.[12] The presiding U.S. district court judge halted the implementation of the DHS's new personnel management system, arguing that the system violated the congressionally bestowed collective bargaining rights of employees. Subsequent appeals have also been decided in favor of the unions.

At the DOD, a lawsuit delayed implementation of its National Security Personnel System (NSPS) for several months while Pentagon officials attempted to review and address the 58,000 public comments they received on the preliminary rules and the counterproposal developed by the labor unions.

The Bush administration also drafted legislation to reform the rest of the civil service, through the Working for America Act (WFAA). But the faltering status of the reform agenda at the DHS and DOD doomed this effort. Unions expressed reservations about WFAA's proposed reforms, fearing that government jobs would be eliminated and questioning why many agencies have failed to use existing flexibilities to address concerns with pay, performance, and hiring. They felt that there was no clear link between the proposed reforms and improved organizational performance.

Bypassing union participation in shaping the reform effort was the fatal flaw of the Bush proposals. The unions have decades of expertise on personnel matters, and yet their input was excluded. As a result, the unions have strenuously and successfully challenged the legality of the new DHS rules and regulations in the courts and on Capitol Hill.

Recent efforts to reduce the scope of bargaining have further soured the relationship. Bob Tobias, former president of the National Treasury Employee Union (NTEU), has pointed out that "the attempt to significantly reduce the scope of bargaining will lead to a reversion to adversarial relationships. When one side has all the power and exercises it without the inclusion or involvement of the other, there is little left to do but fight."[13]

However, the unions themselves have not been creative in developing better people systems. In general, their role has been to react rather than proactively contribute to new solutions, which has led some in Washington to view the unions skeptically. One key congressional staffer told us: "Unions are the major obstacle. Everything else is small in comparison."

Of course, the unions themselves are not monolithic. The proposed reforms have drawn various responses from union leaders and union members. The National Treasury Employees Union, for one, has adopted a flexible attitude toward pay-for-performance proposals, whereas the American Federation of Government Employees is more resistant to them.[14]

Although recent history shows unions blocking reform efforts, this does not reflect the complexity of union perspectives, nor does it prove that unions are unwilling to accommodate reform if they are approached in a more constructive fashion. However, there is no question that one of the big challenges in revitalizing the public service will be to engage, motivate, and involve the unions. Unions want a seat at the table, an opportunity to enrich the work environment for the majority of their members, and they want to improve the quality of supervision in order to limit the risk of reform. In addition, they want pay and growth opportunities for their members. The unions need to be respected. In the last round of reform efforts, the unions were blocked from participation and had to resort to lobbying Congress and seeking court action to prevent what they perceived as a set of adverse actions. But ultimately the unions recognize the problems with the existing system, and it is in their interest to apply their considerable knowledge and expertise to craft serious personnel reforms.

Congress

Getting Congress to pay attention to reform has proved difficult in the past. President Bill Clinton, Vice President Gore, and President George W. Bush tried to engage Congress on this issue, and by and large failed. Gore persuaded Congress to tackle procurement reform, performance budgeting, and other topics but never succeeded in the personnel arena. One of the reasons we wrote this book was to call attention to the specific benefits—in efficiency, cost savings, and better service—that the private sector has achieved by making investments in its workforce. It is the responsibility of Congress to ensure that the U.S. taxpayer enjoys these benefits as well.

The president will need to work hard to overcome the lack of interest and knowledge about human capital reform in Congress, but change is possible. He can use stories about real people in congressional districts to make clear the need for more training and better leadership in government. By making the politics of personnel reform "local," he can motivate members of Congress to respond to issues that are important to their constituents back home. This suggests a targeted campaign, with the help of the unions and civil service employees, to explain why personnel reform is important to them and what specific help they want from their representatives. Progress will be made when Congress understands that performance issues throughout the workforce relate as much to constituent job satisfaction as to the quality of service provided for the broader electorate.

Congressional attention to personnel issues will help assuage concerns about changes to the civil service by increasing accountability around reform proposals. The Bush administration's proposed reforms received the opposite reception in Congress. Constituents and unions had expressed such significant concerns about the Working for America Act that by the time the legislation received a first hearing, Congress had already adopted a "go-slow" approach.

A new level of interest and attention to training will be generated by the creation of a budget line item. Some may be concerned that a budget line item will attract attention to training money, making it an easier mark for cuts. We argue that once appropriators understand the significance and value of training, they will actually work to protect training dollars. The line item will create a hook into the congressional appropriations process through which the appropriating committees can direct resources and require action through the budget report and bills.

An appeal by the White House to the Senate and House leadership to coordinate a bold set of legislative changes would provide the power to overcome the fragmented interest of individual committees, particularly the authorizing committees that control civil service reform and others with government-wide jurisdiction. Congress could initiate hearings on the personnel system in preparation for a legislative initiative for reform. These would draw attention to notable life-saving missions by government employees, scientific discoveries, law enforcement arrests, or engineering accomplishments. They would also highlight the government's pervasive influence on daily life through financial regulation, telecommunications, national research, and security and thereby garner media coverage of the people issue. Mention of the successful (even heroic) efforts of agency employees to serve the public would have a salubrious effect on its views of the career civil service. Employees at the Defense Logistics Agency (DLA) would no doubt welcome the opportunity to publicize efforts that helped save taxpayers $4 billion while improving customer satisfaction in a time of war.

Address Compensation Disparity. Congress should address the issue of federal pay. As noted in chapter 6, the disparity between public and private sector pay at senior management levels is significant and getting worse. Jack Donahue has characterized this as just one consequence of the segregation of the public and private working worlds.[15] The public sector is part of the general economy and market for talent. So if the market values a competent, efficient, and fair government, then government pay must be high enough to attract the right number and quality of people to accomplish its work. This simple principle seems nowhere in evidence at either end of the pay spectrum: the government often pays too much for lower-skilled work and too little for highly skilled work.[16]

Despite the significant difference in pecuniary compensation at the high end of the pay scale, most of today's senior civil servants have stayed in their jobs because of the nonpecuniary aspects of their compensation, including a sense of service, job satisfaction, and a mission that matters. But as Donahue shows, the wage gap is growing so big that many people considering federal employment today may not be able or willing to afford that choice. This is especially true for those working in hard-to-find specialties, such as scientists, engineers, and linguists. If the government does not pay attention to compensation and to nonfinancial benefits such as training and work flexibility, it will increasingly find that only those with above-average means can afford to pursue a long career in the public service. For example, a chemical engineer with four years of experience in biochemical weapons research and an advanced degree is likely to have a choice between taking a position at the CIA for around $79,000 or an equivalent position at one of numerous defense contractors with a starting salary close to $200,000.[17] This initial gap will widen over time with the addition of stock options, bonuses, and valuable training opportunities. Presented with this choice, most job seekers will find it difficult to accept the government's offer, even if the government job is more exciting and interesting.

Political appointees joining government service from the private sector are well aware that similarly skilled executives are paid many times what their public sector counterparts are paid. There are many nonfinancial benefits, but the pay gap is a disincentive to join the ranks of government even for a short time. The relatively low pay keeps out some of the people whom government really needs to attract, such as working parents who cannot afford to take a $10,000 pay cut. In addition, long hours, disclosure of their private financial affairs, and restrictions on their freedom to pursue business opportunities after serving in government make it difficult to attract high-caliber appointees.

Take a New Approach to Political Appointees. Decisive steps must be taken to increase the government's ability to attract senior public sector managers. Paul Light has proposed four sensible reforms: reduce the total number of political positions requiring presidential appointment and Senate confirmation, streamline the confirmation process for appointees, reduce the disclosure paperwork they must fill out, and provide transition assistance so that political appointees from across the country can accept jobs in Washington. We would add compensation reform to lessen the wage gap for highly skilled workers in both career and political positions.

Trimming the number of political appointees would have several benefits. It would reduce layers in government and improve the management environment for career civil servants. In addition, as our surveys indicate, simplifying this complex structure would remove one of the main obstacles to recruiting students who wish to join the government. These cutbacks could also signal a desire to create a strong, stable cadre of agency leaders.

Congress should also consider expediting the confirmation process for new political appointees. According to a new study of the past five presidential transitions, even the best record shows only 25 out of some 400 senior slots filled by April 1 following a presidential inauguration, and more than one-third of these positions still vacant by August 1.[18] The objective should be a smaller number of political appointees who can assume their duties quickly.

Perhaps the single most important change that Congress could make would be to emphasize people management skills during the confirmation process for political appointees. If Congress were to take this qualification more seriously, it would set a much-needed tone in all branches of the government that people skills are valued and noticed.

Today, more than two-thirds of voters say they are fed up with Congress.[19] We believe that part of this is due to their general frustration with government. The public may not connect the dots between government performance and the federal workforce, but Congress should see this link clearly. To reiterate, one of the most direct ways to improve government performance across programs would be to take personnel reform seriously. This would not only have a positive effect on the lives of federal employees in their districts but would also improve the quality of service to their constituents.

The American Public

Other important stakeholders in the personnel system are the customers of the federal government's wide range of services—namely, the public. Unfortunately, the general public has a largely negative image of the civil service and civil servants. Thus it is not so surprising that 60 percent of college students say they would not even consider working for the federal government. The frequent bashing of federal employees in the media, in congressional hearings, and among political leaders has contributed to the myth of the lazy Washington bureaucrat with a guaranteed paycheck and little interest in public service. Many people have lost sight of the hard work and the valuable and frequently demanding work that their civil servants perform.

This constant barrage of negative reports—about the long delays in processing or approving student visas, veterans benefits, patent applications, and so forth, or massive computer failures like those at the FAA that occasionally strand travelers across the nation—makes little mention of the driving force behind the government's inefficiency: its lack of investment in the people who run the system. And, as described in chapter 8, the public itself expects a much higher level of performance from government commensurate with the kind of instant customer service that many companies offer. In short, the public does not perceive the link between the quality of services it wants and the condition of the civil service. Just as any parent knows that constant criticism rarely makes a child perform better, the public needs to recognize that it cannot make government work better by relentlessly disparaging federal employees.

Taxpayers will not see results until federal workers are treated with respect: by providing them with the resources, training, and constructive feedback to carry out their duties well. The nation's fundamental safety, security, and well-being depend on its ability to do this. In the current negative spiral, the public attitude toward federal workers only invites worse results. The public needs to create a positive spiral of support for public servants, so they can deliver the government services it is paying for.

We can offer two examples of healthy respect for certain public sector employees. First, the public holds most local government employees (including firemen, policemen, teachers, school nurses, and librarians) in high esteem. But this opinion does not prohibit well-deserved criticism on a case-by-case basis. Second, Congress and the public have high regard for the military. Both justifiably go to great lengths to acknowledge the courage and service of the men and women in uniform. But they can also deliver blistering critiques of performance when dereliction of duty, poor judgment, or other lapses call for correction. At the same time, this criticism is voiced in the context of a general confidence in and appreciation of the military's service. For local government and the military, the public is able to hold two ideas in mind simultaneously—the high ideal of public service and the potential for human failure—without going overboard in either direction.

Without diminishing the contribution that individual citizens and taxpayers make to the public good, the public needs to recognize that, on a daily basis, federal workers are the guarantors of better security, greater public safety, and a healthier economy.

This balanced view somehow breaks down when the public servant is working for the federal government. Even local public servants manage to escape public wrath, perhaps because they provide immediate, tangible services. By contrast, most federal workers are one step removed from ordinary taxpayers, so it is not easy to see their impact on everyday life. Negative media coverage that paints a picture of unhelpful bureaucrats, as opposed to dedicated public servants doing essential work, certainly does not help either. Whatever the case, it is safe to say that the civil service has by and large lost the affection and respect of the general public.

This relationship between the federal workforce and the general public needs to change. Congress has a responsibility to remind the public that its safety and many of its services depend in large part on the federal workforce. Without diminishing the contribution that individual citizens and taxpayers make to the public good, the public needs to recognize that, on a daily basis, federal workers are the guarantors of better security, greater public safety, and a healthier economy. The general public can help to strengthen the morale of the civil service by adopting a more balanced and respectful attitude toward the federal workforce.

The Media

The media are another stakeholder in people reform. In recent decades, the media have been quick to criticize federal employees, focusing on sensational stories rather than deeper critiques. Even college students tend to be influenced by this criticism. Of the two-thirds of students in our survey who are not considering a government career, more than 50 percent agree that the "media and politicians project such a negative image of the Federal Government that I am less likely to work there."[20] The media's frequent and detailed coverage of congressional investigations into federal government wrongdoing merely reinforces the perception that federal employees are inadequate. Apart from a few specialty publications, such as *Government Executive Magazine* and *Federal Computer Weekly,* many media portrayals of federal workers feature negative stereotypes. Very few articles focus on the extraordinary achievements of federal employees—whether at the Centers for Disease Control, the National Weather Service, or the agencies fighting crime and drugs.

Yet the media do provide more balanced reporting on the military and the private sector. During the early stages of the Iraq War, dozens of journalists were embedded with combat units and sent back moving reports of the heroism and sacrifice of the nation's young men and women. But embedding did not prevent reporting on the torture scandals of Abu Ghraib and profiteering by Halliburton and other contractors. As a result, the public was able to see these scandals in the wider context of the terrible situation faced by U.S. troops.

Media coverage of the private sector is even more positive: it is replete with stories of successful entrepreneurs, dynamic business leaders, technology, and service innovation. Examples of diversity and new thinking are celebrated and widely disseminated. Of course, the media also scrutinize private industry's business ethics, business practices, and its failure to satisfy customer demand or to meet profitability targets. In short, media coverage of the private sector highlights both the good and the bad.

Since the media influence the way federal workers are viewed, the president and the leadership team will need to engage members of the media directly. The government could invite reporters to observe firsthand how the civilian agencies conduct the war on drugs, research new cancer treatments, or forecast hurricanes. The government could urge the media to profile civil servants who are doing cutting-edge work, including scientists, marine biologists, census-takers, or doctors at military hospitals. Some groundwork has been laid by the PPS, which has drawn attention to exceptional achievements by career civil servants. But much more needs to be done to help the media understand the dedication and successes in the federal workforce.

Traditionally, scandals sell more newspapers than tales of midlevel civil servants who spend years doing their jobs. But the objective should be to attract more balanced reporting.

Conclusions

Despite the competing and sometimes conflicting interests of the key stakeholders, they all agree on the need for higher job satisfaction, higher performance, and greater flexibility in government. These goals will be impossible to achieve without presidential leadership and a serious commitment of resources. Indeed, no aspect of public service reform can be achieved—whether it is a matter of deciding on the principles or implementing the change—without putting a significant amount of money into the effort. As outlined in the first part of this book, people factor reforms are likely to produce much higher productivity and better stewardship of taxpayers' money. Therefore the funding required for people reform, as laid out in chapter 10, should be viewed as an *investment in democracy,* not simply as a spending program for federal employees.

10

Funding the
Transition Program

Transforming the government workforce to create the skills necessary for the twenty-first century will require an integrated human capital program. The program we propose is designed to augment the skills of existing civil servants and to make the public sector an employer of choice for high-quality applicants at all levels. This requires a substantial infusion of resources over the next decade to correct for the sustained underinvestment in the federal workforce of previous decades. As Paul Light points out: "The federal workforce will not rebound without a sustained effort to overcome the key barriers to performance embedded in the current system. In a single word, the answer is 'resources.'"[1]

The program requires a $10.3 billion investment spread over five years—a relatively modest amount that is equivalent to less than 1 percent of the government's wage bill over the same period.[2] Continuing the program over ten years, to match the period of analysis for the productivity estimate discussed in chapter 3, this means that an investment in the order of $21 billion would produce a total potential gain of between $225 billion and $625 billion. This makes the program an attractive investment with a substantial payback.

This chapter lays out a straightforward method to fund the program that has a positive net present value. The basic premise is to reduce the size of the government payroll by 2 percent, using the savings to finance the investment in personnel. We believe that the enhanced productivity of the smaller, better-trained workforce will more than compensate for the modest reduction in headcount. Second, a training levy of one-half of 1 percent is imposed on the value of all government service contracts, raising a further $660 million per year.[3] And third, lapsed, unobligated funds within each agency are redirected to pay for the training of federal workers in the first year or two of the program, before the funds from personnel attrition are available. These are funds *already* appropriated to the agencies, a portion of which would otherwise be returned to the general fund. This source would generate close to $2 billion in the first year, more than sufficient to finance expenditures. In addition, Congress will need to provide start-up funding for planning and design of the transformation.

Under this set of assumptions, the five-year cost of the program is $10.3 billion, and savings generated through personnel reductions of 2 percent a year (in other words, replacing 98 percent of the workforce who leave, for a net loss of about 36,000 positions) alone would generate over $10 billion. Taken together with the procurement levy, the cumulative cash generated for the program would equal $13.0 billion. Even projecting that personnel savings will not become available until year two, and that the program will require outlays in the first two years, the program will generate net savings of $2.6 billion. Over ten years, the program produces a highly positive present value in excess of $8.5 billion.[4] These projections are shown in tables 10-1 and 10-2.

> *The program is not designed simply to make incremental changes, but to establish an environment in which people are recognized as the government's core strategic asset.*

However, the chief guarantee of sustainability will be a strong commitment from both the president and Congress to see the program through and to redeploy savings from personnel reduction to this purpose. In addition, some structural and organizational changes will be necessary to administer, monitor, and oversee the transformation effectively.

The main categories of the investment program are spending to enhance recruiting, training, compensation and benefits, and management, to be implemented using an integrated strategy in which all the

T A B L E 1 0 - 1 . Funding Sources for Five-Year Workforce Investment Plan

Dollars in billions

Source	Year 1	Year 2	Year 3	Year 4	Year 5	Five-year total
Personnel attrition savings	0	1.5	3.0	3.0	3.1	10.6
Levy on service contracts		0.3	0.7	0.7	0.7	2.3
Total annual savings	0	1.8	3.7	3.7	3.7	12.9
Total annual expenditures	1.1	2.0	2.2	2.4	2.7	10.3
Net cost/saving	−1.1	−0.07	1.5	1.3	1.0	2.7
Net savings	2.7					
Five year net present value	2.4					
Ten year net present value	6.9					

Number of FTE employees, 1.88 million

pieces reinforce each other. Like the original "people factor" concept described in part 1, the program is not designed simply to make incremental changes, but to establish an environment in which people are recognized as the government's core strategic asset. Table 10-2 lays out the cost of funding each element of the program, including training and education, new compensation and benefits, new human resources (HR) tools, and management and oversight, as well as the cost of delivering the program. Training costs assume that all managers and supervisors will devote a minimum of two weeks a year to training.

Required Expenditures for Human Capital Transformation in Government

While a $10.3 billion investment over five years may seem a large commitment, it needs to be viewed in the context of the federal government's spending on labor costs, which total some $2 billion *each day*.[5] Moreover, the payback from this spending will be large and will show up in the near term. This is consistent with experience in high-performing organizations. That it can deliver results in the government has already been demonstrated at the Defense Logistics Agency (DLA) and General

TABLE 10-2. Costs of Five-Year Workforce Investment Plan

Activity	Number of full-time equivalent (FTE) employees	Cost in dollars of each FTE employee per year	Dollars in billions					
			Year 1	Year 2	Year 3	Year 4	Year 5	Five-year total
Diagnostics and planning for integrated process team	457	10,000	.002	.002	.002	.002	0	.006
Training and education	229,756	4,500	.207	.413	.620	.827	1.03	3.10
New compensation for career staff	7,000	35,000	.245	.245	.245	.245	.245	1.23
New compensation for appointees	2,000	35,000	.070	.070	.070	.070	.070	.350
Transparency and communication	1,881,700	25	.047	.047	.047	.047	.047	.235
Internships and expansion of PMF program	1,000	101,161	.051	.138	.138	.138	.138	.602
Recruiting	500	...	.069	.069	.069	.069	.069	.348
Employee equipment improvement	...	...	.060	.214	.309	.309	.309	1.20
Administration	...	...	.004	.004	.004	.004	.004	.021
Wellness benefits	752,680	750	.283	.565	.565	.565	.565	2.54
Other investments in the federal workforce	...	...	.072	.145	.144	.138	.136	.634
Total			1.11	1.91	2.21	2.41	2.62	10.26

Total costs	$10.3 billion
Five year net present value	$9.6 billion
Ten year net present value	$20.7 billion
Cost per employee	$5,452

Accountability Office (GAO) (see chapter 3). A concerted investment in the federal workforce across the board would certainly achieve a significant gain. We estimate that U.S. taxpayers could recoup $225 billion to $625 billion from three sources: productivity increases (through better operational and managerial practices); cost savings from reduction in waste, fraud, and duplication; and cost savings from better design, supervision, and accountability of contracts.

To illustrate this potential, the federal government spends more than $500 billion a year on outside contracts, a large portion of which are priced on a cost-plus basis. More than half of this activity is spent on services such as consulting, Information technology (IT) development, and administrative support. Despite the fact that the volume of federal contract dollars has more than doubled in the past five years, the size of the acquisition workforce and the training of the overall workforce to manage large contracts have stagnated.[6] If the managerial workforce is trained to design tighter specifications, track and monitor performance more accurately, and evaluate the outputs of these contracts, it is reasonable to project that the benefits to the taxpayer will be significant in terms of avoiding waste, fraud, and misspent dollars. If better management of the services contracts produces savings of just half of 1 percent in contracting dollars, this measure alone will yield savings of nearly $900 million a year.

Our cost calculations are an "order-of-magnitude" estimate based on assumptions that we, as practitioners, believe to be reasonable. In several areas we have erred on the conservative side. The numbers do not include the cost of paying existing salaries and benefits, as they are already included in the federal budget. The budget projections include start-up costs and a ramp in activity to reflect the normal profile of a large project. To arrive at our estimates, we applied the recommended people factor methods described in parts I and II of the book to the full population of relevant government employees. This means that costs are applied largely to the entire managerial and supervisory workforce in the federal government. We assume that the training program (the most expensive item) is rolled out to one-fifth of eligible employees each year until 100 percent are covered after five years. Costs in the early years can be managed by controlling the pace of rollout, which has the additional benefit of allowing the program to be adjusted on the basis of lessons learned as the rollout progresses. Consequently, total implementation costs for the first full year are projected to be approximately $1.1 billion (including initial development and training for the first groups of civil servants), rising to about $2.6 billion a year once the program is up and fully running.

While a $10.3 billion investment [in federal personnel systems] over five years may seem a large commitment, it needs to be viewed in the context of the federal government's spending on labor costs, which total some $2 billion each day.

The largest single element of this investment would be anchored in a Civil Service GI Bill to train and educate government workers to a new national standard.

GI Bill Tuition Payments

The largest single element of this investment would be anchored in a Civil Service GI Bill to train and educate government workers to a new national standard. We model this concept on the original GI Bill for military veterans, one of the nation's most successful pieces of legislation. Based on the premise that Americans have a responsibility to provide opportunities for their veterans, the GI Bill not only enabled 7 million of them to afford an education, but it ultimately benefited the economy as a whole. It succeeded both socially and financially—educating a generation of Americans and boosting the economy by $7 for each $1 invested.[7] Congress has recently re-endorsed this concept by enacting a modern GI bill for military veterans of current wars.

The Civil Service GI Bill would be a nationwide training and education program for investing in public service. (Eventually it could serve as a template for a wider cohort of state, local, and quasi-governmental employees, such as partners in NGOs, but the model described here is for the federal workforce.) Its purpose would be twofold. First, it would send a message to the young people of America that the nation values public service, thereby helping restore some of the prestige, dignity, and magic to jobs in the federal government. Second, it could reshape the fundamental tools, skills, morale, and overall preparedness of the existing workforce. Since 85 percent of federal workers are distributed throughout the United States, this program would draw on an existing infrastructure of community colleges and public and private colleges and universities across the country to deliver classroom and web-based instruction.[8] Course content would support a national curriculum developed in consultation with subject matter experts and tailored to meet the needs of supervisors and managers at different levels and stages of their career development. Under this bill, each employee would have an account for approved course work aligned with the overall needs and requirements of government. The goal of the training would be to retool and improve the management skills of government employees. The investment would benefit employees, raise productivity, and benefit taxpayers in terms of higher-quality services and lower marginal cost.

We have estimated the cost of providing leadership and supervisory training for about 230,000 front-line supervisors, midlevel managers, and senior managers over a five-year period. Each manager and supervisor would have to complete a cycle of managerial and supervisory training for two weeks annually over the five years. This is comparable to the requirements for leading professional associations in areas such as medicine and accounting, which require members to attend forty to eighty hours of training a year to keep current in their respective fields. However, decades of underinvesting in the workforce has made it all the more pressing to improve the skill level of many government employees and will necessitate considerable support. Course work would include theory and practice on topics in leadership and management, supervisory skills, technical training (including procurement), and general transformation, as described in chapter 7. Training would be aimed at adult learners and would accommodate a variety of learning preferences. We have budgeted $4,500 per employee per year for training, including expenses, materials and curriculum. The $3.1 billion over five years for training managers and supervisors would improve general management and leadership skills, enhance the quality of procurement management and oversight, and develop knowledge of specific mission areas related to managing a blended workforce.

Mandatory Training Time

In order to facilitate the recommended training programs, all managers and supervisors should be excused from their responsibilities for two weeks a year. Otherwise, the desire to accomplish the day-to-day mission will trump training time. Admittedly, this requirement will reduce the time that government managers have to accomplish their normal duties. In the long run, however, this effect will be more than offset by the improvement in the quality of management and supervision and associated productivity gains.

We envision an approach to workforce management that would create "float" in the personnel system to make training easier to schedule and accomplish. The U.S. military has such a system, which makes it possible to put new, fully trained personnel directly into key positions. For example, when the navy identifies a replacement for a ship's commanding officer, that individual is given time to attend Prospective Commanding Officer School for instruction in engineering, weapons, navigation, communication, and administration before taking on the new position. Many companies have similar programs for the grooming and intensive training of successors. Even professional sports and major orchestras invest in training replacement personnel to avoid gaps in performance.

The float system would provide the flexibility that workforce managers need to develop staff and invest in their skills. It would also enable staff to prepare for new assignments and assess performance in past assignments and thereby allow the organization as a whole to learn from past successes and failures. This would be most valuable in agencies with law enforcement and public safety missions that require certain numbers of people to be present and "on duty" at all times. In the meantime, the simple device of requiring two weeks of training each year will create the incentives to pursue adequate training.

Expanded Presidential Management Fellow Program and Internships

Fellowships and internships at the entry, mid, and senior levels of government are effective means of opening the government system to involvement by private sector personnel and making new skills available to government. The Presidential Management Fellow (PMF) program has proved an excellent vehicle for attracting top-quality graduates but it is too small. We propose that the program be doubled from 500 to 1,000 participants a year, with a continuing focus on entry-level personnel from elite colleges and universities.[9] The period of PMF fellowships would continue to be two years. The fully loaded annual cost per fellow today is $73,000.

We also propose an additional 500 annual internships at midcareer and senior levels. The fully loaded average cost per intern is approximately $130,000. The cost of both the PMF and midcareer internships is $0.6 billion for the five years.

Compensation and Benefits

The public sector is part of the general economy and competes with the private market for talent. In order to maintain a competent, efficient, and fair government, its workers must be compensated at a level sufficient to attract the right caliber of people. At present, many government jobs overpay lower-skilled positions and underpay the most skilled ones, according to recent comparisons of wages in the two sectors.[10]

In particular, the wages of senior civil servants and top-level political appointees have fallen well behind their private sector counterparts in the past two decades. This disparity was previously offset by a combination of job security and generous retirement benefits. Most workers who joined the government a generation ago are covered by the Civil Service Retirement System (CSRS), which means that upon retirement they will receive a cost-of-living-adjusted annuity equal to about 60 percent of their three highest years of earnings. The value of this benefit is substantial. A government worker covered by CSRS who retires at age sixty-five after thirty-five years of service and lives for an additional twenty years receives about $82,800 a year.[11] Benefits also include health care. Retirees have the right to buy their insurance at the favorable group rates for government. They pay about 28 percent of the premium using after-tax dollars, with the government paying about 72 percent.[12] The health plan options are the same for active and retired employees. CSRS was phased out in the 1980s and is no longer offered to new employees. Government workers are now covered by a far less generous retirement plan. Like most of their counterparts in the private sector, they must rely on savings in 401(k)-type accounts (called the Thrift Saving Plan [TSP]) with no guaranteed pension. They do receive the same health care coverage as

CSRS retirees. However, the large difference in cash value of the retirement makes it important to adjust salaries of senior civil servants today more in line with those of the private sector.

As Donahue points out, however, adjustments to base pay, while sorely needed, will be extremely difficult to make. We propose a one-time market adjustment mechanism for career senior executives that would begin to address the discrepancy between public and private sector pay. The Department of Labor would conduct an annual study to establish a midrange figure for pay and benefits for all senior executive positions by market segment. In particular, the focus would be on compensation of senior civil servants in high-value occupations such as finance and accounting, engineering, science, medicine, information technology, HR, acquisition, and administration. These categories of experts if performing at a satisfactory level or above would then be eligible to receive a one-time market adjustment in their base pay. We estimate this would increase the average pay of the 7,000-member senior executive service by about $35,000 each. The total cost of this over five years would be $1.2 billion.

In order to maintain a competent, efficient, and fair government, federal workers must be compensated at a level sufficient to attract the right caliber of people.

The effort to close the compensation gap would also have a positive effect on the near-term retention of the most experienced government executives. Executives under the CSRS retirement system would have a chance to increase their retirement benefits by staying at least three years to fully adjust their "average of high three years compensation" calculation. Executives under the new FERS system would be able to raise their contribution levels to the Thrift Savings program markedly during this period. Finally, the prospect of future promotion and compensation at the new and higher level just described would act as an incentive for GS-14 and GS-15 managers to stay in government.

Compensation of Political Appointees

The challenge of attracting highly qualified political appointees is more complex. Political appointees joining government service from the private sector must typically take a substantial pay cut. In addition, political appointees face disclosure of their private financial affairs and certain restrictions on their freedom to pursue business opportunities after serving in government. This makes it harder to attract and especially to retain high-caliber political appointees.

Unless financial compensation for political appointees receives close attention, the "churn" in these jobs will continue. As noted earlier, the average tenure of a political appointee is about eighteen months. One reason for this rapid turnover is compensation. Many middle-class appointees find themselves compelled to return to the private sector for financial and family reasons just as they are beginning to be effective in their government jobs. This also creates an incentive to "cash in" on the connections they have made during their tenure. This is not a healthy condition for the public service.

Part of the answer is to streamline the transition from private sector to government. This can be done by reducing the total number of political positions requiring presidential appointment and Senate confirmation, streamlining the confirmation process for them, reducing the disclosure paperwork they have to fill out, and providing relocation assistance so that political appointees from cities and towns across the country can accept jobs in Washington.

As noted in previous chapters, the total *number* of political appointees is excessive and should be reduced. When William Daley was appointed secretary of commerce in 1997, he halved the number of political appointees in the department, from about 200 to about 100. There were no apparent ill effects, and he immediately established strong credibility with the career workforce, which had been traumatized by the loss of senior officials (including Commerce Secretary Ron Brown) in a plane crash a year earlier. Under Daley's leadership, the department was able to reduce material weaknesses on its balance sheet from 87 to 1, and to conduct a highly successful decennial census. The Commerce Department experience suggests that the number of political appointments government-wide could be reduced by at least 25 percent, from about 8,000 to 6,000.[13]

But additional measures are needed to attract well-qualified political appointees for the positions that remain. We propose that compensation for this group be adjusted in line with senior career appointees. In particular, this adjustment needs to be targeted to make public service more affordable for middle-class appointees to reduce the barriers to their participation in government. These benefits should include monetary and nonmonetary provisions. For example, the U.S. military has long provided legal protection to reservists called to active duty so that they can reclaim the jobs they left behind in order to serve their country. The program guidelines apply only to companies above a certain size and require that the reservist return to a "job of similar kind," not the identical job the reservist left. Political appointees called to serve by the president should have the ability to return to jobs at their companies in the same way.

Many middle-class appointees find themselves compelled to return to the private sector for financial and family reasons just as they are beginning to be effective in their government jobs.

Second, a one-time pay adjustment of $35,000 for senior political appointees would help families handle the very expensive cost of living in the Washington area. The nation's capital has one of the highest cost-of-living levels in the country, particularly for expenses such as housing, child care, and nursing home care. To make it possible for individuals of modest circumstances to serve in government, the United States should offer substantial financial assistance. By comparison, most international officials in Washington (for example, those working at the World Bank, International Monetary Fund, foreign embassies, and multilateral institutions) receive subsidies for housing, school tuition, child care, and domestic help, as well as tax benefits and other offsets.

Alternatively, a means-tested general subsidy could be provided. Payments would be based on age and medical conditions of children and parents requiring special education or care during a means-test process conducted during the confirmation process. The means test could employ a ceiling level of adjusted gross income from the appointees' tax filing of the prior year, adjusted for inflation each year. The government could also provide a voucher for a Student Finance Agency loan to cover the costs of higher education for children in the family attending college. These measures would help to ensure that middle-income families asked to serve could handle a sudden relocation, income adjustment, or loss of benefits, and thus could afford to serve in government, and would very likely improve the president's ability to recruit from top minority and women candidates, as well as those serving.

Finally, appointees could elect to continue health care coverage after they leave government service at favorable group rates beyond the eighteen-month limit for plans currently in effect under the Consolidated Omnibus Budget Reconciliation Act (COBRA). (The career civil service is already covered under existing retirement benefits.) Access to the COBRA coverage for periods beyond the eighteen-month limit would provide a bridge for those families that were unable to find employment with adequate coverage. This would reduce the problem of movement between the public and private sector for those families with significant "pre-existing conditions" and other related health care costs.

The combination of these benefits would help to counter the pay gap for highly skilled workers wishing to serve as political appointees for a temporary period in government. Greater participation in government by a more diverse group of middle-class citizens is the goal of this effort. The cost of the pay raise and family-adjustment stipends for political appointees over five years is estimated at $0.35 billion.

Development of New HR Tools

A new set of tools could improve the quality of personnel management in government and thus speed the reform effort.

Recruiting. Active outreach is required to supplement the advantages of better leadership in order to attract new hires. A nationwide recruiting program could employ web-based methods and person-to-person interviews on campuses across the country. We have budgeted for 500 new state recruiters at an average fully loaded salary of $100,000 and an average travel and expense budget of $25,000, as well as $25 million for the development of recruiting materials, advertising, web-based tools, and marketing. We have also budgeted $50 million to assist the government in hiring applicants with high potential through standard recruiting incentives such as signing bonuses, relocation assistance, temporary housing assistance, and student loan repayments. The cost of this item over five years is $0.35 billion (see table 10-2).

Employee Equipment Improvement. Raising the productivity of government workers is, in part, a function of providing them with computing and communications tools. To ensure that all employees who need a computer with web access as well as basic mobile communications will have these capabilities when they join the government service, the program provides funding for all new hires to have access to basic up-to-date IT and communications. We provide an allowance of $1,000 for every new hire to cover these initial costs, including telecommunications upgrades such as monthly voice and data plans. This program will begin as new employees are hired and provide equipment where none was previously budgeted. The cost of this item over five years is $1.2 billion.

Software and System Support. A suite of shared, web-based HR tools is needed to support the new HR best practices for all employees. A new system provided on a shared services basis is required to deliver redesigned business processes (see box 10-1). This improvement, along with the costs of phone and web-based call center assistance and system maintenance will cost approximately $250 per employee and could be rolled out over five years. Further, an HR passport, described in chapter 5, would provide eligible employees with a record to enable them to move between the government, private, and nonprofit sectors using a single, standardized system for capturing their professional achievements, job skills, and competencies during their work in government and beyond in the private sector.[14] The costs of administering the HR passport would cover not only the development of the system but also the infrastructure needed to support the system, including a small central operations staff. These employees would have an average fully loaded salary of $100,000 and provide assistance to private sector job seekers in translating their skills into readily understandable terms for government HR personnel. We have budgeted $20 million for the HR passport, software, and other administrative services.

Wellness Benefits. Studies show that investing in workers' health through wellness programs is highly cost-effective. The government already pays the majority of health care costs for its employees, so it benefits financially from any improvements in their health. Moreover, a healthier workforce improves work performance, job attendance, and productivity. Wellness programs are standard practice among high-performing

BOX 10-1. The Presidential Management Fellows (PMF) Program

The election of Barack Obama as president has brought a surge of interest from people around the country to working in government. More than 300,000 resumes were submitted to the change.gov transition website. But the president only can fill about 4,000 jobs through the appointment process, and these are mostly political positions.

Expansion of the Presidential Management Fellows (PMF) program offers a way to bring thousands more qualified young people into the career ranks of the federal government. The PMF program is the flagship government program for hiring new talent, and it adheres to many of the "best HR practices" described in this book. The program hires graduate students in many disciplines and provides them with two years of rigorous training, including 80 hours of classroom instruction in leadership, communication and teamwork, four- to six-month developmental assignments in different agencies, and training in specific core competencies and technical skills. The PMFs are supervised by career advisers. Before converting to a full-time position, each PMF must be given an Individual Development Plan to guide further career development. Most PMFs go on to enjoy successful careers in government.

The PMF program currently recruits 3,500 top graduate students each year, but offers jobs to only about 500 of them. The government could benefit immediately by opening the program to a larger number of applicants.

corporations. We have budgeted $750 a year per employee for a range of programs aimed at enhancing physical and mental health. This would cover the cost of providing on-site health clinics at major government facilities and other wellness programs. We assume that about one-half of employees will eventually take advantage of this voluntary program. The cost of this item over five years is $2.5 billion.

Management and Oversight

In addition, the government will need to take several steps to leverage its investment in personnel reform. These include planning, budgeting, communication outreach, and other measures.

—*Diagnostics and Planning.* Like any other major initiative, our program will require detailed operational plans and budgets. Resources will be needed to pull together a team of experts from throughout government and to staff the planning phase of this transformation.[15] Each agency will also need a small amount of funding to customize planning to its mission, and it will need to allocate staff to work with the Office of Management and Budget (OMB), Office of Personnel Management (OPM), and auditors who are overseeing the government-wide effort.

—*Transparency and Communication.* We have included funds for building awareness and understanding of the new system among the full population of federal civilian employees. This would cost approximately $25 per employee per year. Support would be provided over the web with targeted updates and would be reinforced in classroom training for managers and supervisors.

—*Other Investments to Measure Performance of the Federal Workforce.* As the demand for training and development increases, resources will be needed to build the systems that support the collection and analysis of measurement data, including data capture, storage, analysis, and visualization. The cost of a performance measurement dashboard that could monitor the progress of the human capital transformation would be about $60 per federal civilian employee per year. We have also budgeted for the establishment of a national commission to develop the performance toolkit, including links to improved workforce planning and analysis. The cost of these items over five years is expected to total $0.63 billion.

Sources of Revenue

Clearly, one of the biggest hurdles facing any major new initiative in government is persuading Congress to provide funding. However, we have designed this program to be self-financing after the first year. Both the authorizing and the appropriations committees in Congress will need to participate in laying the groundwork for personnel reform.[16] In addition to the Civil Service GI Bill, several measures need to be authorized in order to establish the basis for future appropriations.

Reallocate Funds Captured through Workforce Reduction

The first source of reallocation is perhaps the most straightforward to secure. The existing base for current government personnel in the fiscal 2007 president's budget is $331 billion. This figure includes the cost of associated benefits but not retirement. It should be possible to obtain a significant portion of the program costs by capturing some of the savings from personnel attrition.[17] The total workforce should be trimmed by 2 percent distributed rationally throughout the workforce. The resulting savings would be reallocated to training and investing in the remaining workforce.

This reduction of the workforce needs to be managed proactively. The downsizing of the 1990s, achieved largely through attrition, produced a somewhat skewed workforce. As Paul Light has pointed out, junior workers naturally experience greater turnover than middle managers. Consequently, the number of junior employees dropped disproportionately. Many of the lower-level jobs (such as janitors and cafeteria workers) were contracted out, or the job classifications were inflated so as to create more "middle-level clerical workers." This experience suggests that the proposed 2 percent workforce reduction should be executed as part of the overall workforce planning described in part II of the book. This will permit the necessary reductions yet maintain a balanced workforce that will support priority mission areas. The cumulative revenue produced by this item over five years would be about $10.6 billion.

Expand the Use of Existing Procurement Fund

A second source of funding is to designate a fraction of the total procurement budget for service contracts for investments in human capital. A fund of this nature known as the Acquisition Workforce Training Fund was established for the acquisition community in 2004 under the National Defense Production Act. That fund is reserved for acquisition-related training, so its authority would have to be expanded by statute to include training and transformation throughout the government. It reserves 5 percent of fees that pass through certain procurement vehicles for the support of acquisition-related training for government employees. The fund generated $5.2 million in fiscal 2004.[18]

With its authority revised and expanded to include the majority of government services contracts, the fund could be used both for its original acquisition-related purpose and for the broader transformation effort. Rates could be increased to produce more headroom for the program in the initial years. The resulting funds would be used to create training opportunities for acquisition, financial, and human resource personnel to improve their management and supervisory skills. This in turn would improve the government's ability to manage public-private partnerships and major outsourcing projects. The revenue produced by a one-half of 1 percent fee applied to the $264 billion services portion of the $500 billion per year total procurement expenditure, allowing for a period of ramp-up, would generate roughly $2.3 billion over five years.

Each agency would collect these fees on an annual basis patterned after the actual outlays for procurement activity involving services. Money would be planned, tracked, and executed using existing agency budget processes through a budget line item monitored by the OMB for qualified agency programs. Qualified programs would include those reform activities approved by OMB in the annual budget process.

Authorize Agency Use of Lapsed Unobligated Balances for Reform

The savings that are made available through personnel reductions and procurement levies would not be available until year two, and of course the personnel savings would increase over time. To fund the initial outlays in year one and two, we propose that agencies be permitted to capture an additional percentage of lapsed annual appropriations that remain unobligated at the conclusion of the fiscal year preceding launch of the transformation program. Currently, a provision in the Financial Services and General Government Appropriation Bill gives agencies access to 50 percent of their unused program appropriations during the following fiscal year. This existing authority could be expanded to all appropriation acts and the remaining 50 percent captured to fund personnel investments. (The remaining amounts would still remain available to agencies to meet emerging internal program priorities.) This is likely to be on the order of up to $1.7 billion, sufficient to cover initial costs.[19]

Create a Transformation Account

Congress needs to authorize a one-time, no-year transformation account that can be centrally managed to pay for initial planning and diagnostics and to bridge the cash needs for the program during the planning phase and the first year of implementation. However, we believe this will be a modest amount, on the order of $20 million.

Additional Statutory and Legal Reforms

Congress will also need to take two pragmatic steps—one budgetary, the other statutory—to improve the chances of reform.

First, it can adopt and require the executive branch to employ a consistent methodology to account for fully loaded costs for all full-time-equivalent staff (FTEs). At present, the government lacks funds to train and equip its employees. The government budgets for salary and benefits but for the most part fails to budget for the full costs of employing a worker who can perform well, such as the costs of training, computer software and hardware, cell phones, and travel. The federal law enforcement community does this better; it includes the costs of initial training, weapons, and automobiles that certain federal agents need to accomplish their mission. New hires are given the tools they need to succeed from the start. Agencies should budget for the full costs of their personnel, and Congress should fund these costs. During the initial phase of the Iraq War, there was a public outcry over the fact that troops were sent into the theater without proper body armor and life-saving armored vehicles. Just as the nation's troops should not go into battle without adequate equipment, its civilian public servants should not be asked to do their jobs without the basic tools needed to perform effectively, and budgets should be adjusted to reflect these basic necessities.

Second, Congress can take action to adjust and replace sections of Title V using the detailed list of reforms provided in part II of the book and summarized in box 10-2. These will include new flexibilities to

BOX 10-2. **Summary of Proposed People Reforms**

1. Shift the focus of performance management from individuals to teams. The government's ability to devise a more effective system is hampered by 5 USC 4302, which requires the government to evaluate employee performance against standards for the employee's position.[1] The revision should authorize consideration of team performance in performance evaluation processes.

2. Provide a minimum of two weeks a year of leadership and supervisory training for every manager and supervisor. Amend 5 USC Chapter 41 to require OMB, with help from OPM, to develop and prescribe regulations that mandate a specific training and development program for government supervisors and managers. Include reference to curriculum requirements in the law so that training meets standards while retaining ability to change standards over time. The program should be consistent across the government, with the ability for agencies to add to, but not subtract from, the curriculum.

3. Create an employee development program tied to individual training accounts, managed at the work unit level for greatest flexibility, and tracked at the agency level using a "fully funded employee" budget line item. Hiring authority should be granted in conjunction with funding for training and fully equipping the new hire.

4. Create a new Level 7 SES position with several new work and compensation features under the existing SES system; reallocate SES positions to management and policy priorities over time. Increase compensation for SES and senior political appointees through a one-time market adjustment.

5. Repeal the National Security Personnel System (NSPS). NSPS was based on the sound premise that the civil service needed reform. But poor execution has hobbled the effort. The collective bargaining relationship needs to be repaired and set on a sound footing.

6. Correct pay and classification misalignments for upper-grade employees (GS-14, GS-15, and SES) to bring them more into line with the labor market. Use market-based surveys to establish the basis for new salary ranges. Design the compensation system to attract the government's fair share of top talent.

7. Create core-ring positions to increase the flow of talent between the private and public sector. Lower the process barriers for midlevel and senior managers and technologists to serve in government.

8. Flatten the career civil service and political appointee hierarchy within agencies.

9. Create a certification credential requirement for all managers and supervisors. Use the presidential commission suggested in chapter 11 to develop the competencies and criteria for qualification. Develop a system of leadership training for all managers and supervisors that is based on nationally recognized competencies and curricula.

10. Require training for political appointees. Use the models established by the Council for Excellence in Government and leading universities that have developed targeted courses to create a comprehensive curriculum aimed at first-time and returning political appointees.

11. Create a basket of HR best practices, including flex time, telecommuting, wellness programs, child and elder care assistance, and other standard HR best practices. This new capacity will help the government become a better employer by creating a workplace that is appealing and competitive with the best of the private sector.

12. Implement robust performance development plans, measurement, and monitoring. Sequence the requirement to occur after effective leadership and management training are in place and certifications have been obtained by managers and supervisors.

---

1. See http://frwebgate.access.gpo.gov/cgi-bin/getdoc.cgi?dbname=browse_usc&docid=Cite:+5USC4302.

recruit, retain, compensate, and reward government employees and to consider innovative personnel practices, which some agencies are already implementing. Rules should apply consistently across government (as in equal pay for equal work) but allow specific recruiting, training, and management practices to vary, depending on the organization's mission and culture. The new rules will require the president's backing in order to ensure implementation. These significant changes would enable the reform effort to get under way and help it gain additional traction early on by providing necessary flexibilities to the executive branch. All of the following recommendations are predicated on

Just as the nation's troops should not go into battle without adequate equipment, its civilian public servants should not be asked to do their jobs without the basic tools needed to perform effectively, and budgets should be adjusted to reflect these basic necessities.

retaining merit principles. They illustrate the type and range of change that the president might request.

Third, Congress should reorganize the executive branch to provide better direction for the federal personnel system. According to the Volcker Commissions' performance studies, government agencies tend to be organized in a suboptimal fashion that does not support agency missions or induce coordination with other government agencies, nongovernmental organizations, or the private sector.

The most significant structural reason for the current inefficiencies in the government personnel system is the overlap in the roles and responsibilities of the agencies charged with government-wide policymaking, planning, operations, and oversight: namely, the OMB, OPM, and the General Services Administration (GSA). Human capital reform cannot proceed smoothly unless these roles and responsibilities are assigned with clear accountability for planning and executing key human capital management programs.

These roles and responsibilities could be redefined and reassigned in various ways. We present one possible scenario to illustrate the desirable characteristics of a new organizational structure. Given the political and organizational realities of this type of reorganization, it would be up to the president's leadership team to closely examine the options and implications of this reorganization and base its recommendations on that analysis.

Role of Office of Management and Budget

The OMB is currently responsible for formulating and executing the federal budget, but it does not have a central role in federal workforce strategy. As a result, budget authority does not match strategic decisions. Given the importance of this role to the performance of every government agency, policy and budget development should be centralized in one agency. We would assign this role to OMB and the OMB deputy director for management; they would oversee management and personnel, supported by a dedicated and knowledgeable human capital policy staff. The deputy director would be in a position to raise personnel issues with the White House when needed and to influence the budget process.

This OMB office would therefore be responsible and accountable for

—Developing a government-wide personnel strategy and performance goals

—Funding government-wide personnel management programs

—Monitoring budgets so that funds are used appropriately

—Monitoring results against performance goals

—Establishing a reformed government-wide personnel framework

—Setting government-wide personnel management policies on all key points, from benefits to training to customer service.

OMB leadership in the budget process is essential if agencies are to be discouraged from reducing allocations or treating them as "discretionary" expenditures in the case of training and education for the government workforce, pay compensation improvements, and so on, in favor of meeting current program costs. Diverting program funds in this way would seriously undermine the quality and long-term effectiveness of the overall transformation initiative. The conditions must be set for sustained, predictable, and high-quality training if the program is to be effective. The OMB would have to protect funds allocated for the human capital transformation from reallocation either by Congress, as it strives to support high-profile programs with increasingly limited funding, or by agencies, as they distribute and manage their appropriated funds. These vital transformation objectives cannot become reality without substantial support in the budget process.

Role of Office of Personnel Management

OPM has been the key executive branch agency tasked with managing the personnel system. However, it has a limited capability and capacity to transform the personnel system. OPM's mission combines performance evaluation and service delivery in a way that creates conflict between its audit and service functions. The problem is not unlike the conflict of interest that large accounting firms in the private sector experienced before the passage of the Sarbanes-Oxley Act of 2002, when they sold audit services as well as the consulting services required to fix the deficiencies they had identified.

Furthermore, the OPM is driven by process and lacks the necessary authority and creativity to reinvigorate the workforce. So it is in a weak position to lead the reform effort. Moreover, OPM's personnel decisions are not linked closely enough to the OMB budget process, which is the seat of reallocation and management oversight and tends to earmark scarce budgetary resources for presidential priorities. For these reasons, our program calls for a significant transformation of the OPM's roles and responsibilities.

This is not to deny that the OPM has an important role to play. OPM houses most of the government's experts on current personnel practices. These experts should be readily available to agencies in an advisory role as they craft and implement a new model of human capital management. This new OPM would be responsible and accountable for

—Providing technical assistance to agency human capital officers regarding operational matters

—Providing technical assistance to OMB for the development of government-wide policies (this would require a larger cadre of senior subject-matter experts)

—Conducting expert agency reviews and developing improvement plans to strengthen agency accountability for the implementation of reforms

—Integrating human capital and personnel management systems into the OMB budget review, pass-back, submission, and evaluation process, using the Government Performance Results Act (GPRA) and Performance Assessment Rating Tool (PART) procedures already in place.

Needless to say, the agency responsible for monitoring and advising other agencies should not be selling them services as well. Thus our program would have OPM shed its current fee-for-service activities to avoid conflicts with its advisory and oversight roles. These fee-based services could be transferred to the General Services Administration, which is already well established as a provider of fee-based services for government buyers.

Role of General Services Administration

The GSA could conduct a competition for a few government-wide HR line of business providers for state-of-the-art infrastructure and services to support reform. This would speed the implementation of more efficient business processes and technology systems. The GSA should work to eliminate duplication in the delivery of these services and concentrate on building efficient, modern, and standardized systems and on facilitating the strategic management of human capital using a shared services model currently under development in the federal government. Indeed, this is the objective of the Human Resources Line of Business program (see box 10-1).

The GSA (or another government or private sector HR line of business service provider) would be responsible and accountable for

—Providing customer service support on issues including retirement, special approvals, and delegation of authority

—Administering payroll services

—Administering all benefits plans.

Oversight

Since Congress authorizes and appropriates funds to invest in public service, it must also establish mechanisms to ensure that the funds are used properly. The expenditures for human capital transformation can be controlled through a number of proven methods, including performance measurement, reports to Congress, and audits by relevant inspector generals and the GAO. The combined actions of these groups should provide adequate transparency to confirm that funds are being spent for their intended purpose.

Proper tracking of expenses and associated results would ensure that transformation objectives are being achieved and—more important—that the president's promises are being kept. Funds for the transformation could be tracked and controlled in two ways. Initially, the budget should be restructured to clearly track personnel costs with a separate line item for training. This would help ensure that resources are applied to train all designated personnel. The separate line item would provide a clear audit trail for expenditures and help document the result of investments in the transformation effort. The budget activity could be designated a human capital transformation activity and would include all of the costs shown in table 10-2. We recognize that the increased transparency of a line item for training may increase the potential for these funds to be diverted to other programs. We have called for presidential and congressional leadership to protect these funds armed with the knowledge of their far-reaching effect on government performance.

> *The need to adhere to the highest standards will be viewed as even more important once the taxpayer has made a significant investment in training the next generation of employees.*

The second step would be to compile an expenditure report in compliance with the annual performance and accountability report requirements of GPRA. This expenditure report would cover the financial activity of the new Transformation Account, as well as investment results. Key performance indicators would consist of training days completed; trained rating observations on quality and content of instruction, including adherence to the national curriculum; student satisfaction survey results; employee assessment of management performance gathered on an anonymous basis; and surveys of management assessment of the program. These steps would help ensure accountability for transformation funding.

Of course, no amount of external oversight is a substitute for maintaining a high standard of personal ethics among government employees. Government workers are expected to behave in an exemplary way. This includes upholding the law, avoiding relationships that create conflicts of interest, as well as rejecting expensive gifts, nepotism, and abuse of government power. It also means enforcing the government's absolute commitment to nondiscrimination on the basis of gender, race, age, ethnicity, sexual orientation, disability, religion, or national origin. Federal workers must have the personal integrity to conduct all their transactions with honesty and a sense of fairness. The need to adhere to the highest standards will be viewed as even more important once the taxpayer has made a significant investment in training the next generation of employees.

Conclusion

We have called for an investment of about $10 billion in the federal workforce in order to generate gains of up to $625 billion through higher productivity, better oversight of contractors, and reduced duplication and waste. The basic quid pro quo we have proposed is to shrink the workforce slightly, in order to free up funds to create a better trained and more productive and satisfied federal workforce. Given the many competing demands on the federal budget and the huge budget deficits facing the United States, some will view even this amount as impossibly high. But as former practitioners in government who have managed both the budget and large numbers of federal workers, we have concluded that this investment in public service is absolutely vital. As we have shown, no organization can prosper over a long period of time without focusing on the people factor.

11

Concluding Observations on Public Service Reform

A compelling case for reform does not guarantee action. There are dozens of pressing public problems that demand attention, and "investing in the federal workforce" seldom features in the top ten. The economic crisis gripping the United States will make it easy to set aside the public service issue, or to say that the country simply cannot afford it. This would be a serious mistake. Our argument throughout this book is that the best single investment to strengthen the nation is to upgrade the skills and competence of the workforce that will be charged with meeting these challenges. Whether the issue is entitlement spending, energy independence, economic reform, or nuclear deterrence, the need to improve the quality of the federal workforce is a first step in addressing the problem. This chapter explains how to implement a realistic plan for reform. Our major recommendations are summarized in box 11-1.

What will happen if the nation does *not* reform the federal workforce? The answer is an inevitable reduction in the quality of government service combined with rising cost, as more core government activities are contracted out with little accountability to the American public. All government functions will suffer—from national security to environmental standards to airline safety. But this outcome is wholly avoidable if steps are taken to prevent it. These steps must include a massive reinvestment in the people who run the government, especially in state-of-the-art training for program managers and technical experts. Reform on this scale will require coordinated activity by the president, Congress, and the civil service.

The President

The White House will need to take the lead by setting the stage for public service reform and creating a sense of urgency. Securing the necessary legislative action will require a full-scale effort (as we described in chapter 9), with an organized White House campaign to attract bipartisan support. Recent examples of such campaigns are those mounted to enact the North American Free Trade Agreement, the USA-China Trade Agreement, the No Child Left Behind Act, and funding for combating HIV/AIDS in Africa. Success will require a presidential focus comparable to that propelling such historical changes as Roosevelt's New Deal, Johnson's Great Society, and Eisenhower's transportation program. Each required the full panoply of White House powers as well as a major effort in the executive and legislative branches.[1]

To energize the country around this issue, the president might go on a national tour of federal installations (federal laboratories, national parks, veterans hospitals, a weather tracking station, a Coast Guard rescue station, an agricultural safety testing facility, and so forth) to raise awareness of the important yet often unseen role the federal government plays in national life. This tour could provide a platform to call for a new commitment to public service.

Following are some other actions the president might take:

—Convene a national summit for the key stakeholders (described in chapter 9).

—Set concrete and highly publicized goals, such as recruiting 100,000 top candidates in technology, language, medicine, and other disciplines of importance to public priorities.

—Appoint a White House commission on people factor reform.

—Hold a national televised address to report the findings of the commission and to urge adoption of recommendations.

BOX 11-1. Main Recommendations

Reform the culture of public service
1. Starting with the president, launch a national call to public service.
2. Enact reforms to create a more intrapreneurial culture within the federal government that would provide greater scope for creativity, strategic thinking, and personal initiative.
3. Reduce the number of political appointees.
4. Adopt a core-ring model using an "HR passport" to permit an exchange among federal employees, state and local government, nonprofit and for-profit organizations, in order to learn skills related to conducting their missions.

Overhaul Title V and other statutory and executive changes
1. Eliminate Title V restrictions throughout government, except for merit principles.
2. Authorize reforms to flatten civil service hierarchy.
3. Create a certification credential requirement for all managers and supervisors.
4. Double the size of the Presidential Management Fellows program.
5. Establish midlevel and senior internships/fellowships.
6. Reform the senior executive service program.

Invest in training and education of the civil service
1. Enact a national Civil Service GI Bill.
2. Require training for political appointees.
3. Develop a system of leadership training for all managers and supervisors based on nationally recognized competencies and curricula.
4. Develop training for managing the multisector workforce.

—Engage Congress in helping to develop a set of specific legislative proposals to enact the reforms.

—Select political appointees who are "true believers" in the people factor philosophy.

—Establish a high-level White House team to navigate the legislation through Congress, and to ensure that funding is made available to roll out the program.

Establish leading-edge HR practices comparable to those employed by the best U.S. companies
1. Adjust pay and compensation levels.
2. Streamline hiring.
3. Adopt flex time, telecommuting, wellness programs, child and elder care assistance, and other standard HR best practices.
4. Implement robust performance development plans, measurement, and monitoring.
5. Strengthen the process for dealing with poor performers.

Provide financial resources
1. Trim the federal workforce by 2 percent and use the savings to fund investment in the remaining 98 percent.
2. Increase the acquisition derivative fund, include all service-related acquisitions, and use the income to fund personnel investments.
3. Allow agencies to use lapsed, unobligated funds for start-up investment in personnel.

Reorganize government agencies in charge of personnel
1. Locate primary responsibility for investment in personnel at OMB.
2. Eliminate conflict of interest role in OPM by transferring the service function to another agency such as the GSA.
3. Build strategic advisory and research capabilities at OPM.
4. Set up oversight mechanisms for personnel reform.

In order to reach young people, the president needs to communicate in innovative ways, making use of the Internet to reach the target audience. This could include a first-ever web-based national dialogue to showcase and promote the people factor mission, to discuss key issues, and to answer questions. It could include a web-affinity group or social network that could be leveraged for change at a national level. The presidential team could also promote the public service relentlessly through blogsites, presidential podcasts, videos of interesting federal work sites, and so forth. Many public and private organizations would volunteer their help (for example, advertising space on web sites) with enthusiasm. For example, during the past two decennial census efforts, private companies urged people to fill in their census forms as part of their public service.

Another important role for the president is to reenergize the nation's current civil servants. Many of them are overworked and demoralized after decades of incremental reforms that have not achieved real improvement in working conditions. This group, particularly the senior executives, will be the ones tasked to develop and implement many aspects of the reform program. By publicly recognizing the importance of this group (for example, by having groups of senior executives meet with the president and his key team in a series of in-person and nationwide "town hall" meetings), the president can demonstrate an understanding of the challenges they face and communicate directly the importance of the effort to the future well-being of the nation.

Congress

While the president can lead the call to strengthen public service, it will fall short of its goal unless Congress reinforces the message and explains its importance in every state and locality in the country. The need to reinvigorate public service is truly a nonpartisan issue. Regardless of the president's political party, Congress has an opportunity to improve the performance of government for its constituents by partnering with the president on this issue.

The first hurdle is to get Congress to pay attention. With so many topics competing for congressional consideration, it is easy to miss the connection between serving constituents and restoring public service. The point is that the country must address the personnel problem if it is to solve pressing problems related to national security, education, health care, and the economy. Congress must recognize that the public service issue underpins them all.

One important step would be for congressional committees to convene hearings on personnel reform. Such hearings would raise public awareness of the need for reform in the way that hearings on the Internal Revenue

Service (IRS) did in 1996 and 1997; they helped to stir reform efforts by featuring a number of honest taxpayers penalized by the IRS for attempting to ask for help in paying their taxes.

Congress also needs to make the public more aware of the relationship between the people who work for the government and the outcomes that the public wants. In other words, Congress can help to draw the link between economic security, national security, public welfare, environmental protection, the food supply, transportation safety, and infrastructure and the people who work in these occupations. By now it is well understood that the federal government missed certain warning signs before the 9/11 attacks, in part because senior officials failed to investigate concerns expressed by front-line federal employees. We have also seen serious problems in areas ranging from the federal oversight of the financial sector to the flawed intelligence data that contributed to the decision to invade Iraq. Equally important, the country has been spared from attacks on several occasions by the vigilance, initiative, and quick thinking of front-line employees.

Finally, Congress will need to make legislative changes and budgetary appropriations as described in chapter 10. To begin with, it should remove certain Title V restrictions and adopt legislation that would turn the civil service into a dynamic, twenty-first-century organization. That means appropriating funds for the reform program on a sustained basis and implementing the measures described in chapters 4–8 and 10.

The Civil Service

Even with committed leadership by the president and Congress, federal workforce reform needs to be embraced by leaders within the civil service itself. With noteworthy exceptions, the people who make up the civil service have lost a sense of personal responsibility for developing and mentoring subordinates, especially newly hired employees who are many levels below in the organization. As Harvard professor Steve Kelman has pointed out, the only way that fundamental reform can occur in the federal workforce is if the opinion leaders among the senior executives embrace it and participate actively in bringing it about. Without this commitment at the top, new talent may be enticed to join the government, but it will not stay long. The civil service will bear responsibility for implementing the details of people reform, sustaining momentum, and creating a work environment conducive to retaining talent.

Senior executives can take some specific steps to ensure success. They can mentor new hires. They can appoint a team to design an implementation plan that will enrich and incubate the next generation of top government leaders. They can assign a team to work with academics from leading public policy schools to design a national curriculum for management training. They can detail national merit awardees to serve on the National Academy of Public Administration to draw on the talents of current and former civil servants. In short, the senior executives should not only be able to enroll in the new training opportunities, but they also need to help create opportunities for everyone else.

The relationship between the public and the civil service will change once the country is making a substantial, proactive investment in human capital. In recognition of this, there need to be more opportunities for the public to see the range of vital activities that federal workers are performing. For example, the military has adopted a program of embedding journalists with front-line troops, so the public can obtain a more accurate picture of the situation on the ground. Where appropriate, senior civil servants could invite journalists, students, and members of the public to visit and observe their agencies to gain a deeper appreciation of the mission and jobs performed by federal employees.

Conclusion

Throughout this book we have argued that the United States needs to do a much better job of supporting the people who work in the federal government. This commitment to the government workforce is not just the right thing to do; it is also the responsible thing to do from a budgetary perspective. By investing $10 billion in human capital, the government can reap long-term benefits amounting to $300 billion to $600 billion through higher productivity, more efficient contract management, and a significant reduction in waste and duplication.

Government agencies that put the "people factor" principle into practice will pay exceptional attention to traditional human resources issues such as training and career development. They will also offer workers a degree of autonomy in decisionmaking and scope for individual initiative. These strategies have been proven to work not only at leading private sector companies but at enlightened government agencies such as the Government Accountability Office and Defense Logistics Agency.

Beyond the economic benefits, people factor reforms provide an invaluable opportunity to rebuild the relationship between citizens and civil servants—a relationship that has frayed in recent decades. As the generation that heeded John F. Kennedy's call to public service retires from government, the need to energize a new set of Americans to government vocations has seldom been more acute. Restoring trust and respect for the federal workforce is critical in enabling government to attract the next generation of young people to serve the country.

It is never easy to muster the political will to push such reforms through the legislative process or to appropriate the necessary funding to ensure the reforms are sustainable. It requires vision and leadership from the executive branch at the highest level. Yet the case for action is compelling, and the costs of inaction are growing daily. People factor reforms will strengthen the U.S. government and make it more responsive to the complex policy challenges ahead. They will also enable Americans to bequeath a stronger, more resilient, and optimistic country to the generations to come.

Survey of College Juniors and Seniors— Attitudes toward Working for the Public and Private Sectors

Questionnaire

All series are randomized.

Screeners

1. Are you...
   1) Male
   2) Female

2. Are you currently enrolled in a four-year college?
   1) Yes
   2) No   **TERMINATE**

3. What college do you attend?
   OPEN-END

4. Are you a . . .
   1) Freshman   **TERMINATE**
   2) Sophomore   **TERMINATE**
   3) Junior
   4) Senior
   5) Recent Graduate (within the last month)

5. What major(s) are you currently studying? Please list all that apply.
   OPEN-END

6. Which of the following careers are you most likely to pursue when you graduate from school? Please choose all that apply.
   1) Administrative and Support Services
   2) Advertising/Marketing/Public Relations
   3) Agriculture
   4) Architecture
   5) Arts & Humanities/ Entertainment/Media
   6) Business/Financial
   7) Computers/Information Technology
   8) Construction/Engineering
   9) Consulting
   10) Education
   11) Engineering
   12) Law
   13) Medicine
   14) Military
   15) Non-Profit Organizations/ Non-Governmental Organizations
   16) Public Service/Government
   17) Science/Math/Statistics

18) Sports & Recreation
19) Telecommunications
20) Accounting
21) Self-Employment/Family Business
22) Other (Specify)

Favorability

7. For each of the following professions, please rate whether you have a very favorable, somewhat favorable, not very favorable, or not at all favorable opinion of each.

   Doctors
   1) Very favorable
   2) Somewhat favorable
   3) Not very favorable
   4) Not at all favorable

8. Lawyers

9. Journalists

10. Federal Government Employees

11. State/Local/Municipal Employees

12. Military Personnel

13. Teachers

14. Investment Bankers

15. Management Consultants

16. Public Safety (Firefighter, Police Officer, etc.)

17. Non-Profit Employees (e.g., Red Cross, World Wildlife Fund, Save the Children, etc.)

18. Using the same scale, please rate whether you have a very favorable, somewhat favorable, not very favorable, or not at all favorable opinion of the following employers.

IBM
1) Very favorable
2) Somewhat favorable
3) Not very favorable
4) Not at all favorable

19. The Federal Government

20. Wal-Mart

21. U.S. Military/Armed Forces

22. General Electric

23. Procter and Gamble

24. Red Cross

24B. Marriott

24C. State and Local Government

Career Horse-Race

25. When you graduate, are you considering a career with the Federal Government?
    1) Yes
    2) No

26. Do you have any close friends or relatives that work for the Federal Government?
    1) Yes
    2) No

27. Imagine for a second, that you were offered a full-time job that was identical in job description, compensation package, and location at the United States Federal Government and at a private company. Which offer would you accept?
    1) Federal Government
    2) Private Company

28. Why do you say that?
    OPEN-END

29. When you graduate, are you considering a career with a non-profit organization (e.g., Red Cross, World Wildlife Fund, Save the Children, etc.)?
    1) Yes
    2) No

30. Imagine for a second, that you were offered a full-time job that was identical in job description, compensation package, and location at each of the following. Which offer would you accept?
    1) Federal Government
    2) Private Company
    3) Non-Profit Organization

31. If money were not a factor, which do you think would be the best place to make a positive contribution to society, working for the Federal Government or for working for a non-profit organization?
    1) Federal Government
    2) Non-Profit Organization

32. Why do you say that?
    OPEN-END

33. When you graduate, which of the following types of jobs within the Federal Government would you consider a career with? Choose all that apply.
    1) Science
    2) Engineering
    3) Finance/Administration
    4) Foreign Service
    5) Information Technology
    6) Law Enforcement/Intelligence Agencies
    7) Tax Auditing
    8) Legal
    9) Transportation/Aviation
    10) Armed Forces
    11) Peace Corps/Americorps
    12) Other (Specify)
    13) Would not consider any of these

34. Now we would like you to think about each of the following departments within the Federal Government and rate whether working at each would be better, worse, or the same as working for the Federal Government as a whole?
    1) Better
    2) Worse
    3) The Same

REPEAT CODES

35. CIA

36. White House

37. NASA

38. Defense

39. Veterans Affairs

40. Health and Human Services

41. Agriculture

42. Interior

43. State Department

44. Justice Department

45. Treasury Department

46. Transportation Department

47. IRS

48. Environmental Protection Agency

49. Social Security Administration

Career Decision Making Process—Influencers

50. When you are considering job offers, who do you think you will look to the most to give you advice or guidance on whether to accept an offer or not?
    1) Parents
    2) Professors
    3) Friends
    4) Relatives

5) Students/Peers
6) People I know already in the working world
7) Career Counselor

Job Confidence Metric

51. Thinking about the economy in the country as a whole, how would you rate our national economy? Would you say it is in excellent shape, good shape, only fair shape, or poor shape?
    1) Excellent shape
    2) Good shape
    3) Fair shape
    4) Poor shape

52. Now thinking about your own situation. How would you rate your own chances of finding a job that would *satisfy you* after graduating?
    1) Excellent
    2) Good
    3) Fair
    4) Poor

Employer Attributes

You will now be asked to read some factors that people like yourself may or may not look for when choosing a company to work for.

For each of the following characteristics, please rate how important each factor is when deciding what company to work for. Please use a one to ten scale where one is *"Not at all important"* and ten is *"Extremely important."*

Using a one to ten scale, please rate how important this attribute is when choosing a company to work for.

1) 1 – Not at all important
2) 2
3) 3
4) 4
5) 5
6) 6
7) 7
8) 8
9) 9
10) 10 – Extremely important

REPEAT CODES

Remuneration

53. Competitive salary package

54. Strong pension and retirement plan

55. Profit sharing linked to employee/company performance

Credit

56. Receive credit and acknowledgment for accomplishments and good ideas

Access

57. If you have a good idea, management will listen and implement it quickly

58. Senior executives are accessible

Soft Benefits

59. Flexible hours as long as you get the job done

60. Access to a fitness center, cafeteria, and recreation facility

61. Generous allocation of vacation time

62. Organization that really cares about its employees

Freedom

63. Freedom to make your own decisions and do things your own way within your job area

Training and Development

64. Training and development for new employees

65. Commitment to continual, career-long employee training, development, and learning

66. Performance evaluations that offer constructive feedback to help you do your job better

Promotion

67. Opportunity to go as high in the organization as your abilities take you

68. Top-level employees are promoted from within the organization

Lateral

69. Diverse assignments so you can develop a number of different skills

70. Easy to transfer to different jobs, offices, and locations within the same organization

Teamwork v. Working Alone

71. Work mostly in teams with other people

72. Work independently with little supervision

Good for Society

73. Work where you make a positive contribution to society

Casual and Fun

74. Casual and fun work environment

Innovative Culture

75. Trying new things and "thinking outside the box" is rewarded

Work/Life Balance

76. Respects balance between work responsibilities and personal and family life

Ethics

77. Rewards and encourages ethical conduct

Community

78. Company that plays an active role in the community

Diversity

79. Environment that is diverse and free from discrimination

Co-workers

80. Co-workers who you respect, admire, and get along with

Reputation

81. Organization that is respected and admired

82. Organization with a secure and solid future

Challenging Work

83. Challenging and interesting work

Flat v. Hierarchical Chain

84. A flat organization where there are few layers of management

85. A traditional hierarchial structure with many layers of management and a top-down chain of command

Federal Government Gap Analysis

You will now be asked to read some characteristics that could describe a company/employer.

For each characteristic below, please rate whether this attribute applies more to the United States Federal Government or to Private Industry. Please use a one to ten scale, with one meaning that the word or phrase applies "*Much more to the Federal Government*" and ten meaning that the word or phrase applies "*Much more to Private Industry.*"

Using a one to ten scale, please rate whether this attribute applies more to the Federal Government or more to Private Industry.

1) 1 – Applies much more to the Federal Government
2) 2
3) 3
4) 4
5) 5 – Applies to both equally
6) 6
7) 7
8) 8
9) 9
10) 10 – Applies much more to Private Industry

USE same List as above

86. If the United States Federal Government (as an employer) had all the characteristics we just discussed, please rate how likely you would be to accept an offer from the United States Federal Government.
    1) 1 – Would definitely reject the offer
    2) 2
    3) 3
    4) 4

5) 5 – Might reject or accept the offer
6) 6
7) 7
8) 8
9) 9
10) 10 – Would definitely accept the offer

IF YES IN Q28 (Considering Job with Federal Government):

87. You mentioned earlier that you were interested in pursuing a career with the Federal Government upon graduating. Which of the following are the primary reasons you are considering a career with the Federal Government? Please select two from the list below.
    1) Opportunity to serve your country
    2) Make a meaningful contribution to society
    3) Job security
    4) Ease of changing job, location, and department within the Federal Government, while still retaining full benefits and career track
    5) Good pension plan
    6) A wide range of opportunities for professional growth and development
    7) Work with the latest in cutting-edge technology
    8) Recommendation of family/friends/professor/career counselor

IF NO IN Q28 (Not Considering Job with Federal Government):

88. You mentioned earlier that you were *not* interested in pursuing a career with the Federal Government upon graduating. Which of

the following are the primary reasons you are *not* considering a career with the Federal Government? Please select two from the list below.

1) Lower compensation packages than private industry
2) Recruitment process is too long and cumbersome
3) Work environment is bureaucratic and dull
4) Limited bonuses and incentives for personal accomplishments
5) Limited recognition for personal accomplishments
6) Hard to get new ideas implemented, not entrepreneurial
7) Technologically backward, not leading edge
8) Politicized work environment
9) Recommendation of family/friends/professor/career counselor

Working for the Government

89. When you think about working for the Federal Government what kind of thoughts and images come to mind?
OPEN-END

90. Thinking about the kind of workers who may work at the Federal Government. What age do you think best represents the average age of a typical Federal Government employee?
1) 18–24
2) 25–34
3) 35–49
4) 50–64
5) Over 65

91. How much do you think the work environment in the Federal Government has changed over the last twenty-five years?
1) Changed a great deal
2) Changed somewhat
3) Changed a little
4) Has not changed at all

92. How much do you think the work environment in Private Industry has changed over the last twenty-five years?
1) Changed a great deal
2) Changed somewhat
3) Changed a little
4) Has not changed at all

Worker Psychographics

93. Thinking about the first job you will have after you graduate college. How long do you think you will work at that job?
1) Less than a year
2) 1 year
3) 1–2 years
4) 3–5 years
5) 5–10 years
6) More than 10 years

94. How many different employers do you think you will work for throughout your career?
1) One
2) Two to three
3) Four to five
4) Five to seven
5) More than seven

95. After applying for a job, what is the maximum period of time you would wait to find out whether you had received the job offer?
1) Less than 2 weeks
2) 2 to 4 weeks
3) 1 to 2 months

4) 2 to 3 months
5) 4 to 5 months
6) 6 months to 1 year
7) 1 to 2 years

96. At what point would the wait to find out whether you would receive a job offer discourage you from applying for a job?
1) Less than 2 weeks
2) 2 to 4 weeks
3) 1 to 2 months
4) 2 to 3 months
5) 4 to 5 months
6) 6 months to 1 year
7) 1 to 2 years

General Government

97. Do you think the Federal Government hiring process is a fair and open process or is it often based mainly on who you know?
1) Fair and open
2) Based upon who you know

98. Do you think it is easy or difficult to locate and apply for a job with the Federal Government?
1) Easy
2) Difficult

99. Do you think career advancement within the Federal Government is limited or is not?
1) Career advancement limited
2) Career advancement is not limited

Federal Government: Agree/Disagree Statements

The following is a series of statements that you may or may not agree with. Please indicate how strongly you agree or disagree with each of the following statements.

100. Using a 1 to 5 scale, where 1 is "*Strongly Disagree*" and 5 is "*Strongly Agree*," please indicate whether you agree or disagree with the following statement:
I would consider a career with the Federal Government but the pay is not sufficient.
1) 1 – Strongly Disagree
2) 2
3) 3
4) 4
5) 5 – Strongly Agree

REPEAT CODES

101. I would apply for a job in the Federal Government, but the application process is too long and cumbersome

102. I just don't see myself ever working for the Federal Government

103. I would only work for the Federal Government as a last resort

104. The students from my school who go to work at the Federal Government are some of the brightest

105. Media and politicians project such a negative image of the Federal Government that I am less likely to work there

106. What happens in the Federal Government affects my daily life

107. Federal employees do important work

108. The Federal Government is one of the best employers in terms of being free from discrimination and being open to people from all types of backgrounds

109. Generally speaking, it is better to work for the private sector than to work for the Federal Government

110. If you want to contribute to our country, working for a non-profit is a better place to do it than working for the Federal Government

111. It's very hard to get a job with the Federal Government unless you have a friend or relative working there who can help you get in

Federal Government Employment Reforms Section

The following changes have been suggested as ways to improve employment within the Federal Government. For each proposed change, please indicate if this change were adopted by the Federal Government, would it make you much more likely, somewhat more likely, somewhat less likely, or much less likely to pursue a career with the Federal Government?

112. For each proposed change, please indicate if it were adopted, would it make you much more likely, somewhat more likely, somewhat less likely, or much less likely to pursue a career with the Federal Government.

Changing the hiring system so you can apply using your standard resume instead of filling out government forms

If this proposed change were adopted would it make you much more likely, somewhat

more likely, somewhat less likely, or much less likely to pursue a career with the Federal Government?
1) Much more likely
2) Somewhat more likely
3) Somewhat less likely
4) Much less likely

Considering this change, if you were offered a full-time job that was identical in job description, compensation package, and location at the United States Federal Government and at a private company, which offer would you accept?
1) Federal Government
2) Private Company

REPEAT CODES

113. Making the government a "high prestige" employer with excellent pay, special skills training, and similar benefits to America's leading companies

114. Replacing the traditional hierarchical system with a flatter, team-based, flexible system

115. Making it easier for you to go back and forth between government and the private sector (for example, you could work in the government for a while, then go to a private company, then return to the government without losing your pension benefits)

116. Reorganizing so that most people in the government get to do more than one type of job, and can spend time in different geographic locations if they want to

117. Offering cafeteria-style benefits which provide flexibility for full-time employees to pick and choose among benefit options and design plans that fit their needs

118. Changing the government so that each agency can tailor its human resources program to the work force it needs in terms of recruiting and compensation.

119. Appointing a Chief Human Capital Officer for every department who would be in charge of all personnel much like a Chief Financial Officer does for financial companies.

120. Replacing some of the political appointees with career civil servants who rise from the ranks so that more senior jobs go to career civil servants.

121. Thinking about everything you have read, when you graduate are you considering a career with the Federal Government?
    1) Yes
    2) No

    IF NO:

122. What changes would make you consider a career with the Federal Government?

    OPEN-END

Post 9/11

123. Since September 11th, would you say that your interest in working in the Federal Government has increased, decreased, or remained the same?
    1) Increased
    2) Decreased
    3) Remained the same

124. Since September 11th, would you say that your interest in working in community service (i.e., local police, fire, emergency medical departments) has increased, decreased, or remained the same?
    1) Increased
    2) Decreased
    3) Remained the same

125. Since September 11th, would you say that your interest in serving your country has increased, decreased, or remained the same?
    1) Increased
    2) Decreased
    3) Remained the same

Demographics

The following questions are for statistical purposes only:

126. What is your exact age?

127. Which of the following would you say best describes you (please choose all that apply):
    1) White
    2) Black/African-American/Caribbean-American
    3) Hispanic/Latino
    4) Asian
    5) Arab
    6) Native American/Alaskan Native
    7) Other (Specify)
    8) Prefer not to answer

128. Do you consider yourself a strong Democrat, weak Democrat, weak Republican, strong Republican, or Independent?
    1) Strong Democrat
    2) Weak Democrat
    3) Weak Republican
    4) Strong Republican
    5) Independent
    6) Prefer not to answer

129. If you had to choose, would you rather have a smaller government providing fewer services or bigger government providing more services?
    1) Smaller government providing fewer services
    2) Bigger government providing more services

130. Is any member of your immediate family in a Union?
    1) Yes
    2) No

131. Is any member of your immediate family in the Armed Forces?
    1) Yes
    2) No

132. What state do you live in (when not attending school):

133. What is your cumulative GPA to date:
    NUM 0 to 4.0

134. What is your primary source for news and information?

    RANDOMIZE
    1) Television
    2) Newspapers
    3) Magazines
    4) The Internet
    5) Friends/Family
    6) Professors

Note: The survey was conducted by Penn, Schoen and Berland Associates (for Linda Bilmes and W. Scott Gould) among college juniors and seniors nationwide. The margin of error is +/–3.1 percent. For complete results, visit the website www.brookings.edu/~/media/Files/Press.Books/2009/peoplefactor/appendixes.pdf

APPENDIX B

Summary of Laws, Reforms, and Key Demonstration Projects and Test Cases Pertaining to the Civil Service

Item	Summary
Laws and commissions that built the merit-based civil service	
Civil Service Commission (Grant Commission), formed in 1871	Recommended replacing the "spoils system" of awarding civil service positions with a merit-based system.
Civil Service Act of 1883 (Pendleton Act)	Created the merit-based civil service.
Classification Act of 1923	Enshrined the principle of equal pay for equal work in federal law by classifying positions on the basis of duties and assigning salaries to positions.
Ramspeck Act of 1940	Extended reach of competitive service.
Executive Order 10987, issued in 1962	Established an appeals process for nonveteran employees.
Federal Salary Reform Act of 1962	Mandated that the salaries of federal employees should approximate the salaries of private sector employees in similar positions.
Federal Pay Comparability Act of 1970	Changed the system for increasing federal wages to use private sector comparability calculations enacted by executive orders annually.
Reorganization Plan No. 2 of 1978	Abolished the Civil Service Commission and divided its responsibilities between the Office of Personnel Management and the Merit Systems Protection Board.
Civil Service Reform Act of 1978 (CSRA)	Created the Senior Executive Service (SES); established merit pay bonuses for midlevel managers; developed a new performance appraisal system for employees outside of the SES and GS-13, GS-14, and GS-15 grades; and provided research and development authority to OPM.

Item	Summary
Performance Management and Recognition System (PMRS), established in 1984	Created a centralized performance appraisal system with a standardized number of performance levels, reversing the decentralization endorsed by CSRA.
Federal Employees Pay Compatibility Act of 1990 (FEPCA)	Designed to create a fair and competitive way to compensate federal employees by using locality pay, an annual pay adjustment process, and recruitment and relocation bonuses and retention allowances, among other provisions.

Benefits programs

Retirement Act of 1920	Established mandatory retirement ages (by position) and an annuity system for paying retirement benefits.
Federal Employees Health Benefits Act of 1959	Made group-rate, employer-subsidized health insurance available to the federal workforce for the first time.
Federal Employees Retirement System, established in 1987	Replaced the Civil Service Retirement System (CSRS) created in the 1920s with a new three-component program: Social Security benefits, a basic benefits plan, and a thrift savings plan.

Training and employee development

Government Employees Training Act of 1958	Designated responsibility for employee development and authorized funding for training.
Federal Executive Institute and Executive Seminar Centers, initiated in 1963	Provided two-week training sessions on managerial and other needed skills to midlevel government managers and two-month education and training programs to government executives.

Recruiting

Presidential Management Intern Program, initiated in 1977	Helped government recruit young, talented, and well-educated people to government service.
National Commission on the Public Service (first Volcker Commission), 1989	Studied the growing difficulty of attracting the best and the brightest of America's young professionals to government service.

Improving effectiveness

National Performance Review (NPR), initiated in 1993	Intended to reform the overall federal bureaucracy to improve efficiency and performance.
Government Performance and Results Act of 1993 (GPRA)	Required federal agencies and departments to complete extensive strategic plans and annual performance plans, and to devise and report measurable, mission-based performance metrics.
Chief Financial Officers (CFO) Act of 1990	Designed to improve the government's financial management by outlining standards of financial performance and disclosure. Gave OMB greater authority over federal financial management and created the position of CFO for each of twenty-three federal agencies.

Item	Summary
Information Technology Management Reform Act of 1996 (ITMRA, or the Clinger-Cohen Act)	Intended to improve how the government acquires and manages information technology by mandating the use of performance based management principles. Outlines a series of new responsibilities for agency CIOs.
Volcker Commissions on Public Service (1989 and 2003)	The two National Commissions on the Public Service examined federal service reform in the areas of pay, recruitment, and retention. The second of the Volcker Commissions was born of the realization that what the first Volcker Commission termed "the quiet crisis" had become "a roar." The events of September 11 "put a large exclamation point on the need to address the problems" of the federal public service.[a]

Important demonstration projects and test cases

Navy China Lake, initiated in 1980	Established a demonstration project to promote improved employee performance and to better link performance to compensation.
Federal Aviation Administration (FAA) Demonstration Project, initiated in 1996	Exempted the FAA from various provisions of Title V; created a more flexible pay system with broad pay bands, a performance management system with frequent feedback (instead of summary ratings), a comprehensive workforce planning effort that required new hiring authorities, and new policies to promote diversity and an open work environment.
Internal Revenue Service (IRS) Modernization, initiated in 1998	Exempted the IRS from various provisions of Title V; created new pay authorities, workforce-shaping tools, pay bands based on qualifications and performance (instead of longevity), and the ability to rate prospective employees by "category" (rather than by strict numerical score).
Department of Homeland Security (DHS) Personnel Reform, established in 2004	Exempted the DHS from various provisions of Title V, limited the scope of union bargaining, instituted a pay-for-performance system, facilitated disciplining poor performers, limited third-party oversight of employee appeals, and reorganized employees into clusters by professional group and broad pay bands within those clusters.
National Security Personnel System (NSPS), established in 2004	Exempted the DOD from various provisions of Title V; rules very similar to those at DHS.

Source: Authors' compilation.

a. Paul C. Light, Testimony before Senate Governmental Affairs Subcommittee on International Security, Proliferation, and Federal Services, March 19, 2002.

APPENDIX C

List of Interviewees

Name	Title
Jane Alexander	Former Managing Partner, Hewitt Associates
Amy Alving	Former Deputy Director, Defense Advanced Research Projects Agency
Richard Armitage	Executive President, Armitage International
Beverly Ortega Babers	Chief Human Capital Officer, Internal Revenue Service
Roger Blanchard	Assistant Deputy Chief of Staff for Manpower and Personnel, U.S. Department of the Air Force
David Chu	Under Secretary of Defense for Personnel and Readiness, U.S. Department of Defense
Vern Clarke	Admiral, USN (Ret.), and Former Chief of Naval Operations
Claudia A. Cross	Chief Human Capital Officer, U.S. Department of Energy
Ed DeSeve	Professor of Practice and Director, Management, Finance and Leadership, University of Maryland
Don Devine	Vice Chairman of the American Conservative Union
Michael Dominguez	Principal Deputy Under Secretary of Defense, Personnel and Readiness, U.S. Department of Defense
Mike Dovilla	Legislative Assistant for Senator Voinovich
Gordon England	Deputy Secretary, U.S. Department of Defense
Ed Flynn	Senior Partner, Hewitt Associates
John Gage	President, American Federation of Government Employees–AFL-CIO
Steve Goldsmith	Daniel Paul Professor of Government, Harvard Kennedy School, Harvard University
Janet Hale	Under Secretary for Management, U.S. Department of Homeland Security

Name	Title*
Sallyanne Harper	Chief Financial and Chief Administrative Officer, Government Accountability Office
Doris Hausser	Former Director, Office of Personnel Management
Jennifer Hemingway	Staff Director, OGM Subcommittee, U.S. Senate Committee on Homeland Security and Governmental Affairs
Robert Hosenfeld	Chief Human Capital Officer, U.S. Department of Health and Human Services
Pat Ingraham	Director of the Alan K. Campbell Public Affairs Institute, Syracuse University
Clay Johnson	Deputy Director for Management, Office of Management and Budget
Elaine Kamarck	Lecturer in Public Policy, Harvard Kennedy School, Harvard University
Michael C. Kane	Associate Administrator, Office of Management and Administration, National Nuclear Security Administration
Colleen Kelley	President, National Treasury Employee's Union
Steve Kelman	Professor of Public Management, Kennedy School of Government, Harvard University
Don Kettl	Professor of Political Science and Robert A. Fox Professor of Leadership, University of Pennsylvania
John Koskinen	Executive President, U.S. Soccer Foundation
Kenneth Krieg	Under Secretary for Acquisition, U.S. Department of Defense
Nanci Langley	Commissioner, United States Postal Regulatory Commission
Peter Levine	Staff Member, Senate Armed Services Committee
General Frank Libutti	Lieutenant General, USMC (Ret.) and Former Under Secretary, U.S. Department of Homeland Security
Paul Light	Paulette Goddard Professor of Public Service, New York University
Jim Loy	Admiral, USCG (Ret.) and Former Deputy Secretary, U.S. Department of Homeland Security
Dave Mader	Principal, Booz Allen Hamilton and former Deputy Commissioner, Administration, Internal Revenue Service
Robert Mallett	Former Deputy Secretary, U.S. Department of Commerce
Marcia Marsh	Vice President, Partnership for Public Service
Ron Martinson	Staff Director, House Subcommittee for Civil Service and Government Reform
Sharon Mastracci	Assistant Professor, University of Chicago
Chris Mihm	Managing Director, Strategic Issues, Government Accountability Office
Jeffrey Neal	Director of Human Resources, Defense Logistics Agency
George Nesterczuk	Senior Adviser to the Director, Office of Personnel Management
Greg Newbold	Lieutenant General, U.S. Marine Corps (Ret.)
Pat Pizzella	Senior Executive, U.S. Department of the Air Force
Phil Quast	Vice Admiral, USN and Executive Learning Officer, U.S. Department of the Navy
Anne Reed	Chief Executive Officer, Acquisition Solutions Inc.

Name	Title*
Andrew Richardson	Staff Member, U.S. Senate Committee on Homeland Security and Governmental Affairs
Charles Rossotti	Former Commissioner, Internal Revenue Service
Greg Rothwell	Former Chief Procurement Officer, U.S. Department of Homeland Security
Ron Sanders	Associate Deputy Director, National Intelligence
Tania Shand	Clerk, House Subcommittee on the Federal Workforce, Postal Service, and the District of Columbia
Robert Shea	Associate Director, Office of Management and Budget
Eric Shinseki	General, U.S. Army (Ret.), and Former Chief of Staff of the Army
Jackie Simon	Director of Policy, American Federation of Government Employees–AFL-CIO
Hannah Sistare	Vice President for Academy Affairs, National Academy of Public Administration
Linda Springer	Director, Office of Personnel Management
Max Stier	President, Partnership for Public Service
Pat Stillman	Vice Admiral, USCG (Ret.), and Former Program Executive Officer, Deepwater Project, U.S. Coast Guard
Diana Tabler	Staff Member, Senate Armed Services Committee
Andrew Tether	Director, Defense Advanced Research Projects Agency
Tommy Thompson	Former Secretary, U.S. Department of Health and Human Services
James R. Thompson	Commissioner, 9/11 Commission
John Threlkeld	Director, Legislative Affairs, American Federation of Government Employees–AFL-CIO
Bob Tobias	Former President, National Treasury Employee's Union
David Walker	Former Comptroller General, Government Accountability Office
Bob Welch	Former Chief of Procurement, U.S. Department of Commerce
Reginald Wells	Deputy Commissioner and Chief Human Capital Officer, U.S. Social Services Administration

*Titles may have changed since the date of interview.

Federal Election Commission Vacancy Announcement

FEDERAL ELECTION COMMISSION
VACANCY ANNOUNCEMENT

Position Title and Grade	Area of Consideration	Announcement No.
ATTORNEY GS-905-13/14 $79,397-121,967	ALL SOURCES	07-034

Organizational Location	Opening Date	Closing Date
OFFICE OF GENERAL COUNSEL Policy Division	03/26/2007	04/20/2007

THE FEDERAL ELECTION COMMISSION IS AN EXCEPTED SERVICE AGENCY.

THIS IS A PERMANENT, FULL TIME POSITION. THE FULL PERFORMANCE LEVEL IS GS-14. U.S. CITIZENSHIP REQUIRED. THIS IS A MISSION CRITICAL POSITION.

DUTIES AND RESPONSIBILITIES: The incumbent serves as an Attorney in the Policy Division in the Office of General Counsel (OGC) at the Federal Election Commission (FEC).

The FEC is an independent federal regulatory agency established by the Federal Election Campaign Act of 1971, as amended, 2 U.S.C. §§ 431 et seq. (the FECA). It is governed by six Commissioners appointed by the President with the advice and consent of the Senate. The FEC has exclusive jurisdiction for the administration, interpretation, and civil enforcement of the FECA, which requires disclosure of campaign contributions and expenditures by candidates for federal office and committees supporting those candidates, and imposes limitations on the amount and sources of such contributions. The FEC also administers the federal programs that provide public funding to qualified candidates for President and Vice President.

OGC supports the FEC's unique role of regulating the financial aspects of political campaigns for Federal office by directing FEC enforcement activities, representing the Commission in federal court litigation, interpreting the FECA, and advising the Commission on legal matters brought before it. While most questions concern interpretation of campaign finance statutes and regulations, some constitutional issues arise as well, principally First Amendment free speech considerations. Advisory opinions apply a general rule of law to a specific factual situation. These AOs, which are issued by the Commission pursuant to § 437f of the FECA, provide legal protection to the requesting persons. Both draft regulations and AO's are presented to the Commission in public session during a regularly scheduled Commission meeting. All regulations and AOs must be approved by at least four Commissioners.

Attorneys in the Policy Division are engaged in all aspects of the policy development process, including:

- developing and drafting Advisory Opinions (AOs) interpreting the FECA and Commission regulations;
- developing and drafting regulations implementing the FECA, the Bipartisan Campaign Reform Act (BCRA), the Presidential Election Campaign Fund Act (Fund Act), the Presidential Primary Matching Payment Account Act (Matching Payment Act), and other statutes that impact the Commission's operation;
- drafting and researching legal memoranda regarding the FECA and Commission actions;
- presenting and answering questions regarding Policy documents before the Commission;
- drafting and providing advice on proposed legislative amendments to the FECA;
- providing legal review of agency forms and publications;
- representing the agency at conferences and in other public settings.

QUALIFICATION REQUIREMENTS:

Mandatory Requirements: An applicant must meet the following requirements to be eligible for consideration:

(1) An applicant must be a citizen of the United States;

(2) An applicant must hold a law degree from an accredited law school; be a member in good standing of the Bar of a state, the District of Columbia, Puerto Rico, or any territorial court under the Constitution.

GS-13: A law degree, bar membership and two years of professional attorney experience.
GS-14: A law degree, bar membership and three years of professional attorney experience. Applicants must have completed one year of specialized experience; to be creditable, specialized experience must have been at least equivalent to the next lower grade in the Federal service in the normal line of progression.   (See section below, Conditions of Employment, for OGC's policy regarding initial appointments at the GS-14 grade level.)

SPECIALIZED EXPERIENCE

Is experience which directly relate to the line of work of the position to be filled and which has equipped the candidate with the particular knowledge, skills and abilities to successfully perform the duties of the position. Dates of employment should indicate starting and ending month and year so that length of service in each position can be correctly determined. Exceptions to the length of service requirements listed below will be made on a case-by-case basis and will only be made based on outstanding qualifications. Justifications for such exceptions will be submitted in writing to the FEC Human Resources Director based on a review of the candidate's application package.

Time-in-grade requirement: For GS 13, completion of one year of service at GS-12. For GS-14, completion of eighteen months of service at GS-13.

<u>**Knowledge, Skills, and Abilities**</u>:

(1) Ability to write clearly, concisely and persuasively (considered an essential requirement of the position and will be heavily weighted when making final selections for the position).

(2) Ability to research and analyze complex legal issues, including regulatory and constitutional issues.

(3) Ability to make an effective oral presentations

DESIRABLE FACTOR

Knowledge of election law and administrative law (should be also indicated in the applicant's cover letter and/or resume. Experience in writing regulations is desirable and should be highlighted also in the cover letter and/or resume).

SPECIAL FACTORS: Attorney applicants are evaluated in a two-step process. On the basis of written materials submitted in accordance with the vacancy announcement, step one weighs the candidate's legal education and legal experience against a pre-determined set of criteria. The highest rated candidates will be interviewed during a second phase of applicant evaluation. Successful candidates from step two will be forwarded to the selecting official. With their applications, candidates <u>must</u> include <u>one</u> writing sample that reflects the ability to analyze sophisticated legal issues. Applicants, who have held a permanent position as an attorney in the federal government at a GS-14 or higher grade level, or its equivalent, shall be referred directly to the selecting official as an exception to merit promotion procedures. The selecting official may interview or request his or her staff to interview any such applicant at his or her discretion.

EVALUATION METHOD: Final ranking is based on an evaluation of experience, education and training as they relate to the knowledge, skills and abilities listed above, in accordance with a job crediting plan under FEC Personnel Instructions 300.1-A, Appointments & Promotions (Bargaining Unit Positions) and the FEC/NTEU Labor Management Agreement, Article 14. The current performance appraisal, documentation of job related awards or recognition received within the last 3 years, a submitted writing sample, as well as related education, training, and course work will also be used in the evaluation process. For current Federal employees, a copy of the most recent performance appraisal must be submitted. For former Federal employees, a copy of the last performance appraisal must be submitted along with the most recent Notification of Personnel Action (SF50) Applicants must submit a copy of their law school transcript; an unofficial copy is acceptable for the application package.

CONDITIONS OF EMPLOYMENT: Appointment to this position is contingent upon successful completion of the appropriate background investigation. Satisfactory completion of a one-year probationary period is also required. The position is a permanent full-time position. The incumbent will be entitled to life and health insurance, annual (vacation) and sick leave, and retirement benefits. Salary is typically set at the first step of the grade level for which selected. If selected at the GS-13 grade level, the starting salary would be $79,397 per year or GS-13 step 1. If selected at the GS-14 grade level, the starting salary would be $93,822 per year or GS-14 step 1. Highest previous rate will apply to Federal employees when setting initial salary. Based on superior qualifications, appointments may be made above the first step of grade with appropriate documentation and justification approved prior to appointment. The incumbent may be eligible for a transit subsidy up to $110 per month. The position has promotion potential to GS-14 that has a current salary range from $93,822 to $121,967. Selection at the GS-14 level requires exceptional qualifications based on determination by the selecting official. The

Commission's Office of General Counsel generally recommends initial appointment at the GS-13 level even if the applicant meets the basic qualifications for GS-14. However, as noted above, applicants initially appointed at the GS-13 level may be appointed above the first step of

GS-13 and as high as the tenth step. The current salary range for GS-13 is $79,397 to $103,220. Grade requirements and salary expectations may be discussed at time of interview. There is an 18-month review period before consideration for promotion to GS-14.

BARGAINING UNIT STATUS: This position is included in the bargaining unit and will be filled in accordance with the merit staffing provisions of the Labor Management Agreement between the Federal Election Commission and the National Treasury Employees Union, Article 14.

IMPORTANT NOTE
A resume, cover letter, one legal writing sample, and a copy of the applicant's law school transcript are sufficient to apply. Applicants are responsible for addressing the knowledge, skills and abilities section listed above in their resume, cover letter, or supplemental narrative.

All applications/resumes must be submitted to the Human Resources Office by the closing date. Postmarks are acceptable. However, applications postmarked by the closing date and received later than seven days after the closing date will not be forwarded for consideration unless the hiring office requests additional applications. Priority consideration will be given to applications received on a timely basis.

Since the anthrax attacks of October 2001, mail sent to federal agencies has been re-routed outside the Washington, D.C. area to be irradiated and inspected for biochemical substances. Since this may result in a delivery delay of your application package, it is recommended that applicants use e-mail, priority mail, or federal express to send applications. The e-mail address for this announcement is ogcjobs@fec.gov. The subject line must contain the announcement number, (i.e., Announcement 07-034) and the applicant's name. Applications may also be hand delivered. A drop off box is available in the agency's lobby.

HOW TO APPLY: Applicants may apply for this position with the *Optional Application for Federal Employment* (OF-612), the older *Application for Federal Employment* (SF-171), a resume, or other application format of their choice, as long as it contains the necessary information (summarized below) that will give in-depth information on the applicant's background. Applicants should also submit a law school transcript (an unofficial transcript is acceptable). Applicant must specify:

   (4) vacancy announcement number; title and grade(s) of the job for which applicant is applying;
   (5) social security number;
   (6) all relevant educational information, including college/university information: major, and type and year of degree(s). (If no degree, show total credits earned and indicate whether semester or quarter hours.);
   (7) Information about all work experience related to this job, including job titles, duties and accomplishments; employer's name and phone number; number of hours worked per week; starting and ending dates (month and year); annual salary, and reason for leaving;
   (8) Previous Federal civilian experience: indicate highest grade held, the job series, and dates held; Candidates with Federal service must also submit a *Notification of Personnel Action* (SF-50), showing grade and tenure, and a copy of the most recent Performance Appraisal;

   (9) Provide one legal writing sample.

The brochure *Applying for a Federal Job* provides information on the Federal job application process. It is available by calling the number listed below. Applicants whose resumes or applications do not provide all the information requested in the vacancy announcement may lose consideration for this job. Please forward all information to the Federal Election Commission, 999 E Street, NW, Washington, DC 20463. Attn: Human Resources, Room 500, Announcement Number 07-034. For additional information call LaThesia Jones at (202) 694-1080.
 Selectee will be required to complete Form I-9 per the Immigration and Control Act. Relocation expenses will not be paid by the FEC. FEC work areas are smoke free. FEC is an Equal Opportunity Employer.   FEC FORM 92-7 (rev 3/97)

The History of Personnel Reform

The purpose of this appendix is to provide a brief overview of the history of personnel reform as context for comprehensive transformation.

The foundation of the current federal civil service was the Civil Service Act of January 16, 1883, promulgated under President Chester A. Arthur. Before this, government positions were allocated to the supporters of the winning political party after each election in a "spoils" system. The act called for a merit-based civil service in response to the public's growing disgust with the governance issues and scandals caused by the spoils system, as in the case of the notorious Samuel Swartwout, collector of the Port of New York. Despite a proven shortfall of funds during his first term of office under President Andrew Jackson, Swartwout was reappointed under President Martin Van Buren and then took off for Europe with over $1,250,000 of government money.[1] The cost and size of the federal bureaucracy had grown excessively "in attempts to satisfy as many jobseekers as possible," and some positions were even held by absentees who "hired substitutes to do their 'work' at lower salaries."[2]

In 1871 President Ulysses Grant appointed the first Civil Service Commission to look into these and other abuses, and it offered the following recommendations:

—All positions should be classified into groups according to duties and into grades for purposes of promotion.

—Competitive examinations should be held for appointment to all positions within the lowest grade of each group.

—Promotion examinations could be used to fill positions in grades above the lowest.

—A sixth-month probationary period should follow appointment.

—Boards of examiners in each department could examine candidates and maintain lists of qualified applicants.[3]

In 1873, just as the first trials of some of the Grant Commission reforms were being implemented, those with a vested interest in the spoils system persuaded Congress to stop funding the commission. President Grant and his successor, President Rutherford B. Hayes, lobbied Congress to renew the funding, but to no avail.

Public concern about the system resurfaced after President James A. Garfield was shot by a frustrated job-seeker named Charles J. Guiteau. Guiteau believed he had been responsible for President Garfield's victory and in return expected a consulship at Paris.[4] The thought that the spoils system could be directly linked to President Garfield's death horrified the American public, and the resulting pressure for reform led to the Civil Service Act of 1883 (the Pendleton Act). It included the following significant provisions:

—Created the United States Civil Service Commission to develop the rules needed to implement the act; it was made up of three persons representing at least two parties, and they were to be appointed by the president, subject to confirmation by the Senate.

—Required open, competitive examinations for testing the fitness of applicants for the public service.

—Required federal positions to be arranged in classes and filled by selections according to grade from among those graded highest as a result of the competitive examinations.

—Required positions to be apportioned to residents of all the states and territories and the District of Columbia on the basis of population.

—Initiated a period of probation before any absolute appointment or employment.

—Forbade the coercion of any person in public service to contribute to any political fund or to render any political service.

—Forbade public officials from using their authority or influence to coerce the political action of any person or body.

The Office of Personnel Management (OPM) describes the Civil Service Act of 1883 as "a blueprint for a civil service America could respect and trust. Its basic principles, which have not changed in 120 years, have stood both the test of time and the transition of the United States from a pioneer society to one of the most complex in the world."[5] For the first time, merit was becoming the primary value in hiring and managing federal employees.

Initially, only 13,900 out of 132,800 (just over 10 percent) federal civil service positions fell under the new "competitive" system. By 1896, the figure had risen to 42 percent. Staunch support for reform came from President Theodore Roosevelt, who had served as a civil service commissioner from 1889 to 1895. He increased the number of classified positions to almost 64 percent of the federal workforce. By the end of President Herbert Hoover's term in 1932, 80 percent of federal civil positions were classified.[6]

Changes between 1920 and 1970

In the ninety-five years following the Civil Service Act of 1883, the federal personnel management system gradually evolved to meet the needs of government workers and their employer. This evolution was accomplished through new legislation, executive orders, and new rules developed by the Civil Service Commission. Major events in U.S. history, including the two world wars and the Great Depression, helped to shape this evolution. The federal reforms also gradually moved to state and local governments. Following are some highlights of that period.

Retirement Act (1920)

Once the merit-based system was in place, postelection dismissals subsided, and for the first time the government needed assistance in dealing with aging employees. The act mandated retirement ages by occupation; for instance, seventy for clerks, sixty-five for mechanics, and sixty-two for railway mail clerks. The act also provided a retirement/disability annuity plan to employees with a tenure of fifteen or more years. Every employee contributed 2.5 percent of his or her basic salary to the annuity fund. If the employee retired or was disabled before completing the fifteen years required to qualify for the annuity, the employee's contributions were refunded at 4 percent interest.[7]

Changes to the Retirement Act

In 1922 the act was updated to provide annuities to employees over the age of fifty-five and with a minimum of fifteen years of service, should they be involuntarily separated. In 1926 the value of the annuity was increased, the employee contribution percentage rose to 3.5 percent, and the law was altered to allow employees who reached the retirement age before completing fifteen years of service to remain in their positions until they completed their minimum term.

In 1930 the method for calculating the Retirement Act annuities was updated, the eligibility requirement for receiving a disability annuity decreased by five years, and early retirement of two years was offered to employees with thirty or more years of service.[8]

Additional tinkering between 1939 and 1948 granted survivorship benefits, allowed for additional voluntary contributions for the purchase of additional annuities, increased the number of federal employees eligible to participate in the program, and adjusted the various age and tenure requirements for receiving benefits.[9]

Additional changes in 1956 liberalized the calculation and payment of annuities. The employee contribution rate was increased to 6.5 percent, and the various government agencies were required to match their employees' contributions to the retirement fund.[10]

Classification Act of 1923

This act enshrined the principle of equal pay for equal work in federal law by classifying positions "in accordance with their duties and responsibilities, and assigned salaries to such positions."[11]

Hatch Act I (1939)

In a restatement of 1883 restrictions, the Hatch Act prohibited participation of executive branch employees in politics. The only people excepted from this regulation were "the President, Vice-President, employees of the Office of the President, heads and assistant heads of executive departments, and officials appointed by the President and confirmed by the Senate who determine foreign policy, or policy in the nationwide administration of Federal laws."[12]

Hatch Act II (1949)

An extension prohibited political activity by state and local employees whose "activities [were] financed in whole or in part by Federal loans or grants." The only people excepted from this regulation were "Governors, Lieutenant Governors, mayors, elected heads of departments whose positions were not under a merit system, and officers holding elective office."[13]

Ramspeck Act (1940)

The president was now allowed to make all executive branch positions part of the competitive service, except for positions with the Tennessee Valley Authority and the Work Projects Administration, presidential appointees confirmed by the Senate, and assistant U.S. district attorneys. This was important because in the years since 1883 many exceptions to competitive service had accumulated. This act made it possible to reclassify more than 180,000 permanent positions. President Franklin Delano Roosevelt made use of this new power.[14]

Veterans' Preference Act (1944)

The Veterans' Preference Act of 1944 benefited veterans by adding points to their examination scores, giving them work experience credit for time spent in the military, waiving various eligibility requirements and restrictions, and making it more difficult to remove them or lay them off.[15]

Fair Employment Board (1948)

The board was established "to consider appeals from decisions of agencies on complaints of discrimination."[16]

Classification Act (1949)

This act "established new and simplified schedules of grades and salaries; provided for three new grade levels at the top of the classification structure [the new 'supergrades' were GS-16, 17, and 18]; and delegated to each agency the authority to classify its own positions, below the three highest grades."[17]

Schedule C (1953)

President Dwight D. Eisenhower created a new category of federal employees to be exempted from competitive service "because of their confidential or policy-determining character."[18]

Incentive Awards Program (1954)

The new awards program made employees eligible for "cash for suggestions, cash for superior performance, and a variety of honorary awards."[19] According to OPM, "In the first 31 months of operation of the incentive awards program . . . more than $312 million in dollar value benefits accrued to the Government[,] . . . a return of nearly $20 in tangible benefits for every dollar invested in the incentive awards program."[20]

Government Employees Training Act (1958)

The act was designed to resolve ambiguities over who could and should provide training for federal employees. It authorized funds specifically for training and education, with the responsibility for employee development falling to different degrees on both the Civil Service Commission and the various federal agencies and departments. "The act recognized training and employee development as a new, strategic component of modern personnel management."[21]

Federal Employees Health Benefits Act (1959)

This legislation made group-rate, employer-subsidized health insurance available to the federal workforce for the first time. It helped the government compete with the private sector for employees. Some private firms had been offering health benefits since the 1930s.[22]

Federal Salary Reform Act (1962)

The act mandated that the salaries of federal employees should approximate the salaries of private sector employees in similar positions. It also established a methodology for the Bureau of Labor Statistics to use in determining private sector positions and salaries and matching them to federal positions. In addition, advancement was no longer a given; federal employees now had to prove a certain level of competence before they could move to the next grade level. If an employee was an outstanding performer, however, the employee's manager could accelerate advancement by allowing him or her to skip a step.[23]

Executive Order 10988 (1962)

This was the first consistent, government-wide approach to dealing with federal employee unions and affirmed the government's support of voluntary employee membership in unions and employee participation in the development of personnel policies. It required management to negotiate with unions through collective bargaining. However, it also provided conduct guidelines, set eligibility oversight, prohibited strikes and work stoppages, and included a national security override. Furthermore, unions were prohibited from negotiating over issues of "compensation and such management decisions as the work to be done, the budget, the organization, the staffing, and the internal security of organizational units."[24]

Executive Order 10987 (1962)

An appeals process was introduced for nonveteran employees to supplement the process established for veterans in the Veterans' Preference Act of 1944.[25]

Executive Order 11246 (1965)

This order buttressed a 1961 executive order eliminating discrimination from the federal civil service by requiring many more proactive efforts to eliminate discrimination at the agency level, including training programs, outreach to minority communities, and agency-by-agency plans and assessments.[26]

Executive Seminar Centers Program (1963) and Federal Executive Institute (1968)

The seminars program provided midlevel government managers with two-week training sessions on managerial and other needed skills. By 1971 there were three such centers around the country. The Federal Executive Institute initiated two-month education and training programs for government executives (who were then classified as GS-16, GS-17, and GS-18).[27]

Postal Reorganization Act (1970)

This act separated the postal service from the civil service system and removed the postal service from the oversight of the Civil Service Commission.[28]

Federal Pay Comparability Act (1970)

With this change, Congress was no longer required to pass new legislation each time a federal wage increase was necessary. Relying on the existing system for calculating private sector comparability, the president now issued an executive order each year to set pay schedules. Beginning with Richard Nixon, presidents rarely increased salaries by the full recommend amount, and the methodology was rarely used.[29]

The Modern Era of Federal Workforce Management

The modern era of civil service organization and management was ushered in with the Civil Service Reform Act of 1978 (CSRA). CSRA emerged from a desire to make the government more "efficient and businesslike."[30] To achieve this objective, President Jimmy Carter established the Personnel Management Project (PMP) as a component of his Reorganization Project. The intention of the PMP architects was to "modernize human resource management by streamlining the system through simplification and decentralization, to restructure for better management by replacing the Civil Service Commission, creating the Senior Executive Service, and to address such issues as productivity, job quality, workforce planning, recruiting, training, development, compensation and performance evaluation."[31]

The Carter team's good intentions were challenged by the political climate of the post-Watergate era. The public's suspicion of the government was compounded by a campaign for reform. Determined to overhaul what he called the "giant Washington Marshmallow," President Carter promised to clear out fraud, abuse, and underperforming civil servants who were too protected by their permanent status.[32] The PMP team took a radically different approach from that of the many previous commissions and panels that called for more rules and restrictions to keep the civil service insulated from politics. The PMP wanted to simplify the rules and restrictions to make the civil service more responsive to the priorities of the president.[33] As a result, the reforms negotiated represented a compromise between improved management and improved political responsiveness.[34]

Reorganization Plan No. 1, 1978

This attempt at overall reform gave complete authority for equal employment opportunity issues to the Equal Employment Opportunity Commission (EEOC). Discrimination appeals would be heard by both the EEOC and the Merit Systems Protection Board. The Civil Service Commission would no longer have a role in dealing with these issues.[35]

Reorganization Plan No. 2, 1978

Plan 2 took a significant step toward reform by abolishing the Civil Service Commission. The commission's responsibilities were then divided between the OPM and the Merit Systems Protection Board (MSPB). OPM would manage the federal civilian workforce and advise the president on federal civilian personnel issues. Note that this role was to consist of monitoring and advising. OPM was empowered to delegate the administrative role the Civil Service Commission had performed.[36] In another innovation, the director of OPM was to be a presidential appointee.

As a result, OPM had less of a "policing" job and more of a proactive planning and support role.[37] It also made OPM and the federal personnel system in general more responsive to presidential priorities.[38]

True to its name, the MSPB was to protect the merit systems underpinning the civil service from political interference. It was also charged with hearing employee appeals. The MSPB was thus given power to issue subpoenas, initiate disciplinary action, and impose fines. The MSPB was also given an Office of Special Counsel that was charged with protecting whistleblowers and investigating claims of abuse and prohibited practices.[39]

Civil Service Reform Act of 1978

The Civil Service Reform Act of 1978 introduced several key changes:

Senior Executive Service. The Senior Executive Service (SES) was created to replace the "supergrades" in the General Schedule (GS-16, GS-17, and GS-18) and the executive service levels IV and V. These grades comprised the government's senior managers—the layer of employees directly under the political appointees (in fact, up to 10 percent of the SES could be political appointees). Structurally, the SES was to have six pay levels, but no grades, and was not part of the competitive service. The total number of employees in SES positions was to be limited, although OPM was allowed to adjust that number. Most notably, rank in the SES was tied to the person, not to the position, as in the previous system. This structure would make members "more mobile, transferring their managerial skill and expertise to other programs and even other agencies if their political supervisors deemed that appropriate."[40]

The belief was that good managers would be able to work in any environment and quickly pick up the domain's expertise. However, it also meant that the president and his political appointees could transfer a member of the SES to a backwater position if they were displeased with his or her performance. An added risk to government managers was that they could lose their SES status if they were judged to be less than fully successful in their annual performance evaluation.[41] As compensation for these risks and demands, SES members were given high base pay and were eligible to earn performance rewards from their agency or the president. The presidential awards went up to $20,000 and were given out to no more than 1 percent of SES members a year.

Merit Pay. Under CSRA, midlevel managers (grades GS-13, GS-14, and GS-15) were also eligible for performance bonuses. The within-grade salary step increases were abolished for these grades. That money was then used to pay merit bonuses based on annual performance appraisals and ratings. All employees were eligible to earn cash awards for "suggestions, inventions, superior accomplishments, or improvements for governmental operations or . . . special acts or services."[42] With presidential approval, these awards could go as high as $25,000.

Performance Appraisal. The CSRA required each department and agency to develop a new performance appraisal system for employees outside of the SES and GS-13, GS-14, and GS-15 grades, to be negotiated between each supervisor and employee. This reform was intended to increase the importance of performance appraisals, increase responsiveness to managerial directives, and fulfill President Carter's pledge to increase the accountability of individual civil servants.[43] The act also revised the process for bringing and appealing adverse actions, making it easier for managers to remove or demote poor performers.

Research and Development Authority. The OPM was given research and development authority so it could assess new approaches to personnel management in controlled experiments. OPM was empowered to run up to ten demonstration projects at any one time.

Labor Relations and Collective Bargaining. The act's most controversial provisions pertained to labor relations and preference for veterans. The vague language of the labor relations section—made all the more complex by the inability of the unions and Carter officials to effect a compromise—was difficult to interpret. In the final legislation, most of the text replicated the executive orders on labor relations issued since 1962. The key addition was the judicial review of orders issued by the Federal Labor Relations Authority.[44]

Veterans' Preference. The original draft of the CSRA attempted to weaken veterans' preference by proposing time limits on the hiring and reduction-of-force preference for nondisabled veterans. This was scaled back in the final legislation to apply only to those veterans who retired at a rank above major.[45]

The CSRA was difficult to implement. The task of developing performance appraisal processes for 2.3 million people was enormous, as was the SES conversion. Changes in the bonus structure and the "bureaucrat bashing" of the first Reagan administration are two of the factors blamed for the loss of 50 percent of the original members of the SES within the first three years.[46] In addition, the assumption that a government manager could manage equally well in any department or agency proved inaccurate. The mobility management model did not work because government managers tended to be domain specialists, not management specialists.[47]

The merit pay provisions also suffered in implementation. OPM reviews found that merit pay was not motivating individual employees or increasing organizational effectiveness.[48] Within three years, these provisions would be replaced by the Performance Management and Review System (PMRS).

Douglas A. Brook, a former acting director of OPM and editor of *The Future of Merit: Twenty Years after the Civil Service Reform Act*, gives this appraisal of CSRA:

> By [its tenth anniversary], the general conclusion was that CSRA had fallen short of its loftiest objectives. Though CSRA had been successfully implemented as a personnel management system, achievement of its higher goals of greater efficiency and effectiveness, and improved government performance had been less successful. . . . Once the centerpiece of CSRA reform, the SES may now be its greatest disappointment. Beset by early problems in the areas of pay and performance bonuses, conflicting images and objectives, and the political turmoil of a change in administration, the SES did not have a successful launch. . . . The SES continues to be dominated more by technical experts than generalist managers, and the anticipated mobility . . . has failed to materialize.[49]

Presidential Management Intern Program

Another initiative from the same period was the Presidential Management Intern Program (PMI), now known as the Presidential Management Fellows Program (PMF). This program was intended to help the government recruit young, talented, and well-educated people to government service. During their two-year internship, recipients were allowed to rotate through various positions to become exposed to the government's various opportunities. The program has been highly successful and has grown from the original 200 interns a year to 400.

Navy China Lake

Navy China Lake, instituted in 1980 at two naval research laboratories in California, was the first demonstration project under the research and development provisions of CSRA. Originally expected to last for five years, it was extended twice, then made permanent in 1994. The project had 7,600 employees.

The objective was "to create flexible management systems, to give managers more discretion in using those systems, and to reward employees who perform exceptionally well."[50] It was to be a demonstration of "a complete performance evaluation, position classification, and pay for performance system that is designed to give increased responsibility and authority for personnel management to line managers."[51]

China Lake introduced five key innovations: (1) it replaced the General Schedule grades and pay rates with broad pay bands linked to five career paths (professional, technical, administrative, technical assistant, and clerical specialist); (2) made starting salaries within pay bands flexible; (3) replaced fixed-step rates and pay progression with earning "performance-based increments" that adjust base salary and lump-sum bonus payments; (4) made the performance assessment more flexible; and (5) gave line managers the authority to classify positions. In the navy's view,

> Both Demo labs have been more successful in recruitment and retention than have the two control labs. In addition, satisfaction with supervision, performance evaluation, promotion opportunities, and general organizational climate has increased significantly among employees at the Demo labs, slightly among GS employees at the control labs, and not at all for control lab GM [GS-13 and higher] employees. The perceived link between pay and performance increased significantly among employees at the Demo labs, while GM employees at the control labs reported no increase in this link.[52]

The GAO has countered that the project was expensive, however, with salaries permitted to increase approximately 1 percent per year, an escalation unlikely to be repeated throughout government.[53]

The President's Private Sector Survey on Cost Control (The Grace Commission)

When President Ronald Reagan arrived in Washington in 1981, he promised to reduce the size and cost of government. His first step was to create the President's Private Sector Survey on Cost Control, also known as the Grace Commission after its chairman, J. Peter Grace, CEO of W. R. Grace. The commission's extensive report (47 volumes and 21,000 pages) concluded that billions of dollars in waste and fraud could be saved by adopting private sector business practices.[54]

Performance Management and Recognition System (PMRS)

As previously mentioned, the merit pay provisions of CSRA left many midlevel managers dissatisfied. In the Performance Management and Recognition System approved in 1984, Congress attempted to reverse the decentralization under CSRA by creating a centralized performance appraisal system with a standardized number of performance levels.[55] The PMRS structure more closely mirrored the General Schedule pay progression schedule by providing the automatic annual general or comparability increase to employees who received performance ratings above fully successful. These employees could also compete for merit increases and performance awards and bonuses.[56]

However, PMRS was judged unsuccessful and was terminated in 1993, with the midlevel managers folded back into the regular GS system. Like CSRA, the

PMRS did not provide large enough incentive/performance awards to improve employee efficiency and productivity.[57] Thus the PMRS was criticized for increasing system costs without a comparable increase in performance.

Federal Employees Retirement System (1987)

The Federal Employees Retirement System was established in response to widespread concerns about the Civil Service Retirement System (CSRS) in place since 1920. In the main, the CSRS was said to have become an unfunded liability of a half trillion dollars as a result of its growing generosity over the years. Furthermore, these retirement benefits were not portable, so if a federal employee wanted to move to the private sector, he or she would stand to lose significant retirement savings. As a result, employees who would have preferred to leave government service stayed on until retirement. Finally, the public was suspicious of CSRS. Could the public really trust the Social Security System if the people who wrote, signed, administered, and oversaw the program did not participate in it? Why was it not also good enough for members of Congress, the president, and civil servants? This suspicion only increased as questions about the long-term sustainability of the Social Security System became a topic of public debate.[58]

FERS offered federal employees a retirement benefit with three components: (1) Social Security benefits, (2) a basic benefits plan, and (3) a Thrift Savings plan. The Social Security benefit is very familiar to most Americans. The only difference in FERS is that it pays retirees a Special Retirement Supplement if they retire before they are eligible for Social Security (age 62). This supplement approximates the Social Security benefit the employee will be entitled to at the qualifying age.[59]

The second component, the basic benefits plan, is a defined benefit plan funded through government contributions and minimal employee contributions. The third component, the Thrift Savings Plan (TSP), is a tax-deferred retirement savings and investment plan not unlike the 401(k) plans offered to private sector employees.[60] Under TSP, the government automatically contributes 1 percent of base pay annually to an individual's account and matches employee contributions up to designated percentages of base pay.

A 1998 study by the Congressional Budget Office found FERS more generous than most private sector retirement plans. It also found that "for most of the hypothetical employees compared, retirement benefits under FERS have a much higher value than under CSRS."[61]

National Commission on the Public Service (Volcker Commission)

The first National Commission on the Public Service, also known as the first Volcker Commission, was convened to study the growing difficulty of attracting the best and the brightest of America's young professionals to government service. The resulting report, "Leadership for America: Rebuilding the Public Service," summarized the problem as follows: "Too many of our most talented public servants—those with the skills and dedication that are the hallmarks of an effective career service—are ready to leave. Too few of our brightest young people—those with the imagination and energy that are essential for the future—are willing to join."[62]

The report's recommendations focused on three topics: leadership, talent, and performance. Talent, it said, could be acquired if the president and Congress worked to rebuild the public trust in government, eliminate obstacles that hinder attracting talented appointees, make more room for career executives at departments and agencies, give departments and agencies more flexibility in managing personnel and programs, and encourage strong partnerships between career executives and presidential appointees.[63] The commission also recommended that educational institutions and the president develop student awareness and educational training for public service, develop new channels for communicating the opportunities in government service, enhance recruiting efforts and simplify the hiring process, and increase minority representation in public careers.[64] With respect to performance, the commission recommended that the public and its leaders build a competitive and fair pay system, rebuild OPM to give it the strength and mandate it needs, set higher goals for government performance and productivity, provide more effective training and executive development, and improve government working conditions.[65]

Federal Employees Pay Compatibility Act of 1990 (FEPCA)

The Volcker Report's concern about the competitiveness of federal pay was echoed in other quarters:

> A 1987 General Accounting Office survey found that over 60 percent of the SES ranks reported dissatisfaction with pay. The same year, a Congressional Research Service report noted that compensation for the top SES officials lagged behind the private sector by 65 percent. In February 1988, the President's Commission on the Compensation of Career Federal Executives revealed that SES pay had not even kept pace with inflation since 1979. Still, in February 1989, Congress voted down a Reagan administration proposal to increase executive, legislative, and judicial pay.[66]

In the wake of Navy China Lake's lessons and the recommendations of various studies and commissions, the Federal Employees Pay Compatibility Act of 1990 endeavored to develop a fair and competitive way to compensate federal employees. It provided several significant innovations:

> Locality pay, which allows the Government to pay employees at the same grade level different rates of pay based on local labor market conditions in major metropolitan areas.

> An annual pay adjustment process designed to close the overall disparity between Federal and non-Federal pay over a 9-year period.

> Discretionary authority to pay recruitment and relocation bonuses and retention allowances (the "3 Rs") of up to 25 percent of basic pay.

Discretionary authority to pay travel and transportation expense for new hires.

A new pay authority for positions deemed "critical."

New pay systems for administrative law judges and other senior-level employees.

Time off as an incentive award.

Establishment of a committee to study the relationship between pay and performance.

Special pay rates and geographic pay adjustments for law enforcement officers.[67]

The National Performance Review (NPR)

The goal of the National Performance Review, said President Bill Clinton, was "to make the entire Federal Government both less expensive and more efficient, and to change the culture of our national bureaucracy away from complacency and entitlement toward initiative and empowerment. We intend to redesign, to reinvent, to reinvigorate the entire National Government."[68] The team assembled for this task was led by Vice President Al Gore and staffed primarily by career civil servants. President Clinton asked the team to develop a "list of very specific actions we can take now, agency by agency, program by program" within six months.[69] The resulting first NPR report, completed in September 1993, contained 384 recommendations centered on four objectives:
—Cutting red tape
—Putting customers first
—Empowering employees to get results
—Getting back to basics; producing better government for less.
As Patricia Wallace Ingraham notes in *The Foundation of Merit: Public Service in American Democracy,* "Some of these principles or objectives are reminiscent of past reforms; the idea of cutting red tape is certainly not new, nor is that of reducing the cost of government. Empowering employees, on the other hand, directly confronts the tenets of earlier reforms."[70]

However, the NPR team knew its work was not finished: "After the initial report, the NPR team undertook the implementation of the many recommendations, then conducted a second round of reviews in 1995. In the second Clinton-Gore term, NPR changed its mission, approach—and name—to focus on leading a fundamental culture change in the government."[71] All in all, NPR became an eight-year reform effort.

The results of this effort are difficult to quantify because of the complexity and interconnectedness of government operations. For instance, in assessing NPR savings, the GAO found "NPR claimed that about $137 billion in savings has resulted from its efforts to reinvent the federal government, with about $44.3 billion of these savings claimed from recommendations that were targeted toward individual agencies. We reviewed six recommendations representing over two-thirds of this $44.3 billion, and found that the relationship between the NPR recommendations and the savings claims was not clear."[72]

That said, it is widely agreed that NPR made significant contributions to the operations of the federal government. The following are some of the contributions attributed to NPR:

Ending the era of big government by cutting both its size and costs;

Changing government to be more results- and performance-oriented;

Serving the public better;

Changing the ways government works with businesses;

Changing the way government works with communities;

Transforming access to government through technology; and

Making the federal government a better place to work.[73]

1993 Government Performance and Results Act (GPRA)

The 1993 act was designed to increase the performance and accountability of the federal government. Although not the first attempt of this nature, it was the first to achieve legal standing. Today, almost all agencies and departments must comply with GPRA requirements.

GPRA was also unique in its focus on mission: "GPRA sought to shift the focus of Government decision-making and accountability away from a preoccupation with the activities that are undertaken—such as grants dispensed or inspections made—to a focus on the results of those activities, such as real gains in employability, safety, responsiveness, or program quality."[74]

GPRA included strategic plans with a span of at least five years outlining "general goals and objectives, including outcome-related goals and objectives, for the major functions and operations of the agency," along with annual performance plans and reports with performance goals expressed in "an objective, quantifiable, and measurable form."[75]

GPRA heralded a new era of accountability. As Patricia Wallace Ingraham and Donald P. Moynihan note in their study of the act, it marked "the enactment of an individually based, confidential method of accountability, where the accountability measures and appraisal were largely a matter between the manager and employee. The accountability elements associated with GPRA are organizational and very public. . . . This accountability model has . . . enhanced the influence of Congress and other stakeholders whom agencies are obliged to consult when formulating strategic plans."[76]

In our view, GPRA was the big sleeper legislation of the 1990s. It seemed to sneak past the watchful eyes of agency leaders that typically would have raised questions about the resources required to meet its mandates, because many of its requirements did not take effect until several years after it was signed into law. Only much later did the agencies begin to realize the scope of GPRA's implications.

Moreover, few realized how much power the new legislation would give to Congress. Now that agencies had to report on strategy, budget, and performance measures, Congress could suddenly see much more clearly what the agencies were achieving with their congressionally appropriated funds. This had the potential to greatly facilitate oversight.

We believe GPRA has been a vital factor in modernizing U.S. government performance and accountability. Combined with procurement reform and the CFO Act, it has brought the operations of the U.S. government into the twenty-first century. The focus on mission and measurable progress has permeated government thinking. And although much work is left to do in order to realize the full vision of GPRA, especially in the area of strategic human capital reform, GPRA has pushed government toward greater responsibility.

FAA Demonstration Project

The new emphasis on performance and accountability led some agencies and departments to protest various personnel rules that were viewed as restricting their success. In the case of the Federal Aviation Administration (FAA), management was concerned that the inflexibility of Title V of the United States Code, which governs federal civilian personnel management, was constraining "the agency's ability to be responsive to the airline industry's needs and to increase productivity in air traffic control operations."[77]

To test whether exemptions from Title V would give the FAA the flexibility to better meet its objectives, the agency embarked on a demonstration project in 1996 with the focus on (1) compensation and performance management, (2) workforce management, and (3) labor and employee relations.[78]

The first category of changes required Title V exemptions to create a more flexible pay system with broad pay bands and a performance management system that provided employees with frequent feedback instead of summary ratings. With respect to workforce management, the FAA engaged in a comprehensive workforce planning effort. This did not require any exemptions, but some were necessary to develop an independent hiring process. As for labor and employee relations, the FAA established "new groups to represent unions and employees and a new policy initiative to promote diversity and an open work environment."[79] This change did not require exemptions.

When the GAO evaluated the progress of the FAA reforms in 2003, it found, first and foremost, that the reforms were not yet fully implemented. Second, FAA had not collected the data needed to determine if the reforms were effective. GAO's criticism of the FAA clearly echoed the philosophies of NPR and GPRA:

> FAA's lack of empirical data on the effects of its human capital initiatives is one indication that it has not fully incorporated elements that are important to effective human capital management into its overall reform effort. These elements include data collection and analysis, performance goals and

measures, and linkage of reform goals to program goals . . . FAA has also not gone far enough in establishing linkage between reform goals and over-all program goals of the organization.[80]

The GAO also found that "nearly two-thirds of those responding to our struc-tured interview (110 of 176) disagreed or strongly disagreed that the new pay sys-tem is fair to all employees."[81] It was later noted that "dissatisfaction appears to have had dramatic repercussions. For example, since 1995, when legislation was passed giving FAA new personnel authorities, the percentage of employees join-ing unions has increased from 63 percent to 80 percent."[82]

IRS Modernization

The story of the Internal Revenue Service (IRS) in the 1980s up to the late 1990s was one of inefficiency, taxpayer abuse, and repeated failure to reform. The IRS touched 132 million individual taxpayers and 6 million business taxpayers each year. It employed 100,000 people and collected 90 percent of government rev-enue.[83] Its problems were of a high-profile and highly politicized nature.

As Charles O. Rossotti, the commissioner who led the modernization of the IRS in the late 1990s, observed: "The agency needed to be reorganized from top to bottom. . . . This huge reorganization required eliminating and refilling more than two thousand executive and senior management jobs and cutting manage-ment layers and several hundred of these jobs along the way."[84]

After grim congressional hearings into IRS operations and abuses in the fall of 1997 and spring of 1998, Commissioner Rossotti and his team, congressional leaders, and the National Commission on Restructuring the Internal Revenue Ser-vice (the Kerry-Portman Commission) negotiated legislation to modernize and reform the IRS. The IRS Restructuring and Reform Act of 1998 passed the House of Representatives by a vote of 402 to 8.

As part of the act, the IRS, like the FAA before it, was given exemptions to var-ious parts of Title V. Professors James R. Thompson and Hal G. Rainey provide a useful summary of the flexibilities received from these exemptions:

Critical pay authority, to hire up to 40 individuals at a salary not to exceed that of the Vice President of the United States.

Workforce shaping tools, including buyouts and early retirement authority.

Streamlined demonstration project authority, waiving some of the restric-tions that generally apply to personnel demonstration projects.

Authority to assign employees to pay bands whereby pay would be deter-mined according to qualifications and performance rather than longevity.

Authority to rate prospective employees by "category" rather than by strict numerical score, giving managers greater flexibility in hiring.[85]

These flexibilities, say Thompson and Rainey, were "critical to the success" of the overall IRS modernization. They also highlight an important factor that allowed the IRS to use these flexibilities effectively: knowledgeable, effective, and engaged leaders who provided a clear vision of the future and a strategy for moving forward.[86]

The modernization of the IRS has turned one of the most vilified organizations in the United States into one that is widely viewed as a modern, fair, and positive model for change in government.

New Rules for a New Agency: The Department of Homeland Security

The terrorist attacks of September 11, 2001, had an enormous effect on the administration of President George W. Bush. One consequence was the creation of the Department of Homeland Security (DHS). And for the first time in many years, there was a public discussion about the role of civilian federal workers in protecting the United States and its citizens, as well as the federal human capital management system in which they work.

In the draft legislation to create DHS, the Bush administration proposed overhauling Title V to create a new human resources management system for the agency. The stated purpose of this new system was to create a mission-centered, performance-focused, flexible, contemporary system that would generate trust and respect through employee involvement and that would be based on the principles of merit and fairness.

If implemented, the new system would have waived and replaced various statutory provisions of Title V that would otherwise be applicable to DHS employees. For instance, the proposed rules limited the scope of union bargaining, instituted a pay-for-performance system, facilitated the disciplining of poor performers, limited third-party oversight of employee appeals, and reorganized employees into clusters by professional group and broad pay bands within those clusters.[87]

The clash between labor unions, Democrats, and Republicans over the proposal was fierce and was widely blamed for stalling passage of the legislation. The labor unions fought implementation at every step to prevent an anticipated rise in cronyism and loss of annual pay increases, among other complaints. The unions successfully blocked implementation of rules in the new system that would allow senior-level officials to override collective bargaining agreements in federal court.[88] The unions have also managed to work with members of Congress to limit funding for the implementation of the new system. Despite these challenges, the DHS is slowly proceeding with implementation of the new system (excluding the elements blocked by court order).

National Security Personnel System

In 2004 Congress granted the Bush administration the authority to reform the human resources system of the Department of Defense (DOD). It argued that the Title V regulations covering civilian employees at DOD were "too rigid and outdated to respond with agility to modern threats of terrorism."[89] The new National Security Personnel System (NSPS) closely mirrored the regulations proposed for DHS. Not surprisingly, labor unions have been successful in blocking the implementation of the labor relations elements of the regulations through challenges in federal court.[90] However, responding to additional union complaints, the federal judge also blocked implementation of the adverse action and appeals sections of NSPS, a major setback to the initiative.[91] Also like DHS, the DOD is having trouble getting adequate funding appropriated for implementing NSPS.

Working for America Act

In November 2005 the Bush administration unveiled a preliminary proposal for new personnel reform legislation. The Working for America Act (WFAA) was designed to take pay-for-performance reforms similar to those introduced at DHS and DOD to the rest of the federal civilian workforce. The difficulty in implementing the reforms at DHS and DOD slowed the momentum on WFAA, and progress all but ended with the 2007 court decisions affecting DHS and DOD. The difficulties encountered in these cases may be instructive for future reforms.

U.S. Government Merit Principles

United States Office of Personnel Management
SECTION 2301, TITLE 5, UNITED STATES CODE

§ 2301. Merit system principles

(a) This section shall apply to—

(1) an Executive agency; and

(2) the Government Printing Office.

(b) Federal personnel management should be implemented consistent with the following merit system principles:

(1) Recruitment should be from qualified individuals from appropriate sources in an endeavor to achieve a work force from all segments of society, and selection and advancement should be determined solely on the basis of relative ability, knowledge and skills, after fair and open competition which assures that all receive equal opportunity.

(2) All employees and applicants for employment should receive fair and equitable treatment in all aspects of personnel management without regard to political affiliation, race, color, religion, national origin, sex, marital status, age, or handicapping condition, and with proper regard for their privacy and constitutional rights.

(3) Equal pay should be provided for work of equal value, with appropriate consideration of both national and local rates paid by employers in the private sector, and appropriate incentives and recognition should be provided for excellence in performance.

(4) All employees should maintain high standards of integrity, conduct, and concern for the public interest.

(5) The Federal work force should be used efficiently and effectively.

(6) Employees should be retained on the basis of adequacy of their performance, inadequate performance should be corrected, and employees should be separated who cannot or will not improve their performance to meet required standards.

(7) Employees should be provided effective education and training in cases in which such education and training would result in better organizational and individual performance.

(8) Employees should be—

(A) protected against arbitrary action, personal favoritism, or coercion for partisan political purposes, and

(B) prohibited from using their official authority or influence for the purpose of interfering with or affecting the result of an election or a nomination for election.

(9) Employees should be protected against reprisal for the lawful disclosure of information which the employees reasonably believe evidences—

(A) a violation of any law, rule, or regulation, or

(B) mismanagement, a gross waste of funds, an absence of authority, or a substantial and specific danger to public health or safety.

(c) In administering the provisions of this chapter—

(1) with respect to any agency (as defined in section 2302(a)(2)(C) of this title), the President shall, pursuant to the authority otherwise available under this title, take any action including the issuance of rules, regulations, or directives; and

(2) with respect to any entity in the executive branch which is not such an agency or part of such an agency, the head of such entity shall, pursuant to authority otherwise available, take any action, including the issuance of rules, regulations, or directives; which is consistent with the provisions of this title and which the President or the head, as the case may be, determines is necessary to ensure that personnel management is based on and embodies the merit system principles.

Notes

Chapter One

1. Since the subject of this book is the strategic human capital of the federal government, the term "the government" refers to the federal government throughout unless otherwise noted.

2. Based on the financial analysis of total shareholder returns from 1980 to 2005, conducted by Linda Bilmes, Peter Strüven, and Konrad Wetzker for Boston Consulting Group.

3. In 2007 federal expenditures totaled $2.7 trillion, approximately 20 percent of the nation's GDP. Total government spending, including state and local government, is about 28 percent of GDP. Over the past twenty years, federal government spending has averaged 20.9 percent of GDP (Congressional Budget Office [CBO], Budget and Economic Outlook, January 2008, table F-2).

4. The Government Accountability Office identified each of these challenges in its 2005 report, *21st Century Challenges: Reexamining the Base of the Federal Government,* GAO-05-325SP (Government Printing Office, February 2005). For a detailed examination of federal policy toward science and research, see the National Academy of Sciences, National Academy of Engineering, Institute of Medicine, National Research Council, *Preparing for the 21st Century: Science and Engineering Research in a Changing World* (Washington, 1997).

5. Stephen Goldsmith, Daniel Paul Professor of Government and Director of the Innovations in American Government Program at Harvard University's Kennedy School, interview by authors, November 10, 2005.

6. Admiral James Loy, Cohen Group, interview by authors, October 3, 2005. For a complete list of individuals interviewed by the authors, see appendix C.

7. Ronald Coase, "The Nature of the Firm," *Economica* 4 (November 1937).

8. Bob Welch, partner, Acquisition Solutions, Inc., interview by authors, June 8, 2006.

9. Paul C. Light, *A Government Ill Executed* (Harvard University Press, May 2008).

10. Committee on Oversight and Government Reform, "Summary of New Defense Department IG Report," memorandum, May 22, 2007.

11. U.S. Patent and Trademark Office, *U.S. Patent Statistics Chart, Calendar Years 1963–2007* (Government Printing Office [GPO], April 3, 2008).

12. U.S. Patent and Trademark Office, *Performance and Accountability Report Fiscal Year 2006: Management's Discussion and Analysis* (GPO, December 18, 2006).

13. Linda Bilmes, "Soldiers Returning from Iraq and Afghanistan: The Long-Term Costs of Providing Veterans Medical Care and Disability Benefits," Kennedy School Working Paper RWP07-001 (Harvard University, January 2007).

14. Ibid.

15. Loy, interview, October 3, 2005.

16. U.S. Census Bureau, *2007 Statistical Abstract.* For total U.S. population, see www.census.gov/popest/estimates.php; for total federal civilian workers, see CBO, *Characteristics and Pay of Federal Civilian Employees,* March 2007.

17. Light, *A Government Ill Executed.*

18. Data from the U.S. Advisory Commission on Intergovernmental Relations, *Significant Features of Fiscal Federalism,* vol. 2 (Washington, 1994); and U.S. Census Bureau, *Historical Statistics of the United States,* Series Y189-198 (GPO, 1975).

19. On the "shadow government," see Paul C. Light, *The True Size of Government* (Brookings, 1999).

20. Office of Personnel Management (OPM), "Employment and Trends" (www.opm.gov/feddata/html/2007/september/table1.asp [September 2007]).

21. Some of the material in this section originally appeared in Linda J. Bilmes and Jeffrey R. Neal, "The People Factor: Human Resources Reform in Government," in *For the People: Can We Fix Public Service?* edited by John D. Donahue and Joseph P. Nye (Brookings, 2003).

22. There have been two National Commissions on the Public Service, both chaired by former chair of the Federal Reserve Paul A. Volcker. The first convened in 1988 (the first Volcker Commission) and released its report, *Rebuilding the Public Service,* in 1989. The second Volcker Commission released its report, *Urgent Business for America: Revitalizing the Federal Government for the 21st Century,* on January 7, 2003.

23. Title V, U.S. Code, "Government Organization and Employees," was enacted by PL 89-554, sec. 1, on September 6, 1966. Title V and its amendments cover federal civil service functions and responsibilities.

24. The Classification Act of 1949 mandated equal pay for equal work. In order to implement this, the act introduced the principle of classifying job series.

25. OPM, *Handbook of Occupational Groups and Families* (www.opm.gov/fedclass/gshbkocc.pdf [January 2008]).

26. Bilmes and Neal, "The People Factor," p. 118.

27. Claudia Cross, chief human capital officer and human resources director, U.S. Department of Energy, interview by authors, September 26, 2005.

28. OPM, "Federal Human Capital Survey," 2004 (www.fhcs2004.opm.gov/).

29. Ibid.

30. Paul C. Light, "What Federal Workers Want from Reform," *Reform Watch Brief 5* (Brookings, March 2002).

31. Participants in the Kennedy School program for senior executives (SES, GS-14, and GS-15 levels) cited this issue as one of the main reasons that they oppose government reforms in the Defense and Homeland Security Departments. Participants said that their supervisors were unwilling or unable to discipline poor performers, and that this situation was demotivating and frustrating for everyone else.

32. Elaine Kamarck, lecturer in public policy, Belfer Center for Science and International Affairs at Harvard University, interview by authors, October 3, 2005.

33. Light, "What Federal Workers Want from Reform."

34. A survey of federal agencies commissioned by Senator George Voinovich (R-Ohio) found that from fiscal 1997 through 2000, responding agencies said they spent an average of 1.99 percent of their payroll on training, compared with an average of 3.6 percent among private sector companies that have been recognized for training excellence. In fact, Senator Voinovich reportedly had considered adding language creating a budget line-item for agency training costs in the Federal Workforce Improvement Act (S. 2651) but decided not to do so after being told by agency managers that the provision could backfire by allowing congressional appropriators to target agency training funds for elimination. See Michael Dovilla, member of the Senate Governmental Affairs Subcommittee on Oversight of Government Management, Restructuring, and the District of Columbia, remarks to a meeting of American University's Institute for the Study of Public Policy Implementation, Washington, October 29, 2002 (www.american.edu/spa/isppi/news/oct2902clipping.pdf).

35. Brenda Sprague, "International Opinion," *Training Journal,* February 2004; and "Skills Shortage to Drive Training Budget Increases," *Human Resources Development Guide,* April 26, 2004.

36. CBO, "Comparing the Pay of Federal and Nonfederal Law Enforcement Officers," August 2005 (www.cbo.gov/ftpdocs/66xx/doc6619/08-23-LawEnforcementPay.pdf).

37. Stephen Barr, "Federal Law Enforcement Pay, Benefits in Need of Overhaul, Report Says," *Washington Post,* October 26, 2005, reporting on a twenty-five-page paper prepared by staff of House and Senate subcommittees chaired by Senator George Voinovich and Representatives Thomas Davis (R-Virginia) and Jon Porter (R-Nevada).

38. The National Commission on the Public Service, January 7, 2003.

39. GAO, "Human Capital: Preliminary Observations on Final Department of Homeland Security Human Capital Regulations," GAO-05-320T (Washington, February 10, 2005).

40. Jonathan Walters, "Life after Civil Service Reform," IBM Center for the Business of Government, Washington, October 2002.

41. Doris Hausser, interview by authors, October 3, 2005.

42. The National Security Personnel System (NSPS) would enable DOD scientists to adjust pay.

43. "NSPS Modernizes a Fifty-Year-Old Civil Service System, Allowing DOD to Better Attract, Recruit, Retain, Compensate, Reward, and Manage Employees" (http://www.cpms.osd.mil/nsps/whatisnsps.html). See also GAO and National Commission for the Public Service, "Human Capital: Principles, Criteria, and Processes for Governmentwide Federal Human Capital Reform," GAO-05-69SP (Washington, December 2004).

44. Light, "What Federal Workers Want from Reform."

45. By one estimate, the tenure of political appointees lasts eleven to twenty months. See Cheryl Y. Marcum and others, "Department of Defense Political Appointments: Positions and Process" (Santa Monica, Calif.: RAND, 2001). According to another estimate, "the average tenure of presidential political appointees has been steadily declining and is now barely 14 months." See Thomas Mann and Norman Ornstein, "After the Campaign, What? Governance Questions for the 2000 Election," *Brookings Review* 18 (Winter 2000).

46. Light, "What Federal Workers Want from Reform."

47. The phrase "demography is destiny" is usually attributed to nineteenth-century French philosopher and mathematician Auguste Comte, though there are no primary sources to back this attribution.

48. Partnership for Public Service (PPS), "Federal Brain Drain," Issue Brief PPS-05-08 (November 21, 2005).

49. Ibid.

50. Office of Personnel Management (OPM), *2004 Demographic Profile of the Federal Workforce* (GPO, September 30, 2004).

51. OPM, *Fact Book 2005, Senior Executive Service—Member Profile* (GPO, February 2006).

52. Ibid.

53. Ibid.

54. PPS, "Federal Brain Drain."

55. Ibid.

56. "High-three" salary is the average salary for the three consecutive years in which the employee's salary was highest. Employees receive maximum pension benefits of 80 percent after forty-one years, eleven months, of service. Employees covered by CSRS receive life and health insurance benefits, survivor annuities, and annual cost-of-living adjustments. They are not eligible for Social Security. Employees hired after 1984 are enrolled in the Federal Employees Retirement System (FERS), a modern "defined contribution" plan with Social Security, a smaller pension, and a Thrift Savings Plan, which is similar to a 401(k). The pension is equal to 1 percent of the employee's "high-three" salary average multiplied by the years of federal employment. The amount increased to 1.1 percent for employees retiring at age sixty-two or older. The minimum retirement age for FERS employees ranges from fifty-five for employees born in 1958 or earlier to fifty-seven for employees born in 1970 or later. Approximately 32 percent of government employees are now covered by CSRS, including most senior executives, and 68 percent are under FERS.

57. Government retiree health benefits pay an average of 70 percent of monthly health care premiums for retirees and their families for the rest of their lives at top-tier insurers such as Blue Cross/Blue Shield. Given the rate of inflation in health care, this benefit is rising in value faster than the rate of the annuity payments.

58. OPM, "Should I Switch to FERS?" See also the FERS Transfer Handbook (GPO, 2003) (www.opm.gov/fers_election/fersh/h_fers3.htm).

59. OPM, *2004 Retirement Statistics Report* (www.opm.gov/feddata/retire/rs2004.pdf).

60. This projection is based on the following assumptions. The pay of federal employees increases at a compound annual growth rate (CAGR) of 3.2 percent, based

on the average rate from 1994 to 2004. Benefits increase at 4.9 percent CAGR, based on the average rate of the benefits increase from 1994 to 2004. The cost of retirement annuitants increases by 3.9 percent, based on OPM retirement statistics for 2002. Contractors grow at an annual rate of 8.6 percent, based on estimates of contractor growth from 1998 to 2004. See Acquisition Solutions Research Institute, *Knowledge Capture, Transfer and Reuse,* May 2006. Military compensation is projected to grow at 6.5 percent, based on the CAGR of that amount calculated by GAO. We assume the same number of grant recipients as today, with annual salary increases at the rate of inflation (3.5 percent).

61. If retirements rise from 3.9 percent to 4.4 percent.

62. OPM, "Civil Service Retirement System (CSRS) Overview" (www.opm.gov/retire/html/retirement/csrs.html).

63. The Congressional Budget Office (CBO) projects that spending for Medicare, Medicaid, and Social Security together will equal nearly 11 percent of gross domestic product in 2017, compared with a little less than 9 percent in 2007. CBO, "The Budget and Economic Outlook: Fiscal Year 2008" (GPO, January 2007).

64. The government's downsizing was driven primarily by reductions in defense employment. Congress and the administration set a goal for reducing the total federal workforce by 272,900 employees; this was codified into PL 103-226, the Federal Workforce Reduction Act of March 2004. OPM data for fiscal 1994, 1995, and 1996 show that 57,163 reductions were achieved through early retirements ("voluntary early retirements"), 99,079 were achieved through buyouts ("voluntary separation incentives"), and 26,644 were due to reductions in force. The total federal employee population has increased from this low point to the current 1.88 million in large part owing to the decision to hire 50,000 airline baggage screeners as federal employees.

65. Ibid.

66. According to U.S. Census data, there were approximately 80 million persons born between 1946 and 1964 (baby boomers) compared with approximately 58 million born between 1965 and 1980 (Generation X).

67. Light, "What Federal Workers Want from Reform."

68. Nicholas Eberstadt, Henry Wendt Scholar in Political Economy, American Enterprise Institute, interview by authors, February 25, 1992. For additional insights on this topic, see Eberstadt's numerous relevant publications, including "Population Aspects of Communist Countries" (Washington: American Enterprise Institute, January 1, 2003).

69. Rainer Strack and Jens Baier, "'Autumn Leaves' Perspectives" (Boston Consulting Group, 2006).

70. Jeffrey Neal, director of human resources, Defense Logistics Agency, interviews by authors, September and November 2005 and February 2006.

71. According to a PPS study, "Mid-Career Hiring in the Federal Government: A Strategy for Change," released in February 2002, 47 percent of all midlevel federal job vacancies were not open to outside competition.

72. "PPS, "Mid-Career Hiring: Revisiting the Search for Seasoned Talent in the Federal Government" (September 2004); and U.S. Merit Systems Protection Board, "In Search of Highly Skilled Workers: A Study on the Hiring of Upper Level Employees From Outside the Federal Government" (http://www.mspb.gov/netsearch/viewdocs.aspx?docnumber=323118&version=323564&application=ACROBAT[2008]).

73. An OMB application for 2006 asks for proficiency in spreadsheet programs such as Lotus 1-2-3 and Excel and word processing applications such as Word and WordPerfect.

74. A survey of 1,100 college juniors and seniors, designed by Linda Bilmes and Jeffrey Neal, was conducted on their behalf over the Internet by Penn, Schoen & Berland Associates during May 2002. A follow-up survey of 300 students was conducted in January 2006 for the present volume. The sample comprised college juniors (48 percent), seniors (46 percent), and recent (within the preceding month) graduates (6 percent). The 2002 study had a margin of error of plus or minus 3.1 percent, and the 2006 study had a margin of error of plus or minus 5.7 percent. The respondents were chosen from a nationally representative sample of college juniors and seniors, weighted for demographic representation.

75. PPS, "The Hiring Process," Issue Brief PPS-05-06 (July 19, 2005).

76. Formerly called the Presidential Management Intern program and created by President Jimmy Carter, the program was initially capped at 200 students a year but was then raised to 400. President Bush removed the 400-person cap in 2003.

77. In 2005, forty-one students from the Kennedy School applied for the program, but only eleven were accepted.

78. Based on discussions with the Career Services Department at the Kennedy School. Students average $75,000 in debt and on average can expect to wait at least six weeks for a job decision and up to two additional months to begin their work. See also Presidents of the National Academy of Engineering, the Institute of Medicine, and the National Research Council, "Preparing for the 21st Century: Science and Engineering Research in a Changing World" (Washington, 1997).

79. Light, "What Federal Workers Want from Reform."

80. Penn, Schoen & Berland, Survey of College Juniors and Seniors, 2002 and 2006.

81. PPS, "The Class of 9/11: Bringing a New Generation of Practical Patriots into Public Service," PPS05-04 (May 2005).

82. Ibid.

83. Light, *A Government Ill Executed.*

84. Penn, Schoen & Berland, Survey of College Juniors and Seniors, 2002 and 2006.

85. Light, *A Government Ill Executed.*

Chapter Two

1. Linda J. Bilmes and Jeffrey R. Neal, "The People Factor: Human Resources Reform in Government," in *For The People: Can We Fix Public Service?* edited by John D. Donahue and Joseph P. Nye (Brookings, 2003).

2. John Delery and Harold Doty, "Modes of Theorizing in Strategic Human Resource Management: Tests of Universalistic, Contingency and Configurational Performance Predictions," *Academy of Management Journal* 39 (August 1996): 820.

3. Theresa Welbourne and Alice Andrews, "Predicting Performance of Initial Public Offering Firms: Should Human Resource Management Be in the Equation?" *Academy of Management Journal* 39 (August 1996): 891–919.

4. The research was initially conducted by Peter Strüven, Konrad Wetzker, and Linda Bilmes at the Boston Consulting Group Gmbh. Some of the material was later published in their book *Gebt uns das Risiko Zurück: Strategien für mehr Arbeit* (Munich: Carl Hanser Verlag, 1998). Material in this chapter is also drawn from Linda Bilmes, Konrad Wetzker, and Pascal Xhonneux, "Value in Human Resources," *Financial Times,* February 10, 1997.

5. Comparisons were drawn only between similar companies within each sector. For example, pharmaceutical companies were compared with other pharmaceutical companies, not with chemical companies that had some presence in the pharmaceutical industry. Firms that had been acquired by others during the period or that did not have public listings for the entire period were excluded. Thus in the United States only the thirty-six firms of the sample were truly comparable. Standard sources such as the Fortune 500 list and Datastream were used to identify the comparable companies in each sector.

6. To measure relative stock performance, the authors used the highly specific "total shareholder return" (TSR) and its corollary, "relative total shareholder return." TSR measures the actual cash value (share price increases + dividends) of an investment. TSR measures the return that common shareholders receive from stock ownership by incorporating change in stock price (capital gains) and dividend payout. TSR is the best measure of long-term value creation and is easily comparable to the returns investors could have made in other investment vehicles (stocks, bonds, real estate, and so forth). To guard against false cross-industry comparisons, we divided each company's TSR by the average TSR of its peers to create the relative total shareholder return. Stock price data were compiled using Datastream and Reuters databases.

7. Gifford Pinchot coined the term "intrapreneurship" in the Netherlands in 1978. His company, Pinchot & Co., began leading seminars on the topic in 1984. It refers to the creation of entrepreneurship within a large organization, manifested either in individuals who act like entrepreneurs, or in entrepreneurial opportunities throughout. See Bilmes and Neal, "The People Factor," p. 131.

8. "Mini-sabbaticals" refer to the practice, common among leading people companies, especially technology firms, of providing good performers with paid leave of up to six weeks on a standardized basis, such as once every four to five years. They are different from academic sabbaticals in that the employer does not expect the employee to produce any research or other work during this period.

9. Staff of Bilfinger|Berger, interview by Boston Consulting Group, 1996.

10. Rajen Dalal, interview by Linda Bilmes, spring 1996. Rajen Dalal was vice president of Chiron Corporation from 1982 to1992. He served as vice president for business development and strategic planning and, during a period of intense merger and licensing activities, oversaw numerous joint ventures, business collaborations, and technology-licensing agreements in drug discovery, biopharmaceuticals, vaccines, and gene therapy. He then led Chiron through a successful corporate-wide restructuring as vice president of corporate development and was appointed president of Chiron Blood Testing. In 1992 Dalel was named chief executive officer of Guava Technologies Inc., a privately held biotechnology company.

11. Survey of 2,000 male private sector employees, conducted by Penn, Schoen & Berland Associates for Linda Bilmes in 1998 in the United States and West Germany.

The survey was repeated for Linda Bilmes and Scott Gould in 2005 among 250 men and women employed in the private sector in the United States.

12. The attributes were based on what we observed in our interviews with employees at high-performing companies.

13. Paul Light, "What Federal Employees Want from Reform," *Reform Watch Brief 5* (Brookings, March 2002).

14. Watson Wyatt, "Human Capital Index," Human Capital as a Lead Indicator of Shareholder Value Report (New York, 2001/2002).

15. Ibid. Watson Wyatt compared two different correlations. Correlation A represents the relationship between the 1999 HCI score and 2001 financial performance. Correlation B represents the relationship between the 1999 financial performance and 2001 HCI scores. Correlation B should be larger if better financial performance is what creates superior HR practices. Correlation A should be larger if the way companies manage their human capital is driving financial performance. In fact, Correlation A was .41 statistically larger than correlation B, which was .19.

16. Watson Wyatt "Maximizing the Return on Your Human Capital Investment," Human Capital Index Report (New York, 2005).

17. Jeffrey Pfeffer, *The Human Equation: Building Profits by Putting People First* (Harvard Business School Press, 1998).

18. Charles O'Reilly III and Jeffrey Pfeffer, *Hidden Value: How Great Companies Achieve Extraordinary Results with Ordinary People* (Harvard Business School Press, 2000), p. 18-19.

19. Ibid., p. 2

20. Ibid.

21. Brian E. Becker and Mark A. Huselid, "High Performance Work Systems and Firm Performance: A Synthesis of Research and Managerial Implications," in *Research in Personnel and Human Resources Management,* edited by G. R. Ferris (Greenwich, Conn.: JAI Press, 1998), pp. 53–101.

22. Mark Huselid, "The Impact of Human Resource Management Practices on Turnover, Productivity, and Corporate Financial Performance," *Academy of Management Journal* 38 (June 1995): 645.

23. Brian E. Becker, Mark A. Huselid, and Dave Ulrich, *The HR Scorecard: Linking People, Strategy and Performance* (Harvard Business School Press, 2001),

24. Ibid.

25. Jeffrey Neal, director of Human Resources, Defense Logistics Agency, interviews by authors, September and November 2005 and February 2006.

26. Jack J. Phillips, Ron D. Stone, and Patricia Pulliam Phillips, *The Human Resources Scorecard: Measuring the Return on Investment* (Boston: Butterworth-Heineman, 2001).

27. Becker, Huselid, and Ulrich, *The HR Scorecard.*

28. Phillips, Stone, and Phillips, *The Human Resources Scorecard.*

29. Robert S. Kaplan and David P. Norton, "The Balanced Scorecard—Measures That Drive Performance," *Harvard Business Review* 70 (January–February 1992): 71–79.

30. Mark Huselid, Brian Becker, and Richard Beatty, *The Workforce Scorecard: Managing Human Capital to Execute Strategy* (Harvard Business School Press, 2005).

Chapter Three

1. Defense Logistics Agency, "Facts and Figures" (www.dla.mil/facts.aspx [June 12, 2008]).

2. Ibid.

3. Ibid.

4. Ibid.

5. Ray Bracy, vice president of Wal-Mart for federal and international affairs, interview, *Frontline* (PBS), September 17, 2004.

6. Defense Logistics Agency, "Facts and Figures."

7. Ibid. See also Partnership for Public Service (PPS), "DLA: HR Leads Organizational Transformation," March 24, 2005. It reports that customer satisfaction was 4.76 out of 5 with a 95 percent confidence interval as of the fourth quarter of 2003.

8. PPS, "Best Places to Work in the Federal Government" (American University Institute for the Study of Public Policy Implementation, 2005). Note that individual DLA scores were not completely disaggregated from the 218 studied subcomponents of DOD.

9. Jeffrey Neal, interviews by the authors, September and November 2005 and February 2006. See also the numerous studies that have established a positive relationship between employees' job satisfaction and customer satisfaction, including R. J. Burke, "Management Practices, Employees' Satisfaction and Perceptions of Quality Service," *Psychological Reports* 77 (1995): 748–50; Roger Hallowell, L. A. Schlesinger, and Jeffrey Zornitsky, "Internal Service Quality, Customer and Job Satisfaction: Linkages and Implications for Managers," *Human Resource Planning* 19, no. 2 (1996): 20–31; and Benjamin Schneider and David E. Bowen, "The Service Organization: Human Resources Management Is Crucial," *Organizational Dynamics* 21 (Spring 1993): 39–52.

10. This section draws heavily on information from Esther Scott, "Reorganizing the Defense Logistics Agency," case C16-94-1237.0, written for Michael Barzelay, Harvard University, Kennedy School, 1994, and funded by the Department of Defense, Contract MDA-903-90-C-0088 (0294).

11. The DSA did not have the responsibility to buy original equipment, such as helicopters, but it was supposed to buy replacement parts, such as helicopter blades.

12. The Federal Supply Catalog contained listings and descriptions of millions of items used throughout the federal government.

13. Previously, the DLA's headquarters had been funded through the DOD's operation and maintenance appropriation, while the purchase, storage, and transportation of supplies were paid for by a revolving fund, the Defense Stock Fund, which was financed by the sale of goods to users. See Esther Scott, "Reorganizing the Defense Logistics Agency."

14. Ibid.

15. PPS, "DLA: HR Leads Organizational Transformation."

16. The DLA's information operations director has received a CIO 100 award (presented annually by International Data Group's *CIO Magazine*) two times in the past three years.

17. PPS, "DLA: HR Leads Organizational Transformation."

18. Neal, interviews, 2005, 2006.

19. PPS, "DLA: HR Leads Organizational Transformation."

20. Ibid.

21. Defense Logistics Agency, *Transformation Roadmap* (Washington, October 2005).

22. Neal, interviews, 2005, 2006.

23. The Denison Organizational Culture Survey and Denison Leadership Development Survey were developed by Daniel R. Denison and William S. Neale. The surveys and model are based on Denison's more than twenty years of research on the link between organization culture and bottom-line performance measures such as return on investment, return on assets, sales growth and quality, and employee satisfaction. The Denison model—which is made up of four culture traits: mission, consistency, involvement, and adaptability—serves as the basis for the Denison Organizational Culture Survey and the Denison Leadership Development Survey.

24. Neal, interviews, 2005, 2006.

25. Ibid.

26. "The DLA Prime Vendor Program," Hearings before the House Armed Services Committee, 109 Cong. 1 sess. (Government Printing Office, November 9. 2005). At issue was the fact that the DLA refrigerators required more functionality than ordinary household refrigerators.

27. Steven Kelman and Donald Kettl, "Reflections on 21st Century Government Management" (Washington: IBM Center for the Business of Government, 2007).

28. Sallyanne Harper, GAO chief administrative and financial officer, interview by authors, July 12, 2005.

29. GAO Performance and Accountability Report, 2007.

30. Jonathan Walters and Charles Thompson, "The Transformation of the Government Accountability Office: Using Human Capital to Drive Change" (Washington: IBM Center for the Business of Government, July 2005). Among senior executives, an even higher proportion was eligible for retirement.

31. Ibid.

32. See David Walker, "Transforming Government to Meet the Demands of the 21st Century," presentation to the Federal Midwest Human Resources Council and the Chicago Federal Reserve Board, Chicago, August 7, 2007 (www.gao.gov/cghome/d071188cg.pdf).

33. Walters and Thompson, "The Transformation of the Government Accountability Office."

34. Chris Mihm, GAO managing director for strategic issues, interview by authors, July 12, 2005.

35. Harper, interview, July 12, 2005.

36. GAO Performance and Accountability Highlights, 2005 (www.gao.gov/new.items/d062sp.pdf), p. 43.

37. Ibid. The figure for October 2006 is 36.75 percent.

38. David M. Walker, interview by authors, November 3, 2005.

39. Ibid.

40. Harper, interview, July 12, 2005.

41. Lower operating costs, one of the major sources of financial benefits, are usually conceived of as recurring costs; however, the GAO includes the present value of savings for only the first two years after implementation. According to the GAO, agencies have difficulty maintaining a commitment to change over time. There is a strong likelihood of "cost creep" that eats away at the savings; thus rather than forecast operational cost savings far into the future, only the first two years are included. The same is not true for cost reductions associated with multiyear projects. In these instances, the present value of the financial benefit can be included for the life of the project, up to five years after implementation. Likewise, increases in revenues resulting from asset sales or tax and user fee changes are measured over a five-year time horizon.

42. Total government spending increased by 33 percent, from $1.86 trillion in fiscal 2001 to $2.48 trillion in fiscal 2005. Discretionary spending increased by 35 percent, from $664 billion to about $900 billion. Because the GAO's mission is to ensure accountability in government operations, this increase in discretionary spending increases the potential savings to be identified by the GAO and acted upon by Congress or federal agencies. See *Budget of the United States Government: Historical Tables Fiscal Year 2008*, table 8.1, "Outlays by Budget Enforcement Act Category: 1962–2012." Discretionary spending increased from $649.3 billion in 2001 to over one trillion in 2007.

43. The GAO converts all estimates involving past and future years to their net present value and uses actual dollars to represent only the estimates for current years.

44. Walker, interview, November 3, 2005.

45. Some employees have recently joined unions in response to the changes in pay systems.

46. Tony Danker and others, "How Can American Government Meet Its Productivity Challenge?" (New York: McKinsey & Company, July 2006).

47. Ibid.

48. Joseph Stiglitz and Linda Bilmes, *The Three Trillion Dollar War* (New York: W. W. Norton, 2008).

49. Brian M. Riedl, "How Congress Can Achieve Savings of 1 Percent by Targeting Waste, Fraud and Abuse," Backgrounder 1681 (Washington: Heritage Foundation, August 28, 2003).

50. For complete student survey results, see appendix A.

51. This concept—long adopted by industry—means that people with different needs can select among a "menu" of benefits.

Chapter Four

1. David A. Nadler, *Champions of Change: How CEOs and Their Companies Are Mastering the Skills of Radical Change* (San Francisco: Jossey-Bass, 1998); John Kotter, "Leading Change: Why Transformational Efforts Fail," *Harvard Business Review* 73 (March 1995): 61–73.

2. Daniel R. Denison, *Corporate Culture and Organizational Effectiveness* (New York: Wiley, 1990); Edgar H. Schein, *Organizational Culture and Leadership*, 2nd ed. (San Francisco: Jossey-Bass, 1992).

3. Charles O. Rossotti, *Many Unhappy Returns: One Man's Quest to Turn around the Most Unpopular Organization in America* (Harvard Business School Press, 2005).

4. Networks exhibit "one-to-many" and "many-to-many" relationships between stakeholders in a system. These relationships are multifaceted and multidirectional. No one has complete control to achieve significant objectives in the network. This places a premium on collaboration and coordination for those stakeholders who want to achieve a specific result.

5. David M. Walker, interview by authors, November 3, 2005.

6. Greg Rothwell, interview by authors, July 8, 2005.

7. John MacGregor Burns, *Leadership* (New York: Harper & Row, 1978).

8. See http://en.wikipedia.org/wiki/Transformational_leadership.

9. Rossotti, *Many Unhappy Returns,* p. 176.

10. Carol Chetkovich, "Winning the Best and Brightest: Increasing the Attraction of Public Service" (Washington: IBM Center for the Business of Government, 2001).

11. Tom R. Tyler and Andrew Caine, "The Influence of Outcomes and Procedures on Satisfaction with Formal Leaders," *Journal of Personality and Social Psychology* 41, no. 4 (1981): 642–55.

12. Walker, interview, November 3, 2005.

13. Ibid.

14. James R. Thompson and Hal G. Rainey, "Modernizing Human Resource Management in the Federal Government: The IRS Model," Human Capital Series (Arlington, Va.: IBM Endowment for the Business of Government, 2003), p. 28.

15. Jonathan Walters, "Life after Civil Service Reform: The Texas, Georgia, and Florida Experiences" (Arlington, Va.: IBM Endowment for the Business of Government, 2002).

16. T. J. Larkin and Sandar Larkin, "Reaching and Changing Frontline Employees," *Harvard Business Review* 74 (May 1996): 95–104.

17. Max DePree, *Leadership Is an Art* (New York: Dell, 1989); Suzanne L. Geigle, "Sensemaking and Scripts during Radical Organizational Change," Ed.D. diss., George Washington University, 1997.

18. Rossotti, *Many Unhappy Returns,* p. 176.

19. Jennifer Hemingway, staff of Senator Susan B. Collins, interview with authors, August 4, 2005.

20. U.S. Department of Labor, Bureau of Labor Statistics, *The Federal Government,* March 12, 2008 (www.bls.gov/oco/cg/cgs041.htm).

21. Stephen Barr, "Efforts to Change Personnel Rules Move Slowly," *Washington Post,* March 1, 2006, p. D4.

22. Government Accountability Office and National Commission on the Public Service, "Human Capital: Principles, Criteria, and Processes for Governmentwide Federal Human Capital Reform," GAO-05-69SP (December 1, 2004), pp. 10–12.

23. Nadler, *Champions of Change*; Kotter, "Leading Change," pp. 61–73.

24. Denison, *Corporate Culture and Organizational Effectiveness*; Schein, *Organizational Culture and Leadership.*

25. William Bridges, *Managing Transitions: Making the Most of Change* (Reading, Mass.: Addison-Wesley, 1991).

26. David Rooke and William R. Torbert, "Seven Transformations of Leadership," *Harvard Business Review* 83 (April 2005): 71.

27. Walker, interview, November 3, 2005.

Chapter Five

1. Daniel Katz and Robert L. Kahn, *The Social Psychology of Organizations,* 2nd ed. (New York: Wiley, 1978), pp. 76–78.

2. Paul C. Light, "The Troubled State of the Federal Public Service," Center for Public Service Report (Brookings, June 2002), p. 18.

3. Ibid., p. 8.

4. Ibid., p. 17.

5. Ibid.

6. Linda Bilmes and Jeffrey Neal, "The People Factor: Human Resources Reform in Government," in *For the People: Can We Fix Public Service?* edited by John D. Donahue and Joseph P. Nye (Brookings, 2003); James R. Thompson and Hal B. Rainey, "Modernizing Human Resource Management in the Federal Government: The IRS Model," in *Human Capital 2004,* edited by Jonathan D. Bruel and Nicole Willenz Gardner (Lanham, Md.: Rowman and Littlefield, 2004), pp. 12, 31, and 38.

7. National Academy of Public Administration and National Commission on the Public Service Implementation Initiative, "Transforming the Public Service: Progress Made and Work Ahead" (Washington, 2004), p. 13.

8. Texas State Auditor, "State of Texas Classification: Management-to-Staff Ratios, Background and Initiatives in Texas" (www.hr.state.tx.us/systems/fte/Backgroundand Initiatives.html).

9. Ibid.

10. Office of Management and Budget, "The President's Management Agenda: Fiscal Year 2002" (Government Printing Office, 2001) (www.whitehouse.gov/omb/budget/fy2002/mgmt.pdf).

11. Hannah Sistare, interview by authors, October 17, 2005.

12. Public-private collaboration can be implemented through subcontracting and outsourcing models. "In these cases, Government retains responsibility for a service that is totally or partially operated by the private sector. Public-private partnerships (PPP or P3) are emerging as the models of collaboration that trigger the most debate. They are distinct in that they focus on a sharing of resources, risks, and benefits across sectors. And while the service is public, as a general rule, the funds are private. In both cases, Government hands over part of its management responsibilities while retaining enough control to ensure the protection of the public interest. This control is ensured by maintaining a controlling interest or through laws and regulations governing the activities of the corporation" (www.ctg.albany.edu/publications/reports/new_models_ wp?chapter=3). Further suggested reading includes J. D. Donahue, *The Privatization Decision, Public Ends, Private Means* (New York: Basic Books, 1989); Richard Heeks, "Reinventing Government in the Information Age," in *Reinventing Government in the Information Age: International Practice in IT-Enabled Public Sector Reform,* edited by Richard Heeks (London: Routledge, 1999), pp. 9–21; David Osborne and Ted Gaebler, *Reinventing Government* (Reading, Mass.: Addison-Wesley, 1992); and

Economist Intelligence Unit and Andersen Consulting, *Vision 2010: Forging Tomorrow's Public-Private Partnerships* (New York: Economist, 1999).

13. Donald Kettl and others, *Civil Service Reform: Building a Government That Works* (Brookings, 1996).

14. James R. Thompson and Sharon H. Mastracci, "The Blended Workforce: Maximizing Agility through Nonstandard Work Arrangements," Human Capital Management Series (Washington: IBM Center for the Business of Government, 2005) (www.businessofgovernment.org/pdfs/MastracciReport.pdf).

15. Robert Welch, interview by authors, July 14, 2005.

16. Greg Rothwell, interview by authors, 2005.

17. Linda Bilmes, "Soldiers Returning from Iraq and Afghanistan: The Long-Term Costs of Providing Veterans Medical Care and Disability Benefits," Harvard Kennedy School Working Paper (January 2007).

18. Linda Bilmes, "Veterans from Iraq and Afghanistan: Impediments to Securing Disability Benefits and Medical Care," paper presented at the American Economic Association annual meeting, New Orleans, January 2008.

19. W. Scott Gould, "Thoughts on the Blended Workforce," IBM presentation to Senior Executive Association, Washington, D.C., September 21, 2005.

20. Steven Goldsmith and William D. Eggers, *Governing by Network: The New Shape of the Public Sector* (Brookings, 2004), p. 22.

21. Linda Bilmes and Joseph Stiglitz, *The Three Trillion Dollar War* (New York: W. W. Norton, 2008), Afterword, paperback ed.

22. Certain occupations, particularly in high-security and intelligence activities, would not be eligible for the passport program.

23. Penn, Schoen & Berland Associates, Survey of College Juniors and Seniors, 2002 and 2006.

24. Mary Jo Hatch, *Organization Theory* (Oxford University Press, 1997), p. 187.

25. Government Accountability Office, "David M. Walker: Supporting Congress and Making GAO a Model Organization for the Government, 1998 to Present," profile of the comptroller general (www.gao.gov/about/history/gaohistory_present.html [2007]).

26. Air Traffic Organization, "Air Traffic Organization Implementation Strategy" (Washington: Federal Aviation Administration, March 2005).

27. Stephen R. Corey and Patricea W. Hogan, "The Impact of Goal Setting and Empowerment on Governmental Matrix Organizations," Master's thesis, Air Force Institute of Technology, Wright-Patterson Air Force Base, Ohio, September 1993.

28. "FSA Slaps Biggest Fine in Two Years on Credit Suisse," *Dow Jones Financial News,* August 13, 2008.

29. See, for example, Peter Strüven, Konrad Wetzker, and Linda Bilmes, *Gebt uns das Risiko Zurück* (Munich: Carl Hanser, 1998).

30. "Coast Guard Auxiliary Health Care Support Program Wins Award" (www.teamcoastguard.org/2005/July/A050716/health.htm).

31. Chief of Naval Operations, "Sea Enterprise Innovation Awards Program," OPNAV INSTRUCTION 1650.29, April 22, 2005 (neds.daps.dla.mil/Directives/1650_29.pdf).

32. Skip Derra, "ASU, Army Open New Flexible Display Center," Arizona State University (www.asu.edu/feature/includes/spring05/readmore/flexdisplay.html [2007]).

33. David M. Walker, interview by authors, November 3, 2005.

34. GAO, "The Human Capital Strategic Plan: Fiscal Years 2004–2006" (GPO, September 1, 2004).

35. Patrick Pizzella, interview by authors, August 23, 2005.

Chapter Six

1. D. Quinn Mills, "Planning with People in Mind," in *Managing People and Organizations,* edited by John J. Gabarro, updated (Harvard Business School Press, 1991); and David Maister, *Practice What You Preach: What Managers Must Do to Create a High Achievement Culture* (New York: Free Press, 2001).

2. These included coaching and mentoring skills, decisiveness combined with consensus seeking, the ability to face adversity with grace and confidence, and a willingness to take unpopular positions for the good of the team.

3. This material is based in part on interviews with Jeff Neal and on "Processing People," *Government Executive,* December 1, 2004.

4. Keith Hammonds, "Why We Hate HR," *Fast Company Magazine,* no. 97, August 2005.

5. See, for example, Brian E. Becker, Mark A. Huselid, and Dave Ulrich, *The HR Scorecard: Linking People, Strategy, and Performance* (Harvard Business School Press, 2001); and Mark A. Huselid, Brian E. Becker, and Richard W. Beatty, *Workforce Scorecard: Managing Human Capital to Execute Strategy* (Harvard Business School Press, 2005).

6. Mills chose approximately 11 percent of the 2,625 U.S. parent companies listed in *Dun's Directory of American Corporate Families.* Each of the randomly selected 291 companies in his sample had sales of $50 million or more, conducted business in at least ten locations, and had a controlling interest in one or more subsidiaries. He surveyed primarily line managers and had a 77 percent response rate in telephone interviews. D. Quinn Mills, "Planning with People in Mind."

7. Mills, "Planning with People in Mind." In Mills's survey, 72 percent of the respondents who practice HR resource planning were certain that it improved profitability, and 39 percent said they could measure it in the bottom line. However, he points out that companies doing the most comprehensive planning are most likely to measure its impact quantitatively. This has also been the case at the GAO, as discussed in chapter 3.

8. Ibid.

9. R. S. Kaplan and D. P. Norton, "The Balanced Scorecard," *Harvard Business Review* 70 (January–February 1992): 71–79.

10. Partnership for Public Service (PPS), "NASA: Overcoming Mission Challenges" (Washington: Strategic Human Capital Planning, Solutions Center, 2003).

11. PPS, "SSA: Preparing for a Retirement Boom" (Washington: Strategic Human Capital Planning, Solutions Center, 2003).

12. Office of Personnel Management (OPM), "Strategic Management of Human Capital: Third Quarter FY 2005 Update," Message from the Director (www.white house.gov/results/agenda/fy05q3-hc.pdf [July 7, 2005]).

13. Joseph Stiglitz and Linda Bilmes, *The Three Trillion Dollar War* (New York: W. W. Norton, 2008).

14. Maister, *Practice What You Preach,* p. 184.

15. PPS (www.extremehiringmakeover.org/).

16. The 9/11 Commission, Final Report of the National Commission on Terrorist Attacks upon the United States, (Government Printing Office, July 2004).

17. OPM, "Temporary and Term Appointments" (www.usajobs.opm.gov/EI36.asp).

18. See http://jobs-emplois.gc.ca/srp-rpl-rlp/about-rpl_e.htm.

19. United Way of Columbia-Willamette, "Loaned Executive Program" (www. unitedway-pdx.org/yourCampaign/loanedExecutiveProgram.htm).

20. David M. Walker, interview by authors, November 3, 2005.

21. OPM, Federal Hiring Flexibilities Resource Center, "Excepted Service Appointing Authorities" (www.opm.gov/Strategic_Management_of_Human_Capital/fhfrc/FLX05020.asp#itemA1 [June 16, 2008]).

22. For example, the Smithsonian Institution is a hybrid public-private partnership.

23. PPS, "Tapping America's Potential: Expanding Student Employment and Internship Opportunities in the Federal Government," Preliminary Report (Washington, 2002), p. 13.

24. For details, see National Academy of Public Administration (NAPA), Human Resources Management Panel, "A Work Experience Second to None: Impelling the Best to Serve" (Washington, 2001), p. xi.

25. Robert Hosenfeld, interview by authors, October 6, 2005.

26. Patrick Pizzella, interview by authors, August 23, 2005.

27. Michael Beer and Richard E. Walton, "Reward Systems and the Role of Compensation," in *Managing People and Organizations,* edited by John Garbarro (Harvard Business School Press, 1992).

28. Kay Coles James, "A Fresh Start for Federal Pay: The Case for Modernization," White Paper (Washington: OPM, 2002), p. 4.

29. The contractors may in fact be entitled to much lower long-term benefits than the government workers, but this may not be apparent to the federal employee and does not figure into to his or her perception of wage disparity.

30. Stephen Barr, "Pay Discrepancies May Be Dissuading Career Civil Servants from Rising in IG Ranks," *Washington Post,* February 23, 2006, p. B2.

31. Roger Blanchard, interview by authors, September 14, 2005.

32. An economic term, "wage dispersion" refers to the amount of variation in wages encountered in an economy.

33. George Borjas, "The Wage Structure and the Sorting of Workers into the Public Sector," in *For the People: Can We Fix Public Service?* edited by John D. Donahue and Joseph S. Nye (Brookings, 2003).

34. John D. Donahue, *The Warping of Government Work* (Harvard University Press, 2008).

35. Ibid., p. 137.

36. Government Accountability Office (GAO), "Human Capital: Effective Use of Flexibilities Can Assist Agencies in Managing Their Workforces," Report to Congressional Requesters, GAO-03-2 (Washington, December 2002) (www.gao.gov/new.items/d032.pdf).

37. Beer and Walton, "Reward Systems and the Role of Compensation."

38. Tony Danker, Thomas Dohrman, Nancy Killefer, Lenny Mendonca, "How Can American Government Meet Its Productivity Challenge?" (New York: McKinsey and Company, July 2006), p. 4.

39. The Scanlon Plan is based on the historical ratio of labor cost to sales value of production. Because it rewards labor savings, it is most appropriate for companies that have a "high touch labor" content. Ronald J. Recardo and Diane Pricone, "Is Gainsharing for You?" (www.qualitydigest.com/jul/gainshre.html).

40. David M. Walker, "Human Capital: Designing and Managing Market-Based and More Performance-Oriented Pay Systems," statement before the Subcommittee on Oversight of Government Management, the Federal Workforce, and the District of Columbia, Committee on Homeland Security and Governmental Affairs, U.S. Senate, GAO-05-1048T (Washington, September 27, 2005), p. 3.

41. Borjas, "The Wage Structure and the Sorting of Workers into the Public Sector."

42. Stephen Barr, "Agencies Are Increasingly Offering Buyouts, GAO Report Finds," *Washington Post,* April 4, 2006, p. D4.

43. GAO, "Veterans' Benefits. Improvements Needed in the Reporting and Use of Data on the Accuracy of Disability Claims Decisions," GAO-03-1045 (Washington, September 2003). For more information, see GAO, "Veterans Benefits Administration: Better Collection and Analysis of Attrition Data Needed to Enhance Workforce Planning," GAO-03-0491 (Washington, April 28, 2003).

44. For details, see NAPA, "A Work Experience Second to None," p. xi.

45. Marcus Buckingham and Curt Coffman, *First, Break All the Rules: What the World's Greatest Managers Do Differently* (New York: Simon and Schuster, 1999), p. 33.

46. Laurie E. Ekstrand, "FBI Transformation: Human Capital Strategies May Assist the FBI in Its Commitment to Address Its Top Priorities," testimony before the Subcommittee on Commerce, Justice, State, the Judiciary and Related Agencies, Committee on Appropriations, House of Representatives, GAO-04-817T (Washington, June 3, 2004).

47. See GAO, "Human Capital: Effective Use of Flexibilities," p. 15: the GAO found that "agency officials and union representatives cited work-life programs among the most effective flexibilities for recruiting, motivating, and retaining staff." The study offered a list of government-tested programs that are agreed to be valuable. The programs include alternative work schedules, child care centers and assistance, health care, employee assistance programs, and telecommuting.

48. Larry Copeland, "Most State Workers in Utah Shifting to 4-Day Week," *USA Today,* June 30, 2008 (http://www.usatoday.com/news/nation/2008-06-30-four-day_N.htm).

49. For more details, see OPM, "Alternative Work Schedules (AWS)" and "Compressed Work Schedules (CWS)" (www.opm.gov/oca/worksch/HTML/AWScws.asp).

50. Committee on Government Reform, "Government Reform Committee to Examine Telecommuting within Federal Workforce," July 6, 2004.

51. Defense Logistics Agency, "DLA Telework Training for Employees" (Columbus, Ohio, 2004) (www.drms.dla.mil/telework/employeeguide1204.pdf).

52. Daniel Pulliam, "Logistics Agency Expands Telework Initiative," *Government Executive.com,* April 19, 2005 (www.govexec.com/dailyfed/0405/041905p1.htm).

53. Ibid.

54. General Services Administration, "USDA: Work/Life Benefits Set Trends," Federal ETC (Employee Transportation Coordinator) Updates (Spring 2003) (www.mwcog.org/commuter/fedetcinsert4.htm).

55. Department of Justice, "Worklife Program" (www.usdoj.gov/jmd/ps/wlprograms.html).

56. GAO, "Human Capital: Effective Use of Flexibilities," p. 16.

57. All Harvard employees are eligible for a wide range of subsidized health and well-being benefits. They are provided by the university in addition to the benefits and health care plans that employees purchase.

58. GAO, "Human Capital: Effective Use of Flexibilities," p. 16.

59. Walker, "Human Capital: Designing and Managing Market-Based and More Performance-Oriented Pay Systems," p. 6.

60. Alyssa Rosenberg, "Federal Workforce Growing More Diverse, Says OPM," *Government Executive.com,* February 14, 2008 (www.govexec.com/story_page.cfm?articleid=39297&ref=rellink).

61. U.S. Department of Labor, *Futurework: Trends and Challenges for Work in the 21st Century* (Washington, 1999).

62. Mary Ayre, Julie Mills, and Jill Slay, "Equity and Diversity in Science, Technology and Engineering Education" (www.unisanet.unisa.edu.au/flc/staffsvcs/Equity/Equity&diversityinEngScTech.doc [September 28, 2001]).

63. Matti F. Dobbs, "Managing Diversity: Lessons from the Private Sector," *Public Personnel Management*, vol. 25, 1996.

64. Equal Employment Opportunity Commission Task Force (www.eeoc.gov/abouteeoc/task_reports/prac2.html).

Chapter Seven

1. Brenda Sugre and Ray J. Rivera, "State of the Industry: ASTD's Annual Review of Trends in Workplace Learning and Performance" (Washington: American Society for Training and Development, 2005), p. 6.

2. Assumes 2,685,713 active- and reserve-duty personnel, and $6,732.3 million in military spending on noncivilian training and education. Based on DOD, "Fiscal Year 2006 Budget Estimates," Office of the Secretary of Defense, Operation and Maintenance Overview (February 2005), p. 167 (www.defenselink.mil/comptroller/defbudget/fy2006/fy2006_overview.pdf). ASTD data from Sugre and Rivera, "State of the Industry."

3. Roger Blanchard, interview by authors, September 14, 2005.

4. Bureau of Labor Statistics, "Employee Tenure Summary: 2006," September 8, 2006 (www.bls.gov/news.release/tenure.nr0.htm).

5. IBM Intranet (w3-03.ibm.com/manager/quickview/mgrqv.nsf/Content/85256 F11%3A00756195). No public access.

6. IBM Intranet (w3-03.ibm.com/manager/quickview/clusters.nsf/Content/85256 FA5%3a005013BB). No public access.

7. The other leadership competencies were client partnering, embracing challenge, earning trust, enabling performance and growth, developing IBM people and communities, passion for IBM's future, strategic risk taking, informed judgment, and horizontal thinking.

8. See Certified Public Manager Consortium (www.txstate.edu/cpmconsortium/).

9. Ibid.

10. See State of the USA (www.stateoftheusa.org).

11. Sallyanne Harper, interview by authors, July 12, 2005.

12. Robert Hosenfeld, interview by authors, October 6, 2005.

13. Patrick Pizzella, interview by authors, August 23, 2005.

14. Jim Garamone, "Pace Proposes Interagency Goldwater-Nichols Act," American Forces Press Service, September 7, 2004.

15. Ron Sanders, interview by authors, September 16, 2005.

16. See Defense Acquisition University (www.dau.mil).

17. Legislation for the U.S. Public Service Academy was introduced in the House as H.R. 1671 by Representatives Jim Moran and Christopher Shays and in the Senate by Senators Hillary Clinton and Arlen Specter as S. 960.

18. See www.uspublicserviceacademy.org/USPSAessentials.pdf.

19. Ibid.

Chapter Eight

1. David A. J. Axson, *Best Practices in Planning and Performance Management* (New York: Wiley and Sons, 2007), p. 24.

2. Government Performance and Results Act of 1993 (www.whitehouse.gov/omb/mgmt-gpra/gplaw2m.html).

3. "Assessing Program Performance" (www.whitehouse.gov/omb/part/).

4. Title V, *Government Organization and Employees,* 5 U.S.C. 4302 (http://frweb gate.access.gpo.gov/cgi-in/getdoc.cgi?dbname=browse_usc&docid=Cite:+5USC4302).

5. Thomas M. Keane Jr., "The Model City," *Boston Globe,* May 14, 2006.

6. Evaluation Criteria for Performance Excellence (www.quality.nist.gov/Education_Criteria.htm).

7. Watson Wyatt, "Performance Management Programs Need Improvement," press release, November 28, 2005 (www.watsonwyatt.com/news/press.asp?ID=15414). In 2002 the Department of Health and Human Services rated 86 percent of its executives in the top category. Previous research indicates that only about 15–20 percent of performers are actually "stars." Hence at least some among that 86 percent were "strong" but not "top" performers.

8. Government Accountability Office (GAO), "Results-Oriented Cultures: Creating a Clear Linkage between Individual Performance and Organizational Success," GAO-03-488 (Washington, 2003) (www.gao.gov/cgi-bin/getrpt?GAO-03-488).

9. Howard Risher, "Managing for Better Performance: Enhancing Federal Performance Management Practices," *Human Capital Management Series* (Washington: IBM Center for the Business of Government, 2007).

10. Jeff Neal, interview by authors, June 22, 2006.

11. Mary Jo Hatch, *Organization Theory: Modern, Symbolic, and Postmodern Perspectives* (Oxford University Press, 1997), p. 311.

12. Edward Lawler and Michael McDermott, "Current Performance Management Practices," *WorldatWork Journal* 12 no. 2 (2003): 49–60.

13. Sallyanne Harper, chief administrative officer at the GAO, interview by authors, July 2005.

14. Patrick Pizzella, assistant secretary for administration and management, DOL, interview by authors, August 2005.

15. Robert D. Behn, *Bob Behn's Public Management Report,* vol. 3, no. 5 (January 2006) (www.ksg.harvard.edu/thebehnreport/January2006.pdf).

16. Interagency Work Group on Performance Management, *Report to the President's Council on Managing Performance in the Government* (Washington: Office of Personnel Management, February 2000) (www.opm.gov/er/poor/sitemap.asp).

17. GAO, "Human Capital: The Role of Ombudsmen in Dispute Resolution," report to the ranking member, Subcommittee on International Security, Proliferation, and Federal Services, Committee on Government Affairs, U.S. Senate, GAO-01-466 (Washington, 2001), p. 2.

18. Ibid.

19. John B. Gilmour and David E. Lewis, "Assessing Performance Budgeting at OMB: The Influence of Politics, Performance, and Program Size," *Journal of Public Administration Research and Theory* 16, no. 2 (2006): 169–86 (doi:10.1093/jopart/muj002).

Chapter Nine

1. See Doris Kearns Goodwin, *Lyndon Johnson and the American Dream* (New York: Harper and Row, 1976), and Robert A. Caro, *The Master of the Senate: The Years of Lyndon Johnson* (New York: Alfred P. Knopf, 2002), p. 850: "Lyndon Johnson had no choice, and he knew it. Recalling the situation years later, he would say: 'One thing had become absolutely certain: the Senate simply had to act, the Democratic Party simply had to act, and I simply had to act; the issue could wait no longer. Something had to be done.'"

2. Goodwin, *Lyndon Johnson and the American Dream,* p. 152.

3. Ibid., pp. 188–89.

4. David Flitner Jr., "Why the Cynics Are Wrong about Presidential Commissions," George Mason University's History News Network (http://hnn.us/articles/3439.html [February 9, 2004]).

5. In its efforts to downsize after the cold war, the Department of Defense in May 2005 recommended a number of military installations be closed. Congress established BRAC in 2005 to examine the base closure and realignment process. The commission was directed to provide an objective, nonpartisan, and independent review and analysis of the list of military installation recommendations. Their report was submitted to Congress in a complete package, on which members were permitted to vote simply yes or no. This mechanism allowed Congress to approve this controversial realignment without getting bogged down in protracted political negotiations on each site.

6. Steve Goldsmith, interview by authors, November 10, 2005.

7. Robert Tobias, interview by authors, July 6, 2005.

8. George Nesterczuk, interview by authors, July 13, 2005.

9. James R. Thompson and Hal G. Rainey, "Modernizing Human Resource Management in the Federal Government: The IRS Model" (Washington: IBM Endowment for the Business of Government, April 2003), p. 28.

10. Paul C. Light, *The Tides of Reform: Making Government Work, 1945–1995* (Yale University Press, 1997).

11. Brian Friel, "Labor Pains," *Government Executive,* October 1, 2002. The percentage of nonpostal federal workers represented by unions has remained steady at about 60 percent since 1975, after unions launched major organizing campaigns during the 1960s following Kennedy's order. But the number of union members—those who actually pay dues—is significantly smaller, perhaps 25–30 percent of federal workers (which is still much higher than the private sector average). Under the 1978 law, federal employees do not have to be dues-paying members to reap some of the benefits of union representation. While the American Federation of Government Employees (AFGE) represents 600,000 federal workers, only 198,453 are dues-paying members. The National Treasury Employees Union represents 155,000 employees, 74,306 of whom are dues-paying members. The four largest federal employee unions represent 836,123 employees, but only 38 percent, or 318,312, are dues-paying members. The top four unions are AFGE, NTEU, the National Federation of Federal Employees (representing 68,535 employees with just 7,528 members), and the National Association of Government Employees (representing 45,433 employees, 38,025 of whom are members).

12. The four unions were the National Treasury Employee Union, American Federation of Government Employees, National Federation of Federal Employees, and National Association of Agricultural Employees.

13. Tobias, interview, July 6, 2005.

14. Andrew Richardson, interview by authors, August 4, 2005.

15. John D. Donahue, *The Warping of Government Work* (Harvard University Press, 2008), p. 5.

16. Ibid., p. 48.

17. According to the U.S. Bureau of Labor Statistics, the average salary for a microbiologist in the U.S. government in 2007 was $87,206. A starting salary for this position would be from $69,000 to $79,000 under the GS schedule. The government employed 23,000 biological scientists in 2006.

18. Martha J. Kumar, "Getting Ready for Day One: Taking Advantage of the Opportunities and Minimizing the Hazards of a Presidential Transition," *Public Administration Review,* July /August 2008.

19. A *USA Today*/Gallup poll conducted December 14–16, 2007, showed that 68 percent of voters disapproved of Republicans in Congress and 64 percent disapproved of Democrats in Congress.

20. Penn, Schoen & Berland Associates, Survey of College Juniors and Seniors, 2002 and 2006.

Chapter Ten

1. Paul C. Light, *A Government Ill Executed* (Harvard University Press, 2008), p. 231.

2. One percent of total annual federal wages of $331 billion is $3 billion.

3. Total annual contracts paid by the federal government are around $500 billion. See Federal Procurement Data System (FPDS NexGen) (http://fedspending.org/). The

estimate of the total service contracts of $264 billion is from Bob Welch, former chief procurement officer, U.S Department of Commerce.

4. Net present values represent the total amount in today's money. These figures are discounted at 2 percent in this model.

5. Total government labor costs equal $791 billion annually.

6. Light, *A Government Ill Executed,* p. 205.

7. Subcommittee on Education and Health of the Joint Economic Committee, "A Cost-Benefit Analysis of Government Investment in Post-Secondary Education under the World War II GI Bill," December 14, 1988.

8. Congress and individual state legislatures could also consider a more expanded version of such a GI Bill that would include state and local employees who work on implementing federal directives, or who participate in networks that involve the federal government. However, the budget estimates in this chapter pertain only to federal employees.

9. Executive Order 13318 allows the director of OPM to adjust the size of the program.

10. John D. Donahue, *The Warping of Government Work* (Harvard University Press, 2008), p. 48.

11. CSRS computation for retirement is 1.5 percent for the first five years, 1.75 percent for the second five years, and 2 percent for all years after ten. In this example, the final figure would be 66.25 percent applied to the average-high-three-year salary of $125,000, or $82,800.

12. An employee must have participated in the health plan benefit for the final five years before retirement to qualify for this benefit.

13. There are 7,996 positions subject to noncompetitve appointment (www.gpo access.gov/plumbook/2008/p197-199_appendix1.pdf).

14. This would not be applicable to government employees in designated high-security operations.

15. The integrated process team tasked with detailed planning would comprise representatives from across the many agencies and geographic areas of government. We estimate that the square root of the total population of government managers and supervisors is a sound initial estimate to ensure a representative sample. This cohort will form the dedicated group that will plan and provide leadership for the transformation effort. The money will therefore fund about 480 people at varying levels of involvement.

16. The principal committees authorized to oversee personnel management are the House Government Operations Committee and the Senate Government Affairs Committee. Authorizing committees include the Senate Committee on Homeland Security and Governmental Affairs; House Committee on Oversight and Government Reform, Subcommittee on Federal Workforce, Postal Service, and the District of Columbia; and Subcommittee on Government Management, Organization, and Procurement. Appropriations subcommittees with jurisdiction over OPM include the Senate Committee on Appropriations, Subcommittee on Financial Services and General Government; and House Committee on Appropriations, Subcommittee on Financial Services and General Government.

17. According to OPM, the average separation rate for the federal government from 1998 and 2004 was 18 percent.

18. Established in March 2004, the fund grew to $5.2 million by the end of fiscal 2004. For further details, see www.govexec.com/dailyfed/0405/040105k1.htm.

19. The base budget over which the lapsed, unobligated portion is calculated includes government operating costs in 2007 of about $331 billion plus contracting costs of about $500 billion and equipment of about $100 billion, for a total of about $931 billion. Agencies can already keep about 60 percent of this amount through non-year and multiyear funding authorities. This would leave 40 percent available for our calculation. We propose taking 50 percent of that amount, or about $1.7 billion a year, to fund the program.

Chapter Eleven

1. Bills such as this are difficult to move through Congress because members often add provisions with a broad effect, such as incentives to buy American goods. In addition, because civil service reform is under the aegis of the Executive Office of the President, which includes the Office of Management and Budget and Office of Personnel Management, and because the legislation itself would affect all government agencies, the appropriations components are considered and enacted in the Financial Services and General Government Appropriation Bill.

Appendix E

1. Office of Personnel Management, *Biography of an Ideal: A History of the Federal Civil Service* (2002), p. 187.

2. Ibid., p. 194.

3. Ibid., p. 197.

4. Charles J. Guiteau, ibid., p. 200.

5. OPM, *Biography of an Ideal,* p. 206.

6. Ibid., p. 223.

7. Ibid., p. 220.

8. Ibid., pp. 223–24.

9. Ibid., p. 236.

10. Ibid., p. 251.

11. Ibid., p. 222.

12. Ibid., p. 228.

13. Ibid., p. 228–29.

14. Ibid, p. 230.

15. Ibid., pp. 232–33.

16. Ibid., p. 237.

17. Ibid.

18. Ibid., p. 244–45.

19. Ibid., pp. 248–49.

20. Ibid.

21. Ibid., pp. 253–54.

22. Ibid., p. 254.

23. Ibid., p. 257.

24. Ibid., pp. 257–58.

25. Ibid., p. 258.

26. Ibid., p. 259–60.

27. Ibid., p. 262.

28. Ibid., p. 263.

29. Ibid, p. 266.

30. James P. Pfiffner and Douglas A. Brook, eds., *The Future of Merit: Twenty Years after the Civil Service Reform Act* (Washington: Woodrow Wilson Center Press, 2000), p. 2.

31. Ibid.

32. Patricia Wallace Ingraham, *The Foundation of Merit: Public Service in American Democracy* (John Hopkins University Press, 1995), pp. 74–75.

33. OPM, *Biography of an Ideal*, p. 277.

34. Ingraham, *The Foundation of Merit*, pp. 75–76.

35. OPM, *Biography of an Ideal*, p. 278.

36. Ingraham, *The Foundation of Merit*, p. 77.

37. Ibid., p. 77.

38. Ibid.

39. Ibid.

40. Ibid., p. 78.

41. OPM, *Biography of an Ideal*, p. 282.

42. Ibid.

43. Ibid., p. 283.

44. Ingraham, *The Foundation of Merit*, p. 82.

45. Ibid., pp. 80, 82.

46. Ibid., p. 85.

47. Ibid.

48. Ibid., pp. 86–87.

49. Pfiffner and Brook, *The Future of Merit*, pp. 4, 6.

50. Ingraham, *The Foundation of Merit*, p. 88.

51. See www.nawcwpns.navy.mil/~hrd/demogide/background.html.

52. See www.nawcwpns.navy.mil/~hrd/demogide/effective.html.

53. Ingraham, *The Foundation of Merit*, p. 88.

54. OPM, *Biography of an Ideal*, p. 289.

55. Ibid., p. 291.

56. Ingraham, *The Foundation of Merit*, p. 87.

57. Ibid.

58. OPM, *Biography of an Ideal*, p. 292.

59. See www.opm.gov/retire/html/retirement/fers.html.

60. Ibid.

61. See www.cbo.gov/showdoc.cfm?index=821&sequence=0#pt4.

62. National Commission on the Public Service (first Volcker Commission), "Leadership for America: Rebuilding the Public Service" (Washington, 1989), p. 1.

63. Ibid., p. 5.

64. Ibid., pp. 5–6.

65. Ibid., p. 6.

66. OPM, *Biography of an Ideal,* p. 295.

67. Ibid., p. 296.

68. Remarks by President Clinton Announcing the Initiative to Streamline Government, March 3, 1993 (http://govinfo.library.unt.edu/npr/library/speeches/030393.html).

69. Ibid.

70. Ingraham, *The Foundation of Merit,* p. 122.

71. See http://govinfo.library.unt.edu/npr/whoweare/historyofnpr.html.

72. Management Reform: Continuing Attention Is Needed to Improve Government Performance. Statement of J. Christopher Mihm, associate director, Federal Management and Workforce Issues, General Government Division, May 4, 2000 (www.gao.gov/archive/2000/gg00128t.pdf).

73. NPR Archive, "Did NPR Make a Difference?" (http://govinfo.library.unt.edu/npr/whoweare/historypart5.html).

74. U.S. Office of Personnel Management, *Biography of an Ideal: A History of the Federal Civil Service,* pp. 300–01.

75. Government Performance Results Act of 1993, 01/05/93 (www.whitehouse.gov/omb/mgmt-gpra/gplaw2m.html).

76. Pfiffner and Brook, *The Future of Merit,* p. 117

77. GAO, "Human Capital Management: FAA's Reform Effort Requires a More Strategic Approach," GAO-03-156 (February 2003), p. 1.

78. Ibid., p. 3.

79. Ibid.

80. Ibid., p. i.

81. Ibid., p. 24.

82. Shawn Zeller, "Performance Pay Perils," *Government Executive* Magazine, February 15, 2004.

83. Charles O. Rossotti, *Many Unhappy Returns: One Man's Quest to Turn around the Most Unpopular Organization in America* (Harvard Business School Press, 2005), p. 2.

84. Ibid., p. 3.

85. James R. Thompson and Hal G. Rainey, "Modernizing Human Resource Management in the Federal Government: The IRS Model" (IBM Endowment for the Business of Government, April 2003), p. 12.

86. Ibid., p. 7.

87. Shawn Zeller, "DHS Personnel System Unveiled" (GovExec.com [January 25, 2005]).

88. Karen Rutzick, "Appeals Court Hears Arguments in DHS Labor Rights Case" (GovExec.com [May 6, 2006]).

89. Karen Rutzick, "Judge Overturns Defense Labor Relations Reforms" (GovExec.com [February 27, 2006]).

90. Ibid.

91. Ibid.

Index

Hausser, Doris, 19, 154
HCI (Human capital index), 53–54
Health and Human Services Department (HHS), 152, 186, 257
Health care benefits, 8, 251–52
Heritage Foundation, 93
Hierarchical organizational structure, 116–18, 130, 263
Hiring system: challenges of, 27–32; at DLA, 70, 76; at GAO, 79; and HR reforms, 143–52; and negative perceptions of government employment, 32–38; process shortening in, 147–48; talent lost to, 31–32; and Watson Wyatt study, 54
Hispanics and workforce diversity, 169
Homeland Security Department (DHS): and federal law enforcement officers, 18; personnel initiatives at, 15, 21, 112; and public sector leadership, 104; statutory reforms at, 64; student perceptions of, 33; and unions, 233–34
Hosenfeld, Bob, 152
Howard University, 189
Human capital index (HCI), 53–54
Human Capital Institute, 144
Human Capital Office (GAO), 208
Human resources, 135–72; and compensation reforms, 152–60; at DLA, 70; federal government planning, 139–40; federal worker's role defined, 142–43; government needs in, 140–42; and job satisfaction, 163–71; passport system for, 126–28, 256; and people factor scorecard, 44; recruiting and hiring, 143–52; retention of best employees, 160–63; role of, 136–38; transition program development costs for, 255–57; and workforce planning, 138–43
Huselid, Mark, 56–57, 59

IBM: performance management at, 200–02, 205; training at, 177–78; wellness programs at, 166

An Inconvenient Truth film, 221
Individual Development Plan (IDP), 200
Individual performance assessment issues, 83, 197–99
Information assets, 12, 103–04
Information technology (IT), 12, 141–42
Information Technology Exchange Program, 83–84
Innovation, 70, 130–32
Innovation Expo Awards, 130
Intelligence agencies, 188
Interior Department and Lines of Business initiative, 257
Internal Revenue Service (IRS): and cross-training, 187; manager competency training, 181–82; and organizational structure, 118, 119; performance management at, 203; reforms at, 103, 106, 108, 274–75; and SES, 230; wellness programs at, 166
International Broadcasting Bureau, 213
Internship programs, 151–52, 250–51
Intrapreneurship: and BCG study, 42; at Defense Logistics Agency (DLA), 76–77; at GAO, 86; and TSR, 46, 47; at VA, 7
Iraq war: civil service system problems and, 5; and contracting, 11, 126; and media, 241
IRS. *See* Internal Revenue Service
IRS Restructuring and Reform Act of 1998 (RRA), 119, 181
IT. *See* Information technology

Job satisfaction: and child care, 167–69; and compensation, 152–53; at Defense Logistics Agency (DLA), 66, 76; and diversity management, 169–71; at DLA, 71; financial performance linked to, 48–52; and HR reforms, 163–71; and job sharing, 165–66; and staffing schedules, 163–64; and telecommuting, 164–65; and training, 182; and wellness, 166–67; and work schedules, 163–64

NSPS. *See* National Security Personnel System
NTEU (National Treasury Employee Union), 234, 235

Occupational Safety and Health Administration (OSHA), 204
Office of Management and Budget (OMB): Lines of Business initiative, 257; and PART, 196, 215; transition oversight by, 258, 260; transition program role of, 224, 264, 265
Office of Opportunity and Inclusiveness (GAO), 208
Office of Personnel Management (OPM): on compensation system, 153; and GAO, 80; on job sharing, 165; recruiting for, 144; on retirement crunch, 23; survey on workforce underperformance, 17; and training program performance, 180; training spending reported to, 174; transition program role of, 224, 258, 264, 266, 267; on workforce diversity, 169; and workforce planning, 141
OMB. *See* Office of Management and Budget
Ombudsmen and performance management, 213–14
O'Neill, Paul, 103
OPM. *See* Office of Personnel Management
O'Reilly, Charles, 55–56
Organizational structure, 115–34; and adaptability improvements, 116–19; and agility improvements, 116–19; and Chief Human Capital Officer, 132–33; and Chief Operating Officer, 132–33; core-ring model, 120–22; and cross-sector movement, 126–28; and efficiency improvements, 116–19; and innovation, 130–32; matrix structures and teams, 128–30; and multisector workforce, 119–20; and passport system, 126–28; and people factor scorecard, 44; proposal for, 122–26

OSHA (Occupational Safety and Health Administration), 204
Outsourcing of civil service. *See* Contracting
Oversight: and contracting, 11; and public sector leadership, 103; of transition program, 257–58, 267–68

Pace, Peter, 188
Parental responsibilities, 167–69
PART. *See* Performance Assessment Rating Tool
Partnership for Public Service (PPS): on DLA, 66, 68–69, 71; Extreme Hiring Makeover project, 144–48; and media, 242; and political appointee training, 191; and public sector leadership, 112; on recruiting and hiring, 144; as reform advocate, 218; on retirement crunch, 23; on student perception of government employment, 37; and student recruiting, 233; and training program performance, 180; transition program role of, 224
Passport system, 126–28, 256
Patent and Trademark Office (PTO), 12, 160
Pay-for-performance (PFP). *See* Performance-based pay
Pendleton Act of 1883, 15
Pension costs, 8, 23
People factor scorecard: adoption challenges for, 57–60; for Defense Logistics Agency (DLA), 73; development of, 42–48; on GAO, 85–86; in government, 61–97; and leadership of change, 112–14
Performance appraisals: at DLA, 71, 76; at GAO, 83, 84; of individuals, challenges of, 83, 197–99; training supervisors to perform, 184
Performance Assessment Rating Tool (PART): and budget appropriations, 21, 215; and OPM, 267; and performance-based pay, 211; and performance planning, 196–97; and productivity improvements, 92

Linda J. Bilmes is a lecturer in public policy at the Harvard Kennedy School. She has held senior positions in government, including assistant secretary and chief financial officer of the U.S. Department of Commerce, as well as deputy assistant secretary for administration at Commerce. She previously spent ten years as a management consultant with the Boston Consulting Group, where she advised major corporations and governments on organizational and business strategy. Bilmes is coauthor (with Joseph Stiglitz) of the *New York Times* bestseller *The Three Trillion Dollar War: The True Cost of the Iraq Conflict.* She is the author or coauthor of numerous book chapters, academic papers, and newspaper and magazine articles on subjects ranging from municipal pensions to veterans disability benefits. Bilmes has served on several high-ranking commissions, including the National Parks Second Century Commission, and has provided testimony to congressional committees on a variety of public policy issues. She is the recipient of the 2008 Speaking Truth to Power award from the American Friends Service Committee and holds a B.A. and M.B.A. from Harvard University.

W. Scott Gould is vice president for public sector strategy at IBM Global Business Services. Previously, he was CEO of The O'Gara Company, a strategic advisory and investment services firm, and COO of Exolve, a technology services company. Gould has served in the public sector as the CFO and assistant secretary for administration at Commerce and deputy assistant secretary for finance and management at the Treasury Department. As a White House fellow, Gould served in the Export-Import Bank of the United States and in the Office of the White House Chief of Staff. Gould is a veteran of the U.S. Navy. He served at sea aboard the guided missile destroyer *Richard E. Byrd.* As a Naval Intelligence reservist, Captain Gould was recalled to active duty for Operation Noble Eagle and Enduring Freedom. Gould is a fellow of the National Academy of Public Administration and a former member of the National Security Agency Technical Advisory Group and the Malcolm Baldrige National Quality Award Board of Overseers. He holds an A.B. degree from Cornell University and M.B.A. and Ed.D. degrees from the University of Rochester.